Youth: realities and challenges for achieving development with equality

Daniela Trucco
Heidi Ullmann

Editors

UNITED NATIONS

ECLAC

Economic Commission for Latin America and the Caribbean (ECLAC)

Santiago, March 2016

ECLAC Books

137

Alicia Bárcena
Executive Secretary

Antonio Prado
Deputy Executive Secretary

Laís Abramo
Chief, Social Development Division

Ricardo Pérez
Chief, Publications and Web Services Division

This book was edited by Daniela Trucco and Heidi Ullmann, Social Affairs Officers with the Economic Commission for Latin America and the Caribbean (ECLAC), in the framework of the project "Social inclusion of youth in the context of increasing violence and insecurity with a focus on Central America", financed by the United Nations Development Account.

The editors are grateful to Ernesto Rodríguez for his valuable comments on all the chapters, and to Daniela Huneeus for editorial support. They also wish to thank Martín Hopenhayn, former Chief of the Division of Social Development, for his advocacy of youth issues on the agenda of ECLAC and the region, and for his support for this project in particular.

The opinions expressed in this document are the sole responsibility of the authors and do not necessarily reflect the views of the Organization.

Cover design: María Luisa Avaria

United Nations publication
ISBN: 978-92-1-329031-6 (print)
ISBN: 978-92-1-057533-1 (pdf)
ISBN: 978-92-1-358030-1 (ePub)
Sales No.: E.15.II.G.12
LC/G.2647-P
Copyright © United Nations, 2016
All rights reserved
Printed at United Nations, Santiago
S.15-01235

This publication should be cited as: Daniela Trucco and Heidi Ullmann (eds.), *Youth: realities and challenges for achieving development with equality*, ECLAC Books, No. 137 (LC/G.2647-P), Santiago, Economic Commission for Latin America and the Caribbean (ECLAC), 2016.

Contents

Tables

Figures

Boxes

Diagram

Foreword

Over the past few years, the Economic Commission for Latin America and the Caribbean (ECLAC) has called for equality to be viewed as the ultimate aim of development, structural change as the path and policymaking as the instrument for achieving it, an approach developed in the position papers presented at the Commission's three most recent sessions —*Time for Equality: Closing Gaps, Opening Trails (2010); Structural Change for Equality: An Integrated Approach to Development (2012) and Compacts for Equality: Towards a Sustainable Future* (2014).

ECLAC proposes interpreting equality in a way that looks beyond the distribution of resources such as monetary income to encompass the equalization of opportunities and capabilities. This means understanding equality as the full exercise of citizenship, with dignity and mutual recognition between actors. Progress in this direction requires policies that both promote the autonomy of subjects and pay special attention to their vulnerabilities.

It is proposed that equality in this broad, relational sense should be recognized from a rights perspective, while also bearing in mind the need for greater collective solidarity, appreciation of the diversity of groups and identities and the need to combat discrimination, these being crucial for a more cohesive society and sustainable development. This also means subjects having the opportunity to participate actively in decisions affecting collective development rather than as mere beneficiaries of them.

These tenets add strength to our conviction that engaging the youth population in development processes is essential to move towards a more egalitarian society. This book aims to explore that perspective in depth, through the lens of social inclusion of youth.

After a decade of relative economic boom, the region now faces harsher external conditions amid slower growth of the global economy. Accordingly, even more strenuous efforts will be needed to achieve development in a strategic direction through structural change and investment in human capacities.

As ECLAC noted (2014) in its discussion on compacts for equality, Latin America's high-productivity segment produces two thirds of the region's GDP (66.9%), but just under 20% of its employment. Conversely, the less productive sectors employ 50% of workers, but produce just 10% of the region's GDP. Because of this disparity in the contribution each sector makes to output and employment, the distribution of productivity gains between workers is also highly unequal.

The region can hardly expect to implant a development pattern geared towards equality while it has a small group of firms or sectors using the latest technology and competing in global markets, alongside the majority of its firms using knowledge-poor technology yet employing most of the workers in the economy.

Building the capacities of the new generations is understood to be one of the key pillars for turning this state of affairs around, treating young people as essential agents in the production of structural change.

In addition to persistent structural divides, ECLAC has drawn attention to inequalities in capacity-building and the sphere of work, which affect young people in particular and will need to be addressed if progress is to be made along the path of sustainability with equality, on the basis that the position individuals occupy on the social scale is not solely the result of personal circumstances, efforts and decisions. There is a structure of opportunities provided by States, markets, families and communities that are largely beyond the individual's control and that shape prospects for social mobility and access to well-being.

This document addresses the main challenges this important segment of the population faces in relation to development and inclusion in Latin American society, with the intention of contributing to stronger policymaking for youth in the region. It contains the outcomes of several studies conducted in the framework of the project "Social inclusion of youth in the context of increasing violence and insecurity with a focus on Central America", which was financed by the United Nations Development Account and implemented by ECLAC between 2013 and 2015.

Alicia Bárcena
Executive Secretary
Economic Commission for
Latin America and the Caribbean (ECLAC)

Introduction

Young people make up a large segment of the population in Latin America and the Caribbean, and one which has formed the subject of much discussion in relation to development strategies in recent years. As mentioned in the foreword to this book, investing in the young generation is one of the key pillars for advancing a development process geared towards achieving equality. Although the concept of youth is socially constructed depending on the historical context and does not necessarily refer to a particular age range, like other research conducted by the Economic Commission for Latin America and the Caribbean (ECLAC), this book treats youth as referring to the population aged between 15 and 29 years.

Young people often feel that traditional political discourse, spheres and mechanisms do not represent them. Although calls for equity and social justice, environmental protection and cultural diversity resonate with young people, they participate little in decision-making or in discussions on key socioeconomic and political issues. Nonetheless, a number of prominent youth movements have emerged at the global level in the past few years, representing a wake-up call regarding their need to be heard and play an active part in developing the societies in which they live (ECLAC, 2014a). Research has proliferated recently on the role of this population group in development processes.

The research presented in this book is based on a rights-based perspective with equality as its ultimate aim. As argued in ECLAC/UNFPA (2012), the work of the United Nations in the field of youth is grounded in the human rights instruments ratified by the countries of the region, which view young people as bearers of rights. The spheres these instruments are intended to protect include young people's families and their rights to education, employment, health, participation and the development of identity and culture. In this framework, the proposal of ECLAC is geared towards understanding the process of youth inclusion in society from a rights-based perspective, going beyond the basic pillars of education and employment to encompass other dimensions of social inclusion that are also crucial for young people to progress not only in the objective parameters of inclusion, but also in subjective ones, so that they can feel they belong to a society they help to build. Public policies for youth must ensure a set of basic conditions and securities to underpin the development of youth capacities and potential (Alvarado, Rodríguez and Vommaro, 2013). These policies must therefore be approached and designed from a multidimensional and integrated perspective that takes in the spheres of education, employment, health, violence, culture and political participation (see diagram 1).

Diagram 1
Spheres of social inclusion in youth

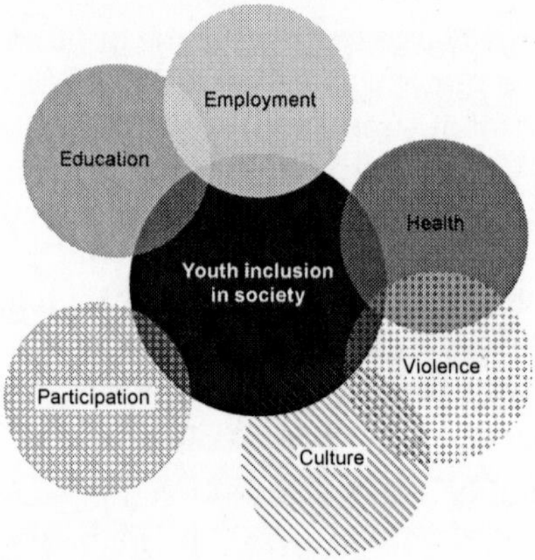

Source: Prepared by the authors.

Notwithstanding this multidimensional and integrated approach to young people's lives, the limitations of the research itself and lack of comparable information have obliged us to restrict the analysis to certain aspects of each dimension. This implies neglecting some issues that are highly significant for youth social inclusion in the region, such as migration, recreation and sport, the environment and religion. We also reflect upon other issues, such as family and communities, in a cross-cutting manner. Although the unit of analysis in the research is the young person, we place him or her within their context and appreciate the importance of that context in fostering or hindering processes of youth inclusion.

This book aims to portray the realities young people face in terms of opportunities for social inclusion, bearing in mind each of the spheres included in diagram 1, but it also seeks to offer recommendations on how to improve these realities through comprehensive public policies. As was recommended recently by experts on public policies for youth (Alvarado, Rodríguez and Vommaro, 2013), this region needs to promote the development and consolidation of youth policies that are comprehensive and integrated (between the different sectors). Public policies must also have a generational perspective, operating transversally and including the largest numbers of young people possible, and in a better way.

On the basis of a general framework for the measurement of social cohesion proposed by ECLAC in 2007, youth social inclusion is analysed in three basic dimensions that are addressed by youth policies and strategies (see table 1). The first is institutional development for the promotion and protection of youth social inclusion. This dimension includes capacity-building for design, coordination and evaluation of coordinating institutions, and openness to the establishment of integrated visions on the part of institutions implementing policies that affect youth. A second dimension focuses on closing objective gaps in social inclusion in key areas for this stage of the life cycle, with an equality- and rights- based perspective, through the implementation of coordinated sectoral policies. Lastly, the third dimension is the subjective sphere of social inclusion, which is about listening to and understanding the needs and visions of young people with respect to their own social inclusion, with a view to including these in policy design and implementation. The three dimensions must be addressed in a holistic manner for successful implementation of comprehensive policies. There are particular aspects to be considered within each dimension, which may be summarized as the sub-dimensions shown in table 1.

Table 1
Dimensions of youth inclusion in society

	Dimensions of analysis		
	Institutional development	Gaps	Perceptions and appreciations
Sub-dimensions	Normative (legal framework)	Employment	Trust
	Planning (sectoral/intersectoral plan)	Education	Expectations
	Coordinating institutions	Health	Identity-building
	Programmes available (implementing institutions)	Violence	Social solidarity
	Access to resources (spending/investment)	Culture	
		Participation	

Source: Prepared by the authors, on the basis of Economic Commission for Latin America and the Caribbean (ECLAC), *Social Cohesion: Inclusion and a sense of belonging in Latin America and the Caribbean* (LC/G.2335), Santiago, 2007.

The mechanisms by which inequality is transmitted between the generations are deeply entrenched in Latin America. The social inclusion of youth may be one of the region's most significant challenges today, not only because of the numbers of young people with respect to the rest of the population, but also because of what this group implies in terms dependency rates, as well as the needs and issues particular to this stage of life. On average, those aged between 15 and 29 represent a quarter of the total population in the region. For the purposes of analysis, the discussions in this book refer to that age group, on the understanding that it represents a highly heterogeneous population and that the term "youth" covers diverse life situations, interests and trajectories. In addition, in some countries, many young people are severely excluded and marginalized from the economic, political and social processes under way.

Following this conceptual framework, this book has been prepared on the basis of an analysis of the main spheres of social inclusion presented in diagram 1, but taking into consideration the various dimensions of analysis proposed in table 1. Chapter I examines the link between education and employment, which is considered the basic pillar of social inclusion at this stage of life, because it represents the step from dependence to autonomy. Chapter II addresses important considerations on youth health. As a related dimension, and one that has come to prominence in the region today, chapter III looks at the issue of violence. Chapter IV reviews youth access to culture in the digital age, while chapter V discusses youth political participation, as another essential sphere for inclusion. Lastly, chapter VI offers a more comprehensive discussion of social policy on youth, taking into account the recommendations arising in each sphere, as well as general considerations regarding institutions, legislation and social investment in the region.

Bibliography

Alvarado, Sara Victoria, Ernesto Rodríguez and Pablo Vommaro (2013), *Informe CLACSO-UNESCO: Políticas de inclusión social de jóvenes en América Latina. Situación, desafíos y recomendaciones para la acción* [online] http://www.celaju.net/informe-unesco-clacso-politicas-publicas-de-juventud-e-inclusion-social-en-america-latina-y-el-caribe/.

ECLAC (Economic Commission for Latin America and the Caribbean) (2014a), *Social Panorama of Latin America, 2014* (LC/G.2635-P), Santiago.

____(2014b), *Compacts for Equality: Towards a sustainable future* (LC/G.2586(SES.35/3)), Santiago, April.

____(2007), *Social Cohesion: Inclusion and a sense of belonging in Latin America and the Caribbean* (LC/G.2335), Santiago.

ECLAC/UNFPA (Economic Commission for Latin America and the Caribbean /United Nations Population Fund) (2012), *Informe Regional de Población en América Latina y el Caribe, 2011. Invertir en juventud en América Latina y el Caribe: Un imperativo de derechos e inclusión*, Santiago.

Chapter I

The master key to the social inclusion of young people: education and employment

Andrés Espejo
Ernesto Espíndola[1]

The concept of equality as defined by the Economic Commission for Latin America and the Caribbean (ECLAC) encompasses much more than simply income distribution; it also refers to equality of opportunity, equality of the capacity to take advantage of opportunities, and equality in capacity-building. Thus, equality is manifested in the full exercise of citizenship, dignity and reciprocal recognition. In order for progress to be made in this sphere, policies are needed that will foster autonomy while helping to shield young people from factors that engender vulnerability. ECLAC therefore sees equality as the horizon, structural change as the path and policy as the toolkit (ECLAC, 2010a, 2012a and 2014a).

Structural change entails the modification and diversification of the production sector in the region's economies in ways that will usher in major technological innovations and set the stage for the creation or growth of high-productivity industries that are driven by the intensive incorporation of knowledge and technical progress. Capacity-building for new generations is one of the main stepping stones along the path to equality and must be paired with changes in the production structure (ECLAC, 2014a).

---

[1] The authors are grateful for the substantive contributions provided by Matías Salces, Heidi Ullmann and Javiera Menchaca.

The region needs to take greater advantage of the demographic dividend and especially of the potential of its young people. There are two major spheres of activity, although they are not the only ones, which are key to progress in this respect: education and employment. These are the two most important links in the chain of the present-day development process and of new forms of development that will give rise to more dynamic, egalitarian societies (ECLAC, 2012a).

In order to ensure that the development process is sustainable over the long term and in order to drive the necessary types of structural change, the young population needs to be more highly educated, have the relevant types of expertise and possess the capacity for innovation and for managing a knowledge-based society. In short, the young people of the region need to be better prepared for life-long learning (ECLAC/OIJ/IMJUVE, 2014). Efforts to strengthen this link must be coupled with improved employment opportunities so that this capacity can be fully taken advantage of in order to boost productivity, enhance innovation and leverage social inclusion processes, since the bridge between education and employment for young people is, in large measure, the path from a dependent life to an autonomous one (Rico and Trucco, 2014).

In addition to these persistent structural gaps, however, there are also stark inequalities in capacity-building, not only in terms of access to education and the completion of schooling, but also as regards the development of skills of a high enough quality to enable those who possess those skills to perform well in the knowledge society. Young people are also faced with a paradox whose implications are more significant now than ever before: great strides have been made in the field of education in recent years and, while further advances are called for, the progress made thus far has not been matched by an improvement in the opportunities for young people to enter and position themselves in the labour market or in the avenues for capitalizing upon the new managerial and innovation capacities being acquired by young people.

In the course of the ongoing discussion about the Sustainable Development Goals (the 2030 Agenda for Sustainable Development), special emphasis is being placed on the younger generations. Proposals concerning ways of providing young people with the tools that they will need as they move forward are focusing on building life skills, especially literacy and other skills that will help young people to establish better positions for themselves in the labour market, reduce youth unemployment and provide access to quality jobs. This chapter will deal with the current situation in terms of education and employment for people between the ages of 15 and 29 and with the situation of persons in that age bracket who, for one reason or another, are not fully participating in one or the other of these areas of activity, which are of such crucial importance for social inclusion and development.

A.   What young people are doing: an analysis

Structurally unequal socioeconomic and spatial conditions, the characteristics of formal and non-formal educational services, the production structure and the surrounding environment all influence the life paths of the region's young people in terms of both the various opportunities for becoming members of society which are open to them and, more generally, their feelings of belonging and the way in which they see life and their future within Latin American society —or elsewhere.

Historically, the transition from childhood to adulthood has been understood as a linear process whereby individuals move from one stage to another, each with its defined social and cultural role (education, entry into the workforce, the establishment of individual independence, marriage, parenthood). The process by which young people became emancipated and autonomous could be clearly tracked as they gradually shed their more youthful roles and took on new ones (Filgueira, 1998, p. 12). The conditions to which younger generations are subject and the opportunities that are open to them have, however, tended to generate a more heterogeneous set of paths for the transition to autonomy. For example, in many cases, the duration of childhood has been extended, with certain milestones associated with the conclusion of that stage being pushed back as the number of years of schooling increases and entry into the labour market and the formation of a family are postponed. As a result, younger persons' life paths are no longer so sequential in terms of their life events; they are less linear than before and are becoming more dynamic (ECLAC/OIJ, 2004; Dávila and Ghiardo, 2005, cited in ECLAC/OIJ/IMJUVE, 2014). Today, we no longer think of all people following the same path of personal development and membership in society; nor does this process exhibit the continuity that it once did. This branching-out of life paths is not only a result of young people's desire to continue their studies and put off certain kinds of roles or activities that people used to undertake earlier in life; it is also —and perhaps mainly— a consequence of structural factors that are beyond individuals' control, including the socioeconomic conditions in which they are raised, as discussed in a recent report on Ibero-American youth (ECLAC/OIJ/IMJUVE, 2014). The surrounding environments for young people in different socioeconomic strata set them on ever-more changeable life paths as they move back and forth between education systems, unemployment, employment, family work, inactivity and other situations. A picture therefore emerges of discontinuous transition patterns in which people shift from one position to another. The classic concept of "continuous learning" makes more sense than ever today as people find it necessary to acquire further education throughout their lives and come to realize that holding the same job or a job in the same company for their entire lives is no longer a feasible proposition.

Some of the reasons for this have to do with the expansion of the coverage of educational systems to include a larger part of the population and with the requirements of more dynamic, global production sectors in which employees need to undergo continuous training. The entry of a growing number of women into the workforce and changing family structures have also prompted people to postpone parenthood, which in turn eases the pressure on young people to attain economic independence at an earlier age. In this context, young people appear to be becoming disconnected from institutions that play a key role in social inclusion, such as education and employment, which is troubling.

This section presents a brief review of the statistics on the distribution of young people between the educational system and paid employment. The reader should bear in mind that the classification of young people on the basis of their ties to these two links in the development chain (education and employment) is a snapshot of the situation at a given point in time (with that point in time varying from country to country). This kind of information provides a picture of the specific situation of each young person, but it masks the fact that participation in education and, above all, in the workforce is the outcome of a process that entails various changes in the principal activity in which each young person is engaged.

In or around 2012, approximately 37% of the people between the ages of 15 and 29 (49.9 million) were attending an institution providing primary education (those who are lagging the furthest behind) or a secondary or post-secondary (vocational school or university) institution. As shown in figure I.1, slightly over 50% of the people in this age group (75.7 million) were employed at the time the survey was conducted. As was to be expected, a majority of the people who were studying were younger (15-19 years) and a majority of the employed persons were older (25-29 years).

A subgroup of 15.3 million young people —just 10% of the total population in this age bracket— were both studying and were gainfully employed.[2]

Another 22% of the people in this age group (29.7 million) said that they were neither in school nor employed. It is important to realize that the fact that these people are not attending school and are not employed does not necessarily mean that they are vagrants or alienated from society. As will be discussed below, most of these youths, especially the young women among them, are care providers and/or are performing unpaid domestic

---

[2]   Employment surveys classify people as having only one principal activity (employment or studying). In this case, the measurements refer to persons whose principal activity is employment who say that they are also attending some kind of educational establishment.

work, are currently unemployed but are seeking work, are waiting for a job or have a disability that prevents them from working or studying, or are in some other position that has nothing to do with criminal behaviour, drug use or gangs —activities that have tended to be the *leitmotiv* of studies on young people.

Figure I.1
Latin America (18 countries): activity status of persons between the ages of 15 and 29, around 2012[a]

(Percentages)

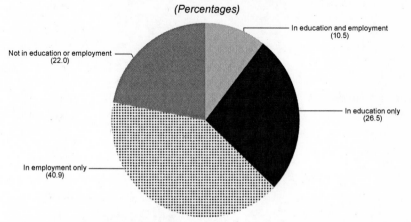

In education and employment (10.5)

Not in education or employment (22.0)

In education only (26.5)

In employment only (40.9)

Source: Economic Commission for Latin America and the Caribbean (ECLAC), *Social Panorama of Latin America 2014* (LC/G.2635-P), Santiago, 2014.
[a] Simple average of the data for the 18 countries.

Examination of the performance of the various countries' education systems, access to those systems, the operation of the labour market, fertility patterns, women's labour force participation and other factors that impact the young population shows up certain differences across countries. For example, in the Plurinational State of Bolivia, Brazil, Guatemala, Mexico, Paraguay, Peru and Uruguay, over 55% of young people are employed (they may or may not also be students), whereas in Argentina, Chile and the Dominican Republic, the figure is below 45%. This is, of course, closely related to the percentage of young people who are in the education system: in Argentina, Chile, Costa Rica, the Dominican Republic and Ecuador, over 44% of all people between the ages of 15 and 29 attend some sort of educational institution, whereas in the Plurinational State of Bolivia, Guatemala, Honduras and Nicaragua, the corresponding figure is below 30%. The largest percentages of young people who are neither students nor employed are found in the Plurinational State of Bolivia, El Salvador, Guatemala, Honduras and Nicaragua (over one fifth of the total population in this age group) —countries with some of the highest levels of poverty and social exclusion.

Table I.1
**Latin America (18 countries): activity status of persons between
the ages of 15 and 29, around 2012**
(Percentages)

	Studies and is employed	Studies only	Only employed	Does not study and is not employed	Total
Argentina, 2012	10.3	36.1	34.3	19.3	100
Bolivia (Plurinational State of), 2011	8.7	14.2	48.5	28.6	100
Brazil, 2012	13.1	22.0	44.0	20.8	100
Chile, 2011	6.5	38.2	32.4	21.8	100
Colombia, 2012	10.7	24.1	42.5	22.7	100
Costa Rica, 2011	15.0	32.2	34.2	18.6	100
Dominican Republic, 2012	11.6	33.6	31.1	23.6	100
Ecuador, 2012	8.8	35.5	38.1	17.7	100
Guatemala, 2006	10.4	13.9	50.0	25.7	100
Honduras, 2010	8.3	20.8	43.6	27.3	100
Mexico, 2012	8.7	23.8	47.0	20.5	100
Nicaragua, 2009	7.3	20.7	43.6	28.4	100
Panama, 2011	9.2	28.8	39.7	22.3	100
Paraguay, 2011	16.9	25.0	40.3	17.8	100
Peru, 2012	12.2	20.2	47.7	19.8	100
El Salvador, 2012	7.8	27.0	40.4	24.8	100
Uruguay, 2011	13.8	27.4	42.4	16.4	100
Venezuela (Bolivarian Republic of), 2012	9.6	33.6	36.3	20.5	100
Latin America (simple average)	**10.5**	**26.5**	**40.9**	**22.0**	**100**

Source: Economic Commission for Latin America and the Caribbean (ECLAC), on the basis of special tabulations of household surveys conducted in the respective countries.

An analysis of the available evidence regarding the master key of social inclusion, i.e., the formal education system and the labour market, provides a clearer picture of the complexity and diversity of the situations and life paths of young people who are studying and/or working and of those who are not. There is a wealth of data that can be used not only to undertake a more in-depth analysis of the situation of young people but also to derive guidelines for the design of better public policies that can bolster existing educational systems, regulate the labour market more effectively and point to other options for bringing young people who are not, at the moment, studying or employed into those spheres of activity.

B. Young people who are studying: access to the education system and progression from one level to the next

In recent studies, ECLAC (ECLAC, 2014b; ECLAC/OIJ/IMJUVE, 2014) has underscored the fact that capacity-building in the formal education system is one of the main avenues for the social inclusion of young people. These studies have found that additional years of study not only provide people with better employment opportunities but also prepare young people to participate more fully in the complex, globalized democratic societies of today. Education is also one of the most effective tools for breaking the cycle of the intergenerational reproduction of poverty.

The primary education completion rate is now so high (94%) that it has ceased to act as a constraint on the expansion of secondary education; thus, for the region's population, there is now a smooth path for the transition from the first of these levels to the next (UNESCO, 2013b).[3] Nonetheless, there are still many young people who are not enrolled in secondary school even though they are in the corresponding age bracket. However, comparable data for 42 countries and territories in Latin America and the Caribbean compiled by the Institute for Statistics of the United Nations Educational, Scientific and Cultural Organization (UNESCO) indicate that the net secondary-school enrolment rate climbed from 60.4% in 2000 to 73% in 2012 (see figure I.2).[4] The expansion of the secondary educational system's coverage has opened up a vast range of educational opportunities for women in the region. The data indicate that the net enrolment rate for women exceeds the rate for men (75.4% versus 70.7% in 2012). This could be due, at least in part, to young men's early entry into the workforce, which tends to erode their current and future opportunities (ECLAC/UNFPA, 2012).

Despite the increase of over 10 percentage points during the past 12 years, these figures are still low and show just how much further the region has to go in order to achieve a 100% secondary-school completion rate, since the lag registered at this level is associated with the school dropout rate.

---

[3] The figure of 94% was computed by ECLAC on the basis of special tabulations of the results of household surveys for 18 countries in the region conducted around 2012.

[4] For information on the countries and territories covered in the data compiled by the UNESCO Institute for Statistics, see [online] http://www.uis.unesco.org/Education/Documents/uis-regions.pdf.

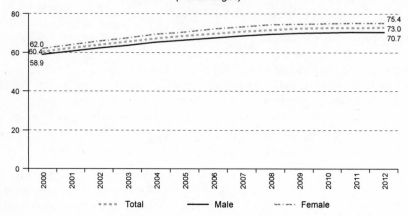

Figure I.2
Latin America and the Caribbean (42 countries): net enrolment rate
for secondary education, by sex
(Percentages)

Source: "Data Centre", UNESCO Institute for Statistics [online] http://stats.uis.unesco.org/.

Generally speaking, two types of secondary schooling are offered in the region: a general sciences/humanities programme, and technical or vocational programmes. The first type of curriculum prepares students to go on to higher education, while the vocational programmes are a secondary-school subsystem that offers students technical degrees that provide them with a way to enter the workforce upon their completion of secondary school (Briasco, 2008). According to the available information on 17 Latin American countries, the great majority of students in the region are enrolled in general sciences/humanities programmes (88.5%). In the Plurinational State of Bolivia, Nicaragua and Peru, practically all secondary-school students are registered in these types of programmes (see figure I.3). Technical education is more widespread —accounting for over 15% of the total number of students registered in secondary schools— in Guatemala (28.1%), Chile (22.5%), Ecuador (21.1%), El Salvador (18.5%), Costa Rica (17.1%) and Mexico (16.6%).

The rise in secondary-school enrolment seen in the past decade is largely attributable to the incorporation of groups that have historically remained outside the school system (Itzcovich, 2014), but there are still definite gaps in the region that correspond to differences in household socioeconomic status. For example, in 2012, whereas 80.3% of adolescents and young people of secondary-school age who were in the highest-income quintile were enrolled in secondary educational institutions, only 57% of their counterparts in the lowest-income quintile were. The situation varies a great deal across countries, however. The differentials between the highest and lowest quintiles are, for example, much smaller in Argentina, the Bolivarian Republic of Venezuela, Chile, Ecuador and Peru than they are in the Central American countries, where the figures reflect lower overall school attendance rates, as well as sharp inequalities between income quintiles (see figure I.4).

Figure I.3
Latin America (17 countries): students enrolled in secondary school, by type of programme, 2012
(Percentages)

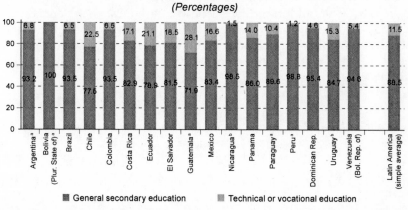

Source: "Data Centre", UNESCO Institute for Statistics [online] http://stats.uis.unesco.org/.
[a] The figures for Argentina, the Plurinational State of Bolivia, Guatemala, Paraguay and Peru are for 2011.
[b] The figures for Nicaragua and Uruguay are for 2010.

Figure I.4
Latin America (18 countries): net secondary-school attendance rates, by highest and lowest income quintiles, around 2012
(Percentages)

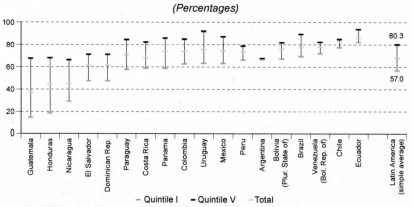

Source: Commission for Latin America and the Caribbean (ECLAC), on the basis of special tabulations of household surveys conducted in the respective countries.

School dropout rates point to another factor that interferes with the normal progression of secondary education and completion of that level.[5] Dropout rates are quite high in many countries of the region, largely because young people find employment opportunities —and are in need of employment— before they finish school. In addition, in many countries this level is not mandatory (ECLAC, 2010b). The secondary-school dropout rate for 2012 in Latin America is estimated at 15.5% (see table I.2). The dropout rate for adolescents and young people in the first quintile is far more than double the rate for those in the highest-income quintile (19.1% for quintile 1 versus 8.2% for quintile 5). Since access to the education system is clearly not enough to ensure that adolescents will complete their formal education, increasing schools' retention capacity, especially in respect of students from the poorest households, is therefore clearly an imperative for the education systems of Latin America.

Table I.2

Latin America (18 countries): secondary-school dropout rates, around 2012

(Percentages)

	Both sexes					
	Total	Quintile I	Quintile II	Quintile III	Quintile IV	Quintile V
Argentina	13.5	18.6	15.0	11.7	9.9	5.5
Bolivia (Plurinational State of)	12.0	16.0	10.6	10.6	13.2	9.4
Brazil	16.2	19.7	19.7	16.2	13.3	5.5
Chile	10.0	12.2	11.8	13.5	7.0	2.2
Colombia	14.6	17.4	18.7	15.9	11.0	6.7
Costa Rica	8.5	7.6	9.5	7.5	10.9	6.4
Dominican Republic	19.3	26.8	24.1	18.8	16.5	9.2
Ecuador	15.5	20.6	18.9	16.4	12.0	4.2
El Salvador	19.3	26.8	24.1	18.8	16.5	9.2
Guatemala	13.0	8.6	10.2	19.9	15.9	8.1
Honduras	16.5	23.8	22.7	16.9	15.8	10.4
Mexico	28.9	37.3	32.6	31.1	27.1	14.8
Nicaragua	19.7	21.5	17.6	18.5	24.3	16.5
Panama	15.7	20.4	14.8	16.1	15.4	9.4
Paraguay	13.6	15.8	16.7	14.2	14.2	5.4
Peru	8.8	7.0	7.5	10.7	9.9	9.3
Uruguay	21.7	30.2	23.9	21.5	17.1	7.0
Venezuela (Bolivarian Republic of)	12.1	14.1	14.1	11.8	10.7	7.8
Latin America (simple average)	**15.5**	**19.1**	**17.4**	**16.1**	**14.5**	**8.2**

Source: Economic Commission for Latin America and the Caribbean (ECLAC), on the basis of special tabulations of household surveys conducted in the respective countries.

---

[5]   A student is considered to have dropped out of school if he or she leaves school for a given year; this does not necessarily mean that the person has left the school system forever.

Here, too, the figures indicate that the situation varies sharply across countries. Costa Rica (8.5%), Peru (8.8%) and Chile (10.0%) have the lowest dropout rates in the region and the smallest differentials between the top and bottom quintiles. Mexico (28.9%), Uruguay (21.7%), Nicaragua (19.7%), El Salvador (19.3%) and the Dominican Republic (19.3%) not only have the highest secondary-school dropout rates, but also exhibit large differentials between the highest-income and lowest-income households.

The high dropout rates seen in so many countries of the region are reflected in a small number of years of schooling completed, which falls far short of the years required to finish the secondary level. Completion of that level is of crucial importance if people are to acquire the basic skills that they need to meet the requirements of a globalized world, to enjoy freedom of action and to be capable of engaging in life-long learning (ECLAC/UNFPA, 2012). What is more, according to ECLAC estimates (2010b), the completion of a secondary education is the minimum, or "floor" value, that is required in most Latin American countries in order for people to be less likely than the average person to be poor. However, in order to have an above-average income, in most of the countries a minimum of 13 or 14 years of schooling (i.e. some post-secondary studies) is needed (ECLAC/OIJ, 2008, and ECLAC/OIJ/IMJUVE, 2014).

The outlook for the region in this respect would therefore appear to be dim, since 4 out of every 10 people between the ages of 20 and 24 have not completed secondary school (see figure I.5) and, if they cannot secure a quality form of employment that provides them with an above-average income, there is an increasing probability that they will continue to be subject to substandard living conditions and that this situation will be perpetuated in the next generation (ECLAC/OIJ/IMJUVE, 2014). Chile and Peru have the highest secondary-school completion rates in the region (nearly 80%), but some countries have far lower rates, such as Honduras and Nicaragua (36% each) and Guatemala (25%).

The low secondary-school completion rates in Latin America and the Caribbean, coupled with the fact that young people need to earn money in order for their households to attain even minimum levels of well-being, translate into quite restricted access to post-secondary (technical-vocational and university) educations, which thus tend to be reserved for a fairly small percentage of young people. Strengthening post-secondary education remains a formidable challenge for the region (ECLAC, 2010b).

It is no easy task to arrive at estimates of the extent of young people's access to post-secondary (or tertiary) education because the age group that may attend this level of instruction is not formally delimited in the same way that the age groups corresponding to the primary and secondary levels are, since people may enter and exit the tertiary level at different points in their lives (UNESCO, 2013b). The gross enrolment rate does, however, provide some idea of the extent of access to this level of education.[6] This indicator shows that enrolment in post-secondary educational institutions in the region has nearly doubled over the past decade, climbing from 22.3% in 2000 to 42.8% in 2012 (see figure I.6). As is also true of enrolment in secondary schools, women have benefited more than men from this increased coverage, since their rate is more than 10 percentage points higher than the corresponding rate for males.

Figure I.5
Latin America (18 countries): completion of secondary school by persons
between the ages of 20 and 24, around 2012
(Percentages)

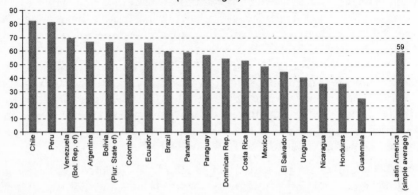

Source: Economic Commission for Latin America and the Caribbean (ECLAC), on the basis of special tabulations of household surveys conducted in the respective countries.

Figure I.6
Latin America and the Caribbean (42 countries): gross enrolment rate
for the tertiary level of education, by sex, 2000-2012
(Percentages)

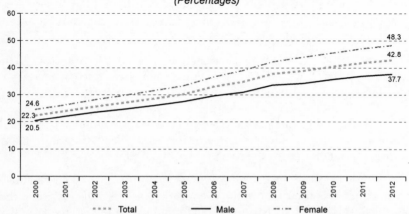

Source: "Data Centre", UNESCO Institute for Statistics [online] http://stats.uis.unesco.org/.

---

6   The age group corresponding to the tertiary level is defined as the five-year range of ages immediately following the age at which a person would theoretically complete his or her secondary education in each country.

Another way of gauging access is to look at the post-secondary attendance rate for persons between 20 and 24 years of age. This indicator shows that, even though attendance rates in the region have risen considerably, post-secondary students continue to be primarily from higher-income groups. This trend is observed in a majority of the countries, although it is stronger in some than in others (see table I.3). There are some countries, such as Brazil, the Dominican Republic, El Salvador, Guatemala, Honduras, Mexico and Paraguay, where tertiary-level attendance rates for the first quintile are as low as around 5% or less.

Table I.3
Latin America (18 countries): tertiary-education attendance rates for persons between 20 and 24 years of age, around 2012
(Percentages)

	Per capita income quintiles					
	Total	Quintile I	Quintile II	Quintile III	Quintile IV	Quintile V
Argentina	37.4	27.2	30.5	38.4	45.2	51.3
Bolivia (Plurinational State of)	34.0	18.0	26.3	35.4	40.5	41.5
Brazil	16.1	4.2	6.1	11.9	20.8	42.1
Chile	33.5	21.1	27.5	26.4	35.9	58.6
Colombia	22.3	6.6	11.3	17.8	29.3	44.8
Costa Rica	32.3	15.1	19.6	26.9	38.1	58.7
Dominican Republic	15.9	2.0	5.1	12.0	20.2	38.7
Ecuador	28.9	14.9	20.3	25.5	30.8	48.8
El Salvador	15.9	2.0	5.1	12.0	20.2	38.7
Guatemala	10.0	0.9	1.9	3.7	8.4	29.1
Honduras	14.3	2.4	3.9	7.5	16.9	31.1
Mexico	22.6	5.6	14.8	16.8	27.4	42.2
Nicaragua	15.5	6.8	8.3	12.2	16.9	29.3
Panama	25.5	8.8	18.3	25.1	31.4	41.7
Paraguay	25.4	5.3	14.9	25.0	27.6	46.3
Peru	22.7	14.8	18.2	21.3	23.2	33.1
Uruguay	25.6	8.1	14.0	23.4	32.7	53.6
Venezuela (Bolivarian Republic of)	37.9	29.9	33.2	38.4	41.0	47.1
Latin America (simple average)	**24.2**	**10.8**	**15.5**	**21.1**	**28.1**	**43.1**

Source: Economic Commission for Latin America and the Caribbean (ECLAC), on the basis of special tabulations of household surveys conducted in the respective countries.

The majority of people between the ages of 20 and 24 who are studying are attending universities (66.3%), but another sizeable group are attending secondary schools (formal courses, adult education programmes or distance learning courses) or attending other types of courses of a duration of less than one year (24.3%), while others are attending technical or vocational programmes (9.4%) (see figure I.7). The situation varies across countries, especially with regard to attendance at technical or vocational programmes. The countries in which the largest percentages of young people are attending these last types of institutions are Peru (27.5%), Chile (21.2%) and Argentina (18.9%). There is another large group of countries (Costa Rica, the Dominican Republic, Ecuador, El Salvador, Honduras, Mexico, Nicaragua, Panama, Paraguay and Uruguay) in which the percentage of students between the ages of 20 and 24 who are attending technical or vocational programmes is marginal.

Figure I.7
Latin America (15 countries): persons between the ages of 20 and 24 who are attending an educational institution, by type of programme, around 2012

(Percentages)

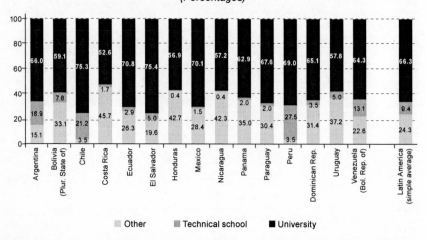

Other   Technical school   University

Source: Economic Commission for Latin America and the Caribbean (ECLAC), on the basis of special tabulations of household surveys conducted in the respective countries.

This indicates that, despite the determined effort that has been made to promote non-university higher education programmes in the various countries of the region, the percentage of young people who are attending these kinds of programmes is still small and is mainly accounted for by young people in the poorest quintiles living in urban areas (ECLAC, 2004). This is due not only to the limited coverage of these types of programmes, but also to the poor quality of these options, which perpetuates the low social status of technical and technological professions in the region (Llisterri and others, 2014) (see box I.1).

Box I.1
Non-university higher education

One of the main challenges for Latin American educational systems today is the development of post-secondary options that will allow persons graduating from secondary school to continue their studies in ways that will prepare them to enter a constantly changing labour market (Jacinto, 2013). Experience around the world has shown that the provision of a wide range of high-quality non-university higher-education options brightens the future prospects of young people once they do become part of the workforce.

The availability of a quality, non-university higher education not only has a considerable effect on the paths chosen by students but also has a strong impact in economic and social terms that takes the form of higher levels of productivity, a narrowing of the gap between skilled labour supply and demand, and reductions in unemployment and in income inequality (Bornacelly, 2013). This type of education thus provides a fitting response to the demands of the countries' ever-changing production systems as they strive to meet the challenges posed by the global economy. The impacts of this are felt in such widely varying spheres as the labour market and information and communications technologies (ICTs) (Jacinto, 2013).

There are two main types of non-university higher education programmes: technical-vocational and technological courses of study. The United Nations Educational, Scientific and Cultural Organization (UNESCO) and the International Labour Organization (ILO) recommend that technical-vocational programmes be focused on deepening students' knowledge about the corresponding technologies and sciences and conveying practical know-how and related attitudes, areas of understanding and theoretical knowledge, as required (Velasco, 2005). Their aim is to provide the kind of specific professional, innovative and operational training that is in demand in the production sector (Bornacelly, 2013). These programmes also accredit and add value to work experience gained as part of the learning process, are more accessible for women and persons with disabilities and help students to develop decision-making capabilities and to adapt to the constantly changing nature of ICTs (Velasco, 2005).

In the course of technical-vocational training programmes, which generally are between four and five semesters in length, students acquire operational and instrumentational skills. The areas of expertise are related to the application of knowledge to highly specific, less complex routine labour activities. Technological training programmes, on the other hand, equip students to perform in diverse settings in which the work usually entails the practical application of expertise in complex, non-routine activities. These courses of study usually are of six or seven semesters in duration (Bornacelly, 2013).

Source: I. Bornacelly, "Educación técnica y tecnológica para la reducción de la desigualdad salarial y la pobreza", *Revista Desarrollo y Sociedad*, No. 71, Bogota, Universidad de los Andes, 2013; C. Jacinto, "La educación post-secundaria técnica: contexto, interrogantes y aportes de la investigación", *Incluir a los jóvenes. Retos para la educación terciaria técnica en América Latina*, C. Jacinto and others, United Nations Educational, Scientific and Cultural Organization (UNESCO), 2013; C. Velasco, *La educación técnica y profesional de nivel medio en siete países de América Latina. Hacia un estado del arte*, Santiago, United Nations Educational, Scientific and Cultural Organization (UNESCO), 2005.

The available information indicates that approximately 10% of persons between the ages of 25 and 29 who have attended tertiary educational institutions are no longer attending them but have not completed their studies (see figure I.8.A).

Given the low enrolment and attendance rates (24% of persons between the ages of 20 and 24) for post-secondary education, as shown in table I.3, in combination with the high percentage of students who then discontinue their studies (nearly half of those between the ages of 25 and 29 who began such studies), the completion rate for tertiary studies is still very low in the region, with only some 10% of young people, on average, finishing this level of instruction (see figure I.8.B). The national completion rates in Latin America vary a great deal, however, ranging from around 20% in Argentina, the Plurinational State of Bolivia and Peru, to less than 5% in the Dominican Republic, Guatemala and Honduras.

Nonetheless, overall, significant progress has been made in terms of access to, attendance, promotion within and completion of the various levels of education in the region. A more detailed analysis does show, however, that there is a great deal of inequality and that it becomes more pronounced as the level of education increases. Many young people do not attend school for economic reasons or because of problems relating to the accessibility or availability of educational services (ECLAC/OIJ/IMJUVE, 2014). Students from poor homes frequently leave school in order to work in what are often poor-quality (low-paying, informal) jobs that do not provide benefits. The wages earned by very young workers are an incentive, since they allow them to achieve an immediate improvement in their households' living standards which would be lost if they were to return to school. Young women may also leave school because they have to take on adult roles involving domestic work or caregiving roles or because they become mothers.

The fact that so few young people have a technical education acts as a constraint on modernization processes and increased competitiveness in the countries of the region (ECLAC/OIJ, 2008). There is thus an urgent need to revamp the technical education system so that it is seen not only as a form of education that will enable someone to obtain a job immediately for the short term but also as one that will provide young people with a platform for life-long learning and for building capacity for innovation and a gateway to other forms of post-secondary education or training (Fretwell, 2004).

Figure I.8
Latin America (12 countries and 18 countries): persons between 25 and 29 years of age who are not studying and who have incomplete or completed tertiary studies [a]

(Percentages)

A. Young people who have not completed their tertiary studies

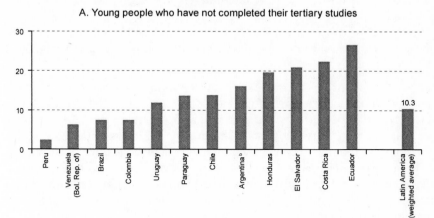

B. Young people who have completed their tertiary studies

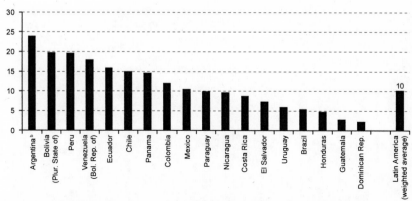

Source: Economic Commission for Latin America and the Caribbean (ECLAC), on the basis of special tabulations of household surveys conducted in the respective countries.
[a] Completion of at least five years of post-secondary studies.
[b] Data are for urban areas.

C. Youth employment

Opportunities for young people to join the labour force are one of the pillars for social inclusion. Paid employment is the main —if not the only— avenue for achieving economic independence for individuals and their families.

Young people hope to find opportunities for quality employment that will enable them to participate fully in their country's civic and productive development, and to attain greater well-being and personal development. The available information on 18 countries indicates that approximately 76 million persons between the ages of 15 and 29 are employed in Latin America. This is equivalent to around 50% of the people in that age bracket, 10% of whom are both studying and gainfully employed (i.e. 20% of employed young people).

The labour-force participation rate for young people in Latin America rises with age (see figure I.9) (ECLAC, 2014; ECLAC/OIJ/IMJUVE, 2014). Around 2012, the participation rate for Latin Americans between the ages of 15 and 19 was 39%, while the rate for those in the 25-29 age bracket was 80%. As noted in the documents just cited, the lower labour-force participation rate of persons between 15 and 19 years of age is not necessarily a cause for concern, since a later entry into the workforce provides more of an opportunity to remain in school and obtain better qualifications for obtaining employment later on.

Figure I.9
Latin America (18 countries): labour-force participation rates for persons between 15 and 29 years of age, around 2012 [a]
(Percentages)

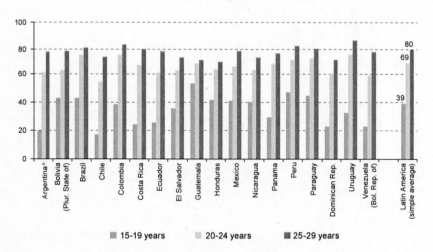

Source: Economic Commission for Latin America and the Caribbean (ECLAC), *Social Panorama of Latin America 2014* (LC/G.2635-P), Santiago, 2014.
[a] The data for the region correspond to the simple average of the data for the countries.
[b] The data refer to urban areas.

Box I.2
Adolescent labour in Latin America

Many young people begin working when they are adolescents (between 12 and 17 years of age) and have to reconcile school attendance with employment (whether in the form of paid or unpaid work). The promotion and protection of their rights are based on the laws of each country and on three international instruments: the Convention concerning Minimum Age for Admission to Employment, 1973 (No. 138), the Worst Forms of Child Labour Convention, 1999 (No. 182) and the Convention on the Rights of the Child. Despite these initiatives, however, in many countries of the region adolescents are working primarily in the informal sector and under very bad conditions.

It is important to point out that not all work done by children should be classified as child labour that is to be targeted for elimination. "Children's or adolescents' participation in work that does not affect their health and personal development or interfere with their schooling is generally regarded as being something positive" (ILO, n/d). The Convention concerning Minimum Age for Admission to Employment does state, however, that "the minimum age ... shall not be less than the age of completion of compulsory schooling" (14-15 years), even though this age may vary from country to country. It also establishes that children between the ages of 13 and 15 may perform light work, provided that it is not likely to be harmful to their health or interfere with their education. Consequently, while adolescents have the same rights as any adult has, their right to work is subordinated to other rights, such as the right to education, the right to health, the right to recreation and so forth (ILO, 2010).

In Latin America (18 countries), approximately one out of every six persons between the ages of 12 and 17 is employed, and more than half of them are having to reconcile their studies with paid employment. When the figures are broken down by smaller age groups, they show that 11% of adolescents between the ages of 12 and 14 are working and, for those between the ages of 15 and 17, the figure is twice as high.

Adolescents work in a wide variety of positions, but the priority is the immediate elimination of dangerous work. This is defined as work that, by its very nature or because of the conditions under which it is performed, is likely to harm the health, safety or morals of the children involved. A recent ILO study (2015) that covers nine countries of the region (Brazil, Costa Rica, Ecuador, El Salvador, Honduras, Mexico, Nicaragua, the Plurinational State of Bolivia and Uruguay) reports that 60% of all employed persons between the ages of 15 and 17 are performing dangerous work. The study also shows that the rates of dangerous work are higher in countries where differentials between urban and rural populations are greater and where agriculture is the predominant economic activity. In addition, males are more likely than females to be engaged in dangerous work, both in relative and absolute terms.

Box I.2 (concluded)

Latin America (18 countries): persons between 12 and 17 years of age who are employed, by age group, around 2013[a]

(Percentages)

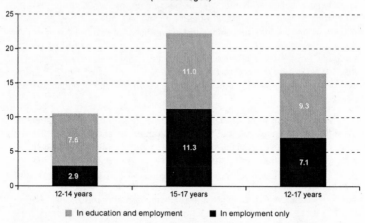

◼ In education and employment   ◼ In employment only

Source: Economic Commission for Latin America and the Caribbean (ECLAC), on the basis of special tabulations of household surveys conducted in the respective countries.
[a] The data for the region correspond to the simple average of the data for the countries.

Many adolescents (primarily females) are engaged in unpaid domestic work. As noted by Rico and Trucco (2014), this is the stage at which gender-based labour specialization tends to emerge, with young males working in economically productive activities while young women devote their efforts to unpaid domestic work. These authors also observe that female adolescents devote, on average, around three times as many hours per week to domestic activities than male adolescents do and that this can be assumed to detract from the scholastic achievement of girls and young women, who, if they live in rural zones, are also often involved in small animal husbandry and family farming.

Given the substandard and insecure conditions under which many adolescents in the region live, there is an urgent need to provide better ways of helping them to remain in school, to introduce policies that will provide flexible arrangements that allow them to reconcile the demands of employment, education and recreation, and to ensure that the types of work to be performed by adolescents are governed by special national legal regimes that will protect their rights in line with the relevant instruments of international law (ILO, 2010).

Source: International Labour Organization (ILO), *World Report on Child Labour 2015: Paving the way to decent work for young people*, Geneva, 2015; *Decent Work and Youth in Latin America 2010*, Lima, Promoting youth employment in Latin America (PREJAL), 2010; "What is child labour", International Programme on the Elimination of Child Labour (IPEC) [online] http://www.ilo.org/ipec/facts/lang--en/index.htm; and María Nieves Rico and Daniela Trucco, "Adolescentes: derecho a la educación y al bienestar futuro", *Políticas Sociales series*, No. 190 (LC/L.3791), Santiago, Economic Commission for Latin America and the Caribbean (ECLAC).

The trend in the unemployment rate is just the opposite of the trend in the labour-force participation rate, since the former tends to descend at higher age brackets. As a result, the rate eventually converges with the overall rate for the adult population. On average, however, the youth unemployment rate is twice as high as the rate for the adult population (see figure I.10). This is a long-standing trend that reflects a worldwide structural problem (ECLAC/OIJ/IMJUVE, 2014). In addition, although the economic crisis of the mid-2000s did not have a stronger impact on the youth unemployment rate than it did on the rate for adults, during the ensuing recovery (2009-2011), the adult employment rate bounced back faster than the youth employment rate did. This would appear to indicate that, in 2007-2011, the reduction in youth employment was offset by the fact that more young people (especially those in the 15-19 age bracket) remained in the educational system (ECLAC, 2014b).

Figure I.10
Latin America (18 countries): unemployment rates, by age group [a]
(Percentages)

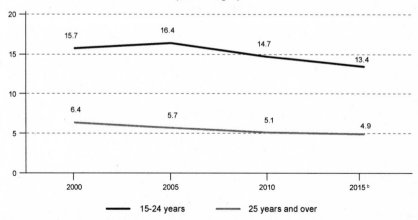

— 15-24 years   — 25 years and over

Source: International Labour Organization (ILO), 2013 Labour Overview. Latin America and the Caribbean, Lima, ILO Regional Office for Latin America and the Caribbean, 2013.
[a] Simple average of the data for each country.
[b] The data for 2015 are projections.

The data reviewed by Weller (2007) indicate that there is no major difference between the amount of time that young people and adults spend looking for work. Yet, while young people as a whole do not have more difficulties in finding work than adults do, the same cannot be said for the younger members of that group, who account for a large percentage of persons seeking work for the first time and those who have the hardest time entering the labour market and finding quality jobs.

There are many other factors, apart from their youth, that influence young people's employment prospects; one of the most influential is the socioeconomic status of the household in which they grow up. As shown in table I.4, unemployment rates in the different countries tend to decline in the higher-income groups. The fact that these groups are also the ones that attain a higher level of education attests to the importance of education as a factor in promoting entry into the labour market and, as a corollary, reductions in the amount of time that people are unemployed and in the periods of economic inactivity of persons who encounter serious difficulties in finding employment (discouraged workers). At the regional level, it can be seen that the average unemployment rate for young people in the higher-income quintiles is just a third of the rate for those in the poorer quintiles —and, in some countries, there is as much as an eightfold difference (Costa Rica).

Table I.4
Latin America (18 countries): unemployment rates for persons between 15 and 29 years of age, by quintiles, around 2012 [a]

(Percentages)

Country	Quintile I	Quintile II	Quintile III	Quintile IV	Quintile V
Argentina [b]	28.8	18.3	14.3	9.3	4.6
Bolivia (Plurinational State of)	5.0	5.5	5.5	4.7	3.6
Brazil	23.9	16.3	9.8	6.2	5.5
Chile	39.9	18.2	14.2	8.2	7.3
Colombia	25.4	20.9	19.1	14.3	10.3
Costa Rica	36.9	21.5	11.5	10.0	4.3
Dominican Republic	32.2	17.5	12.7	9.6	6.6
Ecuador	14.4	11.5	9.3	9.2	5.3
El Salvador	15.1	13.4	10.1	9.2	5.4
Guatemala	1.2	2.6	3.4	3.4	3.8
Honduras	3.3	7.6	8.2	8.3	6.9
Mexico	10.6	7.8	8.1	7.1	4.4
Nicaragua	14.3	10.2	11.5	8.6	8.1
Panama	9.5	17.4	8.5	7.0	4.3
Peru	7.2	9.0	7.9	7.3	6.5
Paraguay	17.6	13.0	12.6	8.1	6.1
Uruguay	24.0	16.1	11.7	8.4	7.3
Venezuela (Bolivarian Republic of)	29.9	17.3	13.6	7.7	5.5
Latin America	**19.3**	**13.9**	**10.4**	**7.6**	**5.7**

Source: Economic Commission for Latin America and the Caribbean (ECLAC), on the basis of special tabulations of household surveys conducted in the respective countries.
[a] The data for the region corresponds to the simple average of the data for the countries.
[b] The data are for urban areas.

Most persons between the ages of 15 and 29 who work are employed as wage earners (79%), while a smaller percentage (19%) are independent or own-account workers. The breakdown for persons 30 years of age or more who are gainfully employed is less uneven: 56% and 37%, respectively (see figure I.11).[7] This pattern is widespread: as people grow older and gain more

---

[7] These are just the two largest categories.

work experience, they are more likely to become independent by either engaging in own-account work or by starting up a business of their own since, at that point, they know a great deal about their area of activity and about the suppliers and clients in that specific line of business. This has implications for the design of training programmes, inasmuch as, while encouraging young people to become entrepreneurs and helping them to develop the corresponding skills are important, this is not likely to have significant effects on a large scale, and these programmes should therefore be provided as a supplementary component of programmes designed to prepare young people for wage work.

Figure I.11
Latin America (18 countries): youth employment, around 2012 [a]
(Percentages)

A. Occupational status, by age group

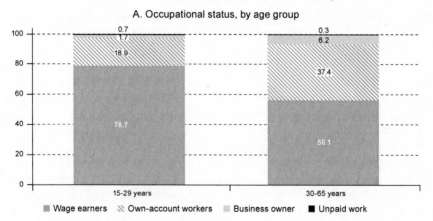

B. Branch of activity for persons between the ages of 15 and 29, by sex

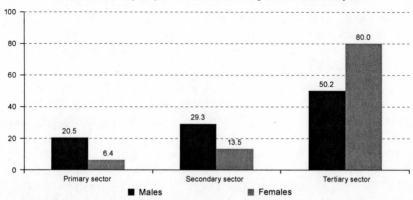

Source: Economic Commission for Latin America and the Caribbean (ECLAC), on the basis of special tabulations of household surveys conducted in the respective countries.
[a] Simple averages of the data for the countries.

The breakdown of youth employment by branch of economic activity shows that most young people are working in the tertiary sector, where most jobs have a high turnover rate. This situation does not appear to be attributable to the traits of the young people themselves but rather to the characteristics of these branches of activity (Pérez, 2007). As noted by Weller, the occupational structure for young people reflects a decline in the proportions of employment accounted for by the agricultural sector and the manufacturing sector (Weller, 2001 and 2003). This situation gives rise to a polarization of the tertiary structure with, on the one hand, a large number of highly productive and generally well-paid jobs (in financial services, business services, telecommunications, energy and social services) and, on the other, low-productivity jobs with low entry barriers (in informal commerce and certain kinds of personal services). Women with high and intermediate levels of education predominate in both segments.

The marked income gap between young people and adults is primarily due to the value of work experience. As is to be expected, the gap narrows as workers' age and experience increase (ECLAC/OIJ/IMJUVE, 2004). The youngest cohort (15-19 years) earn, on average, one third of the mean earnings of adults; people in the 20-24 year age group earn approximately half as much, and those in the next-oldest group (25-29 year) earn more than three fourths as much as their adult counterparts (see figure I.12.A). The data also indicate that the gap is considerably wider for men than for women. While this phenomenon has been studied extensively, there are two factors that warrant attention. The first is that there is no wage gap between the sexes when people are starting out on their working careers, but a gap then begins to appear and widens further as they grow older. This could be accounted for, in part, by the fact that women accumulate less work experience because they tend to shoulder greater workloads as caregivers and thus have less continuous work histories. Another factor appears to be that, even though women, as a group, attain higher educational levels than men, this does not translate into higher levels of labour income. This situation is attributable to the social and cultural patterns that are associated with gender-based wage discrimination.

Another approach to the analysis of this situation is to look at the association between labour income and level of education. Figure I.12.B depicts a correlation between the two variables: as workers become older, their incomes rise. There is a sharp change in the curve for people who complete their tertiary education, when income levels climb more steeply. This appears to be pointing to what is referred to as the "sheepskin effect" in the specialized literature, which refers to the increases in labour market earnings associated with the award of a degree or diploma or, in this case, the completion of tertiary education. In Latin America (18 countries), members of the employed labour force earn an average monthly wage of around

US$ 900 (at 2005 purchasing power parity values), which is more or less 30% more than young people's average monthly incomes (approximately US$ 640). An analysis of the different educational levels shows that people between the ages of 15 and 29 who have completed their primary education or have an incomplete primary education have an average income of less than US$ 430, whereas those who have completed their tertiary education have an average wage of over US$ 1,400 per month.

Figure I.12
**Latin America (18 countries): average monthly labour income
of the employed population, around 2013** [a]
(Purchasing power parity in 2005 dollars)

A. By age group and sex

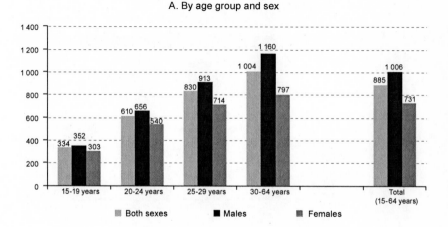

B. By age group and educational level

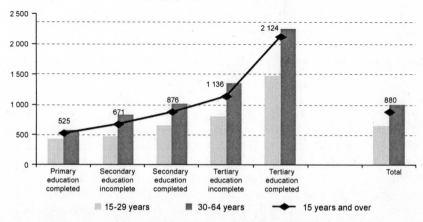

Source: Economic Commission for Latin America and the Caribbean (ECLAC), on the basis of special tabulations of household surveys conducted in the respective countries.
[a] Simple averages of the data for the countries.

As observed in other studies conducted by ECLAC and the Ibero-American Youth Organization (OIJ) (ECLAC/OIJ, 2004 and 2008), the presence of economically dependent young people in a household may place a burden on the family. If they are employed, they can contribute to the well-being of the family and help their households to avoid lapsing into poverty or to lift themselves out of poverty. The available evidence for 18 countries of the region indicates that the labour incomes of the youths in the household amounts to approximately 32% of the total and increases as they grow older, rising from 22.6% for the younger members to 40% for those in the 25-29 age bracket (see figure I.13). In addition, the percentage of total income provided by young heads of household is more or less the same as for adult-headed households (about 80%).

Figure I.13
Latin America (18 countries): percentage of household income accounted for by the labour income of young workers, by relationship [a]

(Percentages)

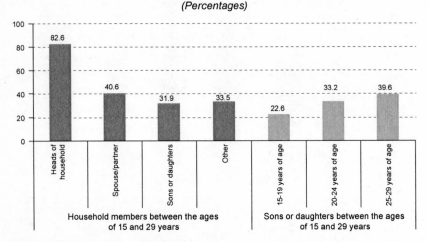

Source: Economic Commission for Latin America and the Caribbean (ECLAC), on the basis of special tabulations of household surveys conducted in the respective countries.
[a] Simple averages of the data for the countries.

The quality of the type of employment obtained by young people and adults do differ, as the majority of young people are employed in precarious jobs of one sort or another. One reflection of this is the percentage of young wage earners who are covered by the social security system. The young population, especially those who are under 20 years of age, have much less coverage that their older peers. While 27.5% of wage earners between the ages of 15 and 19 are covered by the social security system, the corresponding figure for adults is about 70% (see figure I.14). Coverage increases at the higher age brackets, which suggests that a large part of the young population that is employed but lacks social security coverage will only be without such protection temporarily (or will be working for a limited amount of time). This nonetheless clearly constitutes a form of discrimination against young workers (ECLAC, 2014b). The seriousness of this situation lies in the fact that this is a period in the life cycle during which contributions to social security systems are of particular importance given the effect on the length of time when such contributions will be accumulating and, hence, the returns on those funds.

Figure I.14
Latin America (18 countries): wage earners covered by the social security system, by age group, around 2012 [a]
(Percentages)

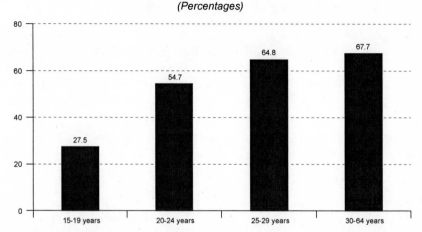

Source: Economic Commission for Latin America and the Caribbean (ECLAC), *Social Panorama of Latin America 2014* (LC/G.2635-P), Santiago, 2014.
[a] Simple averages of the data for the countries.

Young people's participation in the labour market therefore tends to be characterized by a high turnover rate, segmentation and precarious conditions. However, as noted by the Organization of Ibero-American States (OEI, 2012), many young people view this state of affairs as the "new normal" which, in some cases, meets their expectations in terms of the autonomy that they are seeking. The fact of the matter, however, is that today's labour market does not allow most young people to build career paths that give them upward mobility or establish stable employment relationships. According to the International Labour Organization (ILO), this situation poses a political challenge, since young people's aspirations to paid employment an independence are thwarted by a labour market in which unemployment is high and informality is commonplace (ILO, 2013a). In short, this picture of the situation on the ground reaffirms the view, as expressed in the ECLAC/OIJ/IMJUVE (2014) report, that employment is the most pivotal link in the chain of social inclusion for young people. Ten years ago, ECLAC and OIJ warned that, despite the fact that young people tend to be better able to adapt to organizational changes and new forms of communication than adults are, the major strides made in the region in the area of education had not translated into comparable changes in the area of employment (ECLAC/OIJ, 2004). In order for young people to have access to decent employment opportunities, quality job creation has to be expanded and has to be coupled with the provision of training to young people that will enable them to take advantage of that expansion (ECLAC/OIJ, 2008).

D.   Young people who are not attending school and are not in paid employment

It is estimated that approximately 30 million young people in Latin America (22% of the total) are not positioned within either of the main channels of social inclusion: the education system and the labour market. This not only puts them at a serious disadvantage, both now and in the future, in terms of their ability to remain or rise above the poverty line; it also brands them with a stigmatizing label ("not in education, employment or training" or "NEET").

The stigma associated with not being part of either the education system or the labour market has to do with the idea that young people in this position constitute an at-risk population that is prone to vagrancy, criminal behaviour and alcohol and drug abuse. The actual fact of the matter is that these young people are an extremely heterogeneous group; it is therefore necessary to shed light on the complexity and diversity of the people in that group and on the many different reasons why they are in their present position so that other paths for their integration into society can be identified.

As demonstrated in a recent ECLAC study (2014b), a majority of the young people who are not participating in either the educational system or the labour market are women (73.5%) and live in urban areas (63.5%), except in Guatemala and Honduras, where a majority of these young people live in rural zones. The differences between age groups are not large, but there are more people between the ages of 20 and 24 in this category (37.5%) than there are people between the ages of 25 and 29 (30.1%); this fact highlights the changing, transitory nature of this phenomenon. The gaps between income quintiles are more striking, since nearly 50% of the young people who are neither in school or employed are in the two lowest-income quintiles.[8]

More than half (55%) of the young people who are not studying and are not employed are engaged in unpaid domestic work and caregiving (see figure I.15). This observation shows up the existence of a gender distinction,

---

[8]   For more detailed information on young people who are neither in school nor employed, see ECLAC (2014).

since the great majority of young people engaged in these activities are women, and they devote far more time to these tasks than their male counterparts do.[9] The high future opportunity cost of this situation for these women should not be overlooked either, since their position makes them economically dependent on other people and hampers their entry into the labour market. Young men who leave the education system do not have to pay the same price, since they make up for their lack of formal education by amassing more work experience, on which the labour market places a fairly high value (Rico and Trucco, 2014).

Figure I.15
Latin America and the Caribbean (18 countries): activity status of persons between the ages of 15 and 29 who are neither in school nor employed, around 2012
(Percentages)

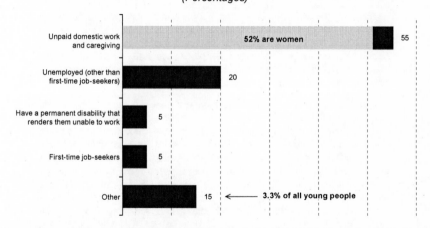

Source: Economic Commission for Latin America and the Caribbean (ECLAC), *Social Panorama of Latin America 2014* (LC/G.2635-P), Santiago, 2014.

As may be seen from the above figure, some 20% of the young people who are neither in school nor employed have worked before and are now looking for a job, while another 4.5% have left school and are seeking work for the first time. It is probable that this will be a temporary situation for these young people and that they will succeed in finding employment at some point in the future.

Another group of young people who are economically inactive and about whom awareness should be raised is made up of people with some sort of permanent disability that renders them unable to work and that often makes it impossible for them to study as well. Although the surveys that were used do not provide information on types of disability, the available information for 18 countries indicates that 5% of people between the ages of 15 and 29 who are neither in school nor employed are in this position (see box I.3).

---

[9]   For further information on this subject, see Rico and Trucco (2014).

Box I.3
Young people and disability

Young people with disabilities are among the poorest and most marginalized members of the youth population. They face the same challenges as the rest of their peers in gaining access to education, employment, health care and social services but, in their case, they are also faced with much more formidable challenges. The stigmatization and discrimination to which they are subject make it much more difficult for them to attend school, find work and participate fully in society.

As noted by ECLAC (2014b), until recently young persons with disabilities were hidden away and ridiculed and, in many cases, were victims of violence. Thanks to changes in the way disability is perceived and to the ratification of the Convention on the Rights of Persons with Disabilities by 23 countries of the region, the situation of persons with disabilities has improved somewhat, but much remains to be done.

Ensuring the participation of young people with disabilities in the education system and the labour market poses an important challenge for all the countries of the region. Recent estimates indicate that 6% of the population between 13 and 19 years of age, or 6.5 million people of secondary-school age, have at least one disability. A majority of these youths have a visual or hearing disability; learning difficulties are the next-most common disability.

Education is of fundamental importance in enabling these young people to realize their full potential. However, children with disabilities are less likely to attend school than other children and must overcome major hurdles in order to stay in school and progress through the various levels of education (WHO/World Bank, 2011). Information on the amount of time spent in attendance at centres of instruction by persons with disabilities between the ages of 13 and 18 in the region reveal marked differences across countries and by type of disability. Overall, however, the available information indicates that the average as of 2011 was no more than three years of studies in Latin America and only slightly more than that in the English-speaking Caribbean (ECLAC, 2013). Educational institutions are not as accessible as they should be, lack appropriate facilities and do not provide the necessary accommodations or aids for students with disabilities. Having inclusive, accessible schools is of fundamental importance in promoting social inclusion, acceptance and equality of opportunity in schools and colleges for young people with disabilities. Awareness-raising and training programmes are needed for teachers and other school and university staff, and the lack of such programmes often leads to the exclusion of students with disabilities from certain activities (WHO/World Bank, 2011).

Unless young people with disabilities can acquire the skills and capabilities they need in order to participate in the labour market, they will have very few chances of obtaining decent work and becoming independent. While low levels of educational achievement and a lack of skills may make them less competitive in the labour market, negative attitudes about disability and discrimination are the main obstacles that they face in finding a job. Negative ideas about persons with disabilities, mistaken beliefs on the part of employers —such as the idea that they are less productive than other workers, will require too much help or will tarnish the employer's image— or concerns about the initial costs of hiring persons with disabilities (e.g., the cost of building ramps) are

Box I.3 (concluded)

formidable barriers for young persons with disabilities who are looking for work, despite studies that demonstrate that persons with disabilities are just as productive and reliable as persons without disabilities and, in fact, tend to have lower absenteeism rates (Du Pont, 1993; Zadeck and Scott-Parker, 2003). The situation is even worse for young women with disabilities, since they must deal with prejudice and discrimination because of their disability and their gender. Even highly educated young women with disabilities take longer to find employment than their male counterparts (Roggero and others, 2005).

Latin America and the Caribbean (31 countries): distribution of the population with disabilities in the 13-19 age group, by type of disability, around 2010

(Percentages)

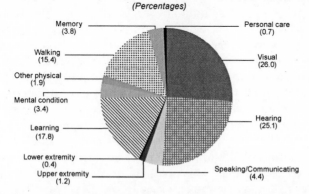

Memory (3.8)
Walking (15.4)
Other physical (1.9)
Mental condition (3.4)
Learning (17.8)
Lower extremity (0.4)
Upper extremity (1.2)
Personal care (0.7)
Visual (26.0)
Hearing (25.1)
Speaking/Communicating (4.4)

Source: Prepared by the authors on the basis of: Argentina (National Population, Household and Housing Census, 2010); Aruba (Population and Housing Census, 2010); Bahamas (Population and Housing Census, 2010); Bolivarian Republic of Venezuela (National Population and Housing Census, 2011); Cayman Islands (Population and Housing Census, 2010); Chile (Population and Housing Census, 2002); Costa Rica (National Population and Housing Census, 2011); Curaçao (Population and Housing Census, 2011); Dominican Republic (National Multi-Purpose Household Survey, 2013); Ecuador (Population and Housing Census, 2010); Grenada (Population and Housing Census, 2001); Mexico (National Household Income and Expenditure Survey (ENIGH), 2012); Panama (Population and Housing Census, 2010); Paraguay (preliminary results of the National Population and Housing Census, 2012); Peru (First National Specialized Survey on Disability, 2012); Saint Vincent and the Grenadines (Population and Housing Census, 2001); Suriname (Population and Housing Census, 2012).

So long as young persons with disabilities are discriminated against because they are different, are poor and/or socially isolated, face prejudice and ignorance and must cope with a lack of services and support, they will not be able to exercise their rights and live full lives. This situation, which blocks persons with disabilities from realizing their full creative and productive potential, not only has an adverse social and economic impact on the persons themselves and their families, but also has a high cost for society as a whole.

Source: Economic Commission for Latin America and the Caribbean (ECLAC), *Social Panorama of Latin America 2012* (LC/G.2557-P), Santiago, 2013; *Social Panorama of Latin America 2014* (LC/G.2635-P), Santiago, 2014; Du Pont, *Equal to the Task II: 1990 Du Pont Survey of Employment of People with Disabilities*, Wilmington, Du Pont de Nemours and Company, 1993; World Health Organization (WHO)/World Bank, *World Report on Disability, 2011* [online] http://www.who.int/disabilities/world_report/2011/report/en/; P. Roggero and others, *Employment & Youth with Disabilities: Sharing Knowledge and Practices*, Washington, D.C., World Bank, 2005; S. Zadeck and S. Scott-Parker, *Unlocking Potential: The New Disability Business Case*, London, Employers' Forum on Disability, 2003.

For another fairly large segment of the group of young people who are neither in school nor employed, however, there is no clear reason why they are in this position (denoted as "other" in figure I.15). This segment, which represents nearly 15% of the young people who are neither in school nor employed (some 4.8 million young people in Latin America and the Caribbean), is what ILO has called the "hard core" of social exclusion (OIT, 2013a).

These are the young people that existing strategies for bringing people into the education system or the labour market have thus far failed to reach, those who, for a variety of reasons, remain outside the main channels for the social inclusion of young people (ECLAC, 2014b). The existence of this hard-core group is thought to be largely attributable to the structural conditions associated with socioeconomically disadvantaged groups, but the presence of exclusionary, discriminatory social institutions that sideline anyone who does not meet certain expectations is another influential factor. As their educational and employment opportunities are cut short, these young people's chances of being embraced by society are diminished. This situation is compounded by the fact that these are also the people whose rights tend to be violated the most and who are the most prone to joining alternative, socially unaccepted organizations and groups. An analysis of this group indicates that, unlike the larger group of all those who are not in school and not employed, it is made up primarily of men (59.8%) living in urban areas (70.8%) who are between 15 and 19 years of age (49.1%) and are in the lowest-income quintiles (24.5%).

A more in-depth analysis points to other reasons why these young people are not participating in the education system or the labour market. The available information for nine Latin American countries (the Bolivarian Republic of Venezuela, Chile, the Dominican Republic, Ecuador, Honduras, Nicaragua, Panama, Peru and Uruguay) indicates that the young people in this hard-core group say that the main reason why they are not in school is because they are not interested in studying or do not think that it serves any purpose to be in school at their age (19.7%) (see figure I.16). These views would appear to be linked to a belief that secondary education is not beneficial and to an education system that is out of touch with the day-to-day lives of young people in the region (Rico and Trucco, 2014).

Another reason cited by the young people who were surveyed is that they have completed their schooling (16%) and do not wish to continue on with further studies. The people in this category feel that their position is a temporary one and that they will soon join the workforce (this situation will be analysed further later on in this chapter). Approximately 13% of the members of this hard-core group stated that they had difficulty paying for school and have therefore left the education system. This comes as no surprise, since nearly 50% of the young people in this group belong to one of the two lowest-income quintiles. It is therefore understandable that, since they were unable to pay their tuition, they have left school in order to look for a job and contribute to their household's economic upkeep. The problem is that they do not always succeed in obtaining paid work because of a lack of preparation or experience.

Figure I.16
Latin America and the Caribbean (11 countries): reasons why the young people in the "other" category are not attending school, around 2012

(Percentages)

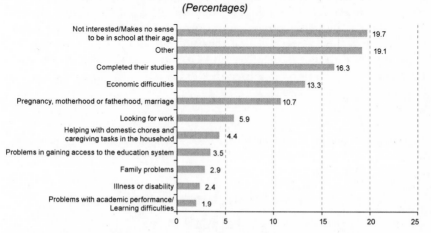

Source: Economic Commission for Latin America and the Caribbean (ECLAC), on the basis of special tabulations of household surveys conducted in the respective countries.

An additional reason for not attending an educational institution that was given by 10.7% of the survey respondents was pregnancy, motherhood or fatherhood. Latin America and the Caribbean is the region with the second-highest adolescent fertility rate, surpassed only by sub-Saharan Africa (Rodríguez, 2014), and the persistence of high rates of pregnancy (especially unwanted pregnancies) and births among adolescents is a public health issue for the region that is closely linked to a failure to uphold young people's reproductive rights and to social exclusion (ECLAC/OIJ, 2008). In many cases, this leads young people to leave school and thus helps to perpetuate poverty.

Finally, a cluster of unspecified reasons (categorized as "other") were given by around 19% of the economically inactive survey respondents who are not attending school, as were a series of reasons that were cited by fewer respondents, such as family problems; problems in gaining access to the school system; the need to help with domestic chores and caregiving for children, older adults or other persons; illness or disability; and learning or performance problems that made it necessary for the person to leave school.

With regard to employment, the available information for 10 countries of the region (the Bolivarian Republic of Venezuela, Chile, Colombia, the Dominican Republic, Ecuador, Honduras, Nicaragua, Panama, Peru and Uruguay) shows that 20.7% of survey respondents said that they had grown tired of looking for paid work. These young people have become discouraged about their future employment prospects and have not only been sidelined in the labour market but may also have difficulties in pursuing their studies or training programmes. This kind of situation has negative long-term implications, since persons in this position experience reductions in personal income and are stigmatized if they remain economically inactive or outside the workforce for a lengthy period of time (ILO, 2010). Along similar lines, 5.6% of the respondents said that they are not looking for work because they do not think that they have a chance of securing a job, either because they lack education or work experience or because of their age, sex or race (see figure I.17).

Figure I.17
Latin America and the Caribbean (10 countries): reasons for not seeking paid work cited by young people in the "other" category, around 2012
(Percentages)

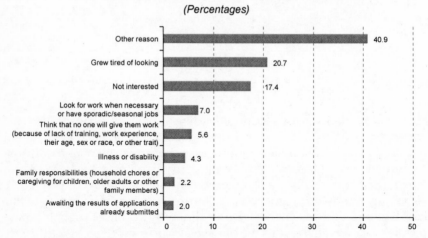

Source: Economic Commission for Latin America and the Caribbean (ECLAC), on the basis of special tabulations of household surveys conducted in the respective countries.

Another reason cited by 17.4% of the respondents was that they were not interested in working. Although no first-hand information on this aspect is available, this lack of interest might be attributable to the fact that many young people still live with their parents and, for the time being, have no wish to become independent. Some of these respondents may also constitute a hard-core group of persons who do not wish to be involved in social inclusion mechanisms and reject the system (whatever this is understood to mean); these people may instead choose to become part of alternative subcultures, some of which are connected with drug use, gang activity and criminal behaviour.

Finally, a full 40.9% of the respondents gave "another reason" for not being employed. This category includes a large number of different reasons that need to be taken into account in order to arrive at an understanding of this phenomenon, with the reasons cited ranging from poor working conditions and very low wages to having other sources of income (unemployment benefits, monthly allowances, profits or government transfers) or not having the papers needed to work (birth certificates and identification documents).

The situations described above place young people in an extremely difficult situation, since employment not only provides well-being and a regular source of income and, in some cases, access to health-care and social security systems, but also helps to give young people a sense of belonging insofar as they view their work as contributing to the collective good (ECLAC/OIJ, 2008). All of this creates a conducive environment for furthering interpersonal development, building self-esteem and enhancing mutual recognition between similar collectives —all of which play a key role in fostering social cohesion (ECLAC/OIJ, 2008). The fact that young job-seekers become discouraged and, even worse, believe that they will not be able to find a job should be regarded as a problem in terms of social inclusion, solidarity and trust among different social groups and as factors that hinder young people, especially those from low-income groups, from feeling like they are an important part of society.

There are nearly 4.8 million young people in the region who are neither in school nor employed, and part of the reason for this is demotivation and a lack of interest in studying or looking for work. In order to mount an effective, well-aimed effort to support young people and encourage them to continue their studies or to look for work, social inclusion strategies need to be designed in such a way as to address national and local sets of conditions and the living situations and specific life paths of the young people involved (ECLAC, 2014b). At the same time, efforts should be made to shape educational institutions and the labour market in ways that will be conducive to the entry of young people. This is the only way to craft policies that make sense to young people and that will enable the region to make headway in reducing the hard core of social exclusion.

E.   Policy recommendations

An examination of the wide range of policies and programmes relating to the youth population points up the need to develop and consolidate integral and integrated policy approaches for the young population of the region and to endow sectoral policies with a cross-cutting generational perspective

(ECLAC/UNFPA, 2012; Alvarado, Rodríguez and Vommaro, 2013; ECLAC/ OIJ/IMJUVE, 2014). Policies focusing on education and employment need to be more fully coordinated, not only so that they will be more effective, but also in order to ensure that they are aligned with young people's family life and the caregiving required by the dependent population.

In the analysis and design of integral policies in the areas of education and employment, consideration must be given to the institutional development that is so necessary in order to link these two spheres; in order to accomplish this, the various programmes' design, coordination and evaluation capacities will have to be strengthened and the institutions responsible for implementing those policies will need to become more open to comprehensive approaches to youth-related issues. There is also an urgent need to work to close the gaps that exist in education and the labour market on the basis of an approach that places priority on equality of rights and the protection of those rights based on the implementation of coordinated policies on education and training, employment, youth entrepreneurship, access to social security coverage and other aspects. The persons and agencies responsible for designing and implementing the policies and programmes focusing on these areas must also stand ready to hear the views and understand the needs and aspirations of young people regarding their own involvement and inclusion in society and to incorporate those elements into those policies and programmes.

A number of specific policy lines dealing with the areas addressed in this chapter are outlined in the following sections. These recommendations draw on normative concepts and good practices in various countries and initiatives.[10]

1.   Flexible, relevant educational and training services

In order to continue to provide more educational opportunities to young people in the region, the diversity of their life paths needs to be taken into account, and they need to be given the opportunity to continue their studies on a flexible basis. This is why it is important to offer an array of formal and non-formal forms of instruction that include non-traditional approaches that can be adapted to the specific situations of different groups of young people (e.g., those in remote rural areas and those in poor, marginalized areas). Non-discriminatory programmes need to be provided that will allow young people to both study and work, that will accommodate the special needs of different groups (e.g., young people with disabilities), that will reduce segregation and that will include compensatory mechanisms (scholarships, school meal programmes, conditional cash transfer programmes for young students), modules designed to encourage young people to stay in school

---

[10]   For a review of noteworthy experiences and programmes dealing with the social inclusion of young people, see Alvarado, Rodríguez and Vommaro (2013).

or to return to it if they have left, and measures that will allow students to reconcile their studies with the demands of caregiving and other roles (ECLAC/OIJ/IMJUVE, 2014).

The young people of today are the product of a society that, on the one hand, exalts them in advertisements, the media and consumerist publicity and, on the other, isolates and stigmatizes them. As a result, they increasingly tend to socialize among themselves without the presence or guidance of adults. Youth culture has a growing sense of its members' rights which, in the school context, translates into demands for better treatment and a different type of relationship with adults (and teachers, in particular). They are also demanding a type of education that makes sense to them, one that provides them with a sense of identity and belonging that links the youth culture to the wider society by means of a more meaningful and relevant learning process (Rico and Trucco, 2014). The relevance of what is being taught takes on special importance in rural areas, particularly for indigenous groups. Educational programmes should not only take the customs and world visions of these young people into consideration, as well as their daily lives, but also their own languages, and there is therefore a need for teachers who can speak and teach in indigenous languages and who, ideally, come from the same peoples as their students.

The linkages among the various educational and training subsystems also need to be improved so that, in addition to fitting in with the variety of life paths that young people are choosing today (including those involving early motherhood and fatherhood), institutions will be in place that can accommodate a suitable transition between training, technical education, vocational education and university programmes so that young people can continue or resume their studies in order to update their knowledge or to specialize in different areas throughout their lives.

A number of success stories or different types of successful initiatives can help to inform efforts to make formal education systems more flexible:

- Roving classrooms designed primarily to meet the needs of rural youths and to fit in with farm-work cycles by gearing the curricular demands of their programmes to those conditions by instituting weekend reading assignments or seasonally adjusted curricula. A single one of these roving classrooms or "mobile schools" can serve various areas.

- In areas with low population densities and widely scattered settlements, these roving classrooms or mobile schools can be combined with multi-grade or one-teacher schools (or schools with a few teachers) to meet the primary and especially secondary education needs of inhabitants of rural areas.

- Night schools, which have traditionally been designed to provide adult education programmes, can be revamped to include school-age students and can offer them concentrated (two or three years of study in one) programmes or extended programmes.

- Flexible education programmes geared to the needs of young people in situations of social vulnerability can be designed and implemented that will strengthen their students' bonds with the school community by means of programmatic and extra-programmatic activities (e.g., soccer clubs, reading groups, music workshops) and thereby provide alternative means for them to join or rejoin the wider society using the school (one of the institutions that has the greatest local presence in all the countries of the region) as a vehicle for their integration.

In respect of non-formal education systems and job training programmes:

- Training programmes can be diversified to meet the demands of the labour market more successfully and can be expanded to provide fuller coverage. One of the avenues for making progress in this direction is the strengthening of the institutional framework for the regulation and coordination of the various public training programmes so that better information tools can be developed for the coordinated planning of many different types of training modules to meet the needs of the labour market and provide coverage for all potential beneficiaries.

- Public-private partnerships can be leveraged to heighten the relevance of training programmes by ensuring that they are suited to existing and future production structures at the local level. This will allow the content of training curricula in each location to be aligned with the demands of local labour markets rather than providing content that is out of sync with students' employment prospects and with the needs of local production systems.

- In addition to the programmatic diversity of vocational training, programmes should be of varying lengths and should provide the options of studying during or after working hours (day programmes and night programmes). It is also a good idea to coordinate the different training programmes in a given area of specialization so that certain subjects can be applied to one or another programme (transferability of credits from one programme to another). This opens up the possibility for young people and adults to accumulate knowledge and training on an ongoing basis through regular attendance at such programmes.

- Employment skill certification programmes can be developed or strengthened and those certifications can be aligned with the programmes outlined above. This will make it possible to provide accreditation for on-the-job acquisition of specialized skills that will support employer recognition and improvements in the associated wage and non-wage benefits. These kinds of programmes will encourage additional, continuing specialization by young (and adult) workers.

National technical-vocational training systems also need to be strengthened:

- Technical-vocational education programmes can be developed or strengthened by reinforcing the underlying institutional structure composed of national agencies that provide, coordinate or regulate the technical instruction services provided at the secondary and post-secondary levels.

- Technical-vocational programmes should meet the present and future needs of national production systems, and in order to accomplish this, public-private partnerships must be in place and must undertake joint analyses of labour market needs and projections of future labour demand. This will set the scene for the appropriate planning of programme offerings in terms of programme content, programme diversity and the structuring of those services in terms of levels of specialization and the actual potential for the labour market's absorption of the persons graduating from those programmes.

- Just as in the case of training programmes, technical secondary, technical post-secondary, professional and tertiary (university) programmes need to be aligned so that young people (and adults) can continue their studies by entering compatible, interchangeable programmes that also offer accredited intermediate exit options. People should also be provided with ways to build up expertise without having to complete the requirements of an entire programme if they have already completed areas of specialization in previous programmes.

2. Facilitating the transition from education to more suitable, higher-quality jobs and promoting the formation of a legal and public policy framework that will provide young people with opportunities to obtain decent work and establish career paths

The links between the education system and the labour market should be reinforced through the introduction of more opportunities for technical and vocational training, especially for persons completing their secondary education (ECLAC, 2014b). Strategies are needed to increase young people's employability by providing them with education, training, skills-building opportunities, internships and apprenticeships, entrepreneurship programmes and own-account employment preparation programmes (ILO, 2013a). These kinds of initiatives should be designed to pull together these different sorts of educational and training programmes and align them with the different types of projected skill demands of the labour force, as mentioned earlier. Youth entrepreneurship programmes, the extent of their diversification and baseline analyses of the scope of their impact should all be evaluated as a basis for adjusting the programme curricula and improving the linkages between these programmes and other training programmes and the actual demands of the market.

Legal frameworks are also needed that will ensure the inclusion of young women, members of indigenous groups, persons of African descent and persons with disabilities, and that will underpin public policies to support these groups. Efforts need to be made to advocate for the recognition of the difficulties faced by young women in reconciling education and employment opportunities with motherhood and with domestic and caregiving responsibilities. As part of this effort, unpaid domestic work and the caregiving economy need to be recognized for what they are and included in policies to promote shared responsibility by men and women for these tasks and to advocate for a work-life balance for both sexes.

It is also very important to design programmes and incentives for sheltered employment positions for young people that provide social security coverage and health-care and unemployment benefits.

A number of specific recommendations relating to youth employment policies and programmes are set out below.

- The various initiatives undertaken as part of this effort should be subsumed under a consolidated, permanent institutional structure or, at the least, a coordinated structure that will avert the fragmentation that has long been a characteristic of the various employability, job creation, self-employment and entrepreneurship programmes and that will improve the working conditions, the formalization and the social protection afforded to young workers. Along these same lines, national youth employment plans should be drawn up within the framework of the explicit or implicit national development plans that governments put in place and should serve as a means of linking up and consolidating youth employment policies and strategies and of averting any dispersion or duplication of effort.

- Laws to promote decent work and employment for young people must be aligned with general laws on youth and with other labour laws. Legislation should also be drafted that will open up different opportunities for gaining work experience and experience in setting up business ventures, as well as other kinds of opportunities.

- Youth employment policies should be aligned with national macroeconomic and economic growth policies and with policies on education, labour and youth development, since the creation of jobs for young people and other groups often requires structural reforms in order to spur formal job creation and ensure that the education system provides young people with the skills that are in demand in the market.

- Employment programmes for disadvantaged young people should be modelled on comprehensive programmes; rather than being confined to training and job entry, they should also address psychosocial issues. This is because, in order for young people to become more employable, in addition to acquiring specific technical skills, they also need to improve the way they relate with those around them and particularly with employers, supervisors, co-workers and subordinates. This also includes the development of "soft skills" for the workplace, such as social skills, leadership, empathy and assertiveness.

- In order for youth employment programmes to have the necessary linkages, they have to be designed and implemented in such a way as to involve employers', workers' and youth organizations, the lead agencies in the field of youth employment, and the public and private sectors in general. Steps also have to be taken to strengthen the various mechanisms for consultation, feedback and social dialogue with these stakeholders during the formulation and operation of the programmes.

- Programmes to promote entrepreneurship and self-employment should provide the young people in these programmes with access to the various types of financial services, particularly loans, seed capital and credit guarantee schemes. Depending on the nature of the financial system, in some cases it may be necessary to create new financial products geared to the needs and activities of young entrepreneurs in order to help them consolidate their business ventures.

- Finally, policies, programmes and measures are needed to formalize existing informal forms of employment and to create new jobs in the formal sector for young people. These initiatives should include social protection mechanisms and means of upholding labour rights (for independent workers as well as employees). As part of this effort, measures for encouraging and assisting young people to obtain social security coverage should be put in place and steps should be taken to strengthen labour inspection systems.

3.   Promoting the creation of information systems to support evidence-based coordination between the education system and the labour market

Building institutional capacity is a more important task than ever before. Steps have to be taken to build capacity not only for arriving at accurate baseline analyses but also for monitoring the progress of young people taking part in the various educational programmes and those in the labour market. The region has made a great deal of headway in improving information systems that deal with the formal educational system and, to a lesser extent, its labour and social security monitoring mechanisms. However, in addition to the data needed in order to analyse the situation on the ground, information is required that can be used to project future labour-market requirements so that planning can be improved and so that educational institutions can be encouraged to offer course content that is in line with the current and future needs of the region's production systems. This is important not only as a way of responding to those demands but also as a means of closing the productivity gaps existing between different economic sectors. In order to forge suitable links between the education system and the labour market, inter-connected information systems are needed that can support a feedback loop between the two that can then be used to inform the design of inter-linked policies for these two sectors.

Bibliography

Alvarado, Sara Victoria, Ernesto Rodríguez and Pablo Vommaro (2013), *Informe CLACSO-UNESCO: Políticas de inclusión social de jóvenes en América Latina. Situación, desafíos y recomendaciones para la acción* [online] http://www.celaju.net/informe-unesco-clacso-politicas-publicas-de-juventud-e-inclusion-social-en-america-latina-y-el-caribe/.

Bornacelly, Iván (2013), "Educación técnica y tecnológica para la reducción de la desigualdad salarial y la pobreza", *Revista Desarrollo y Sociedad*, No. 71, Bogota, Universidad de los Andes.

Briasco, Irma (2008), "¿Hacia dónde va la educación técnico profesional en América Latina?", *Andamios*, No. 1, Buenos Aires, Fundación UOCRA, April-June.

Bucheli, Marisa (2006), "Mercado de trabajo juvenil: Situación y políticas", *Estudios y Perspectivas series*, No. 6 (LC/L.2642-P), Montevideo, ECLAC office in Montevideo.

Dávila, Oscar and Felipe Ghiardo (2005), "Trayectorias, transiciones y condiciones juveniles en Chile", *Revista Nueva Sociedad*, No. 200, November-December.

ECLAC (Economic Commission for Latin America and the Caribbean) (2014a), *Compacts for Equality: Towards a Sustainable Future* (LC/G.2586(SES.35/3)), Santiago.

____(2014b), *Social Panorama of Latin America 2014* (LC/G.2635-P), Santiago.

____(2012a), *Structural Change for Equality: An Integrated Approach to Development* (LC/G.2524(SES.34/3)), Santiago.

____(2012b), *Eslabones de la desigualdad. Heterogeneidad estructural, empleo y protección social* (LC/G.2539), Santiago, July.

___(2010a), *Time for Equality: closing gaps, opening trails* (LC/G.2432(SES.33/3)), Santiago.

___(2010b), *Social Panorama of Latin America*, 2010 (LC/G.2481-P), Santiago.

___(2004), *Social Panorama of Latin America*, 2004 (LC/G.2259-P), Santiago.

ECLAC/OIJ (Economic Commission for Latin America and the Caribbean/Ibero-American Youth Organization) (2008), *Juventud y cohesión social en Iberoamérica. Un modelo para armar* (LC/G.2391), Santiago, October.

___(2004), *La juventud en Iberoamérica. Tendencias y urgencias* (LC/L.2180), Santiago.

ECLAC/OIJ/IMJUVE (Economic Commission for Latin America and the Caribbean/Ibero-American Youth Organization/Mexican Youth Institute) (2014), *Invertir para transformar. La juventud como protagonista del desarrollo*, Santiago, October.

ECLAC/ILO (Economic Commission for Latin America and the Caribbean/International Labour Organization) (2012), "Youth employment: crisis and recovery", *The Employment Situation in Latin America and the Caribbean*, No. 7, Santiago, Chile, October.

ECLAC/UNESCO (Economic Commission for Latin America and the Caribbean/United Nations Educational, Scientific and Cultural Organization) (2009), "Impacto social y económico del analfabetismo: modelo de análisis y estudio piloto", *Project documents*, No. 299 (LC/W.299), Santiago.

ECLAC/UNFPA (Economic Commission for Latin America and the Caribbean/United Nations Population Fund) (2012), *Informe regional de población en América Latina y el Caribe 2011: Invertir en Juventud* (LC/G.2391), Santiago.

Feijoó, María del Carmen and Margarita Poggi (coords.) (2014), *Educación y políticas sociales: sinergias para la inclusión*, Buenos Aires, International Institute for Educational Planning (IIPE)- United Nations Educational, Scientific and Cultural Organization (UNESCO).

Filgueira, Carlos (1998), "Emancipación juvenil: Trayectorias y destinos" (LC/MVD/R.154.Rev.2), Montevideo, ECLAC office in Montevideo, June.

Fretwell, David (2004), "Enseñanza secundaria: Preparar a los jóvenes para el mercado del trabajo en la economía del conocimiento", *Las reformas de la enseñanza técnica y de la formación profesional en la economía del conocimiento*, Paris, International Centre of Pedagogical Studies (CIEP).

ILO (International Labour Organization) (n/d), "What is child labour", International Programme on the Elimination of Child Labour (IPEC) [online] http://www.ilo.org/ipec/facts/lang--en/index.htm.

___(2013a), *Trabajo decente y juventud en América Latina. Políticas para la acción*, Lima, ILO Regional Office for Latin America and the Caribbean.

___(2013b), 2013 *Labour Overview. Latin America and the Caribbean*, Lima, ILO Regional Office for Latin America and the Caribbean.

___(2010), "Youth employment in crisis. A background paper for the Informal Meeting of Ministers of Labour and Social Affairs during the 99th Session of the International Labour Conference", Geneva, 15 June.

ILO/OIJ (International Labour Organization/Ibero-American Youth Organization) (2014), "Trabajo decente para los jóvenes: El desafío de las políticas de mercado de trabajo en América Latina y el Caribe", *Boletín OIJ-OIT*.

Itzcovich, Gabriela (2014), "La expansión educativa en el nivel medio. América Latina, 2000-2010", *Cuadernos*, No. 19, Information System on Educational Trends in Latin America (SITEAL).

Llisterri, J. and others (2014), "Educación técnica y formación profesional en América Latina. El reto de la productividad", *Políticas Públicas y Transformación Productiva series*, No. 13, Development Bank of Latin America (CAF).

Martínez, Rodrigo, Daniela Trucco and Amalia Palma (2014), "El analfabetismo funcional en América Latina y el Caribe: Panorama y principales desafíos de política", *Políticas Sociales series*, No. 198 (LC/L.3841), Santiago, Economic Commission for Latin America and the Caribbean (ECLAC).

OAS (Organization of American States) (2012), "Estado del arte sobre empleo juvenil en América Latina y Europa", paper presented at the Intersectorial Meeting of Interchange and Programming "Inserción laboral de los jóvenes. Estrategias innovadoras para facilitar la transición escuela-trabajo".

OIJ/ECLAC/UNDP/UNFPA/UNESCO (Ibero-American Youth Organization/ Economic Commission for Latin America and the Caribbean/United Nations Development Programme/United Nations Population Fund/United Nations Educational, Scientific and Cultural Organization) (2012), *20 buenas prácticas en políticas públicas de juventud*, November.

Pérez, Pablo (2007), "El desempleo de los jóvenes en Argentina. Seis hipótesis en busca de una explicación", *Revista Estudios del Trabajo*, No. 34, Buenos Aires.

Rico, María Nieves and Daniela Trucco (2014), "Adolescentes: Derecho a la educación y al bienestar futuro", *Políticas Sociales serie*, No. 190 (LC/L.3791), Santiago, Economic Commission for Latin America and the Caribbean (ECLAC) [online], http:// www.unicef.org/lac/Adolescentes_derecho_educacion_bienestar_futuro.pdf.

Rodríguez V., Jorge (2014), "La reproducción en la adolescencia y sus desigualdades en América Latina. Introducción al análisis demográfico, con énfasis en el uso de microdatos censales de la ronda de 2010", *Project Document* (LC/W.605), Santiago, Commission for Latin America and the Caribbean (ECLAC).

UNESCO (United Nations Educational, Scientific and Cultural Organization) (2013a), "Regional progress toward Quality Education for All in Latin America and the Caribbean", *Education Post 2015*, No. 1, Santiago, October.

___(2013b), *The State of Education in Latin America and the Caribbean: Towards Education for All – 2015*, Santiago, UNESCO Regional Office for Education in Latin America and the Caribbean.

UNESCO/IESALC (United Nations Educational, Scientific and Cultural Organization/ International Institute on Higher Education in Latin America and the Caribbean) (2006), *Informe sobre la educación superior en América Latina y el Caribe 2000-2005. La metamorfosis de la educación superior*, Caracas.

Weller, Jürgen (2007), "Labour insertion of youth: characteristics, tension and challenges", *CEPAL Review*, No. 92 (LC/G.2339-P), Santiago, August.

___(2003), "La problemática inserción laboral de los y las jóvenes", *Macroeconomía del desarrollo series*, No. 28 (LC/L.2029-P), Santiago, Economic Commission for Latin America and the Caribbean (ECLAC).

___(2001), "Procesos de exclusión e inclusión laboral: La expansión del empleo en el sector terciario", *Macroeconomía del desarrollo series*, No. 6 (LC/L.1649-P), Santiago, Economic Commission for Latin America and the Caribbean (ECLAC).

Chapter II

Health and young people in Latin America and the Caribbean

Heidi Ullmann[1]

Introduction

Understanding and addressing the health needs of young people is crucial because health furthers capacity-building by facilitating school attendance and labour market integration, and thereby fosters social inclusion. And, as ECLAC has noted, social inclusion provides the progressive compliance and fulfilment of rights critical to attain many of the aspirations of a safe, healthy and prosperous society throughout the world, guaranteeing high levels of food and nutrition security, health and well-being (ECLAC, 2014a).

The concept of health has been defined and redefined over the years, going from the idea of absence of disease to a state of complete physical, mental and social well-being enshrined in the constitution of the World Health Organization (WHO) (WHO, 1948). Health is multidimensional in nature, in that it involves the individual in interaction with his or her sociocultural context. This conceptual definition has enabled a debate, not only on the definition of health but also on health-oriented policies and programmes.

[1] The author acknowledges contributions by Matías Salces, Sebastián Moller and Alicia Sánchez, as well as bibliographic support from Mirian Ramírez.

While disease and death rates tend to be lower among young people than among persons in other stages of life, the health risks they face associated with exogenous factors are higher. And many of the harmful health habits acquired in youth do not manifest as morbidity and mortality until years later (Maddaleno, Morello and Infante-Espíndola, 2003).

Health is strongly influenced by genetic factors, but economic and social environments play a substantial role in the development of diseases and in their identification and treatment. Poverty, inequality and social exclusion have a significant impact on the health of young people. In rich and poor countries alike, young people in situations of exclusion and low socioeconomic status (whether measured by income, by education or by other variables) have poorer health and higher mortality rates than more advantaged young people do. Moreover, the most unequal societies tend to have worse health indicators (Marmot and Wilkinson, 2006).

The main paradigm for understanding these socioeconomic inequalities is that of the social determinants of health. There is an extensive literature that explores the social determinants of a number of health conditions as well as analysing the relationship between socioeconomic status and health at the individual level. One example is the fundamental causes theory put forth by Link and Phelan (1995).

Research on the social determinants of health has emerged as a core public health focus, but much remains to be done to achieve the effective implementation of measures to reduce health inequities. The situation is particularly sensitive among adolescents and young people, since much of the research has focused on how the social determinants of health in early childhood impact adulthood, but do not consider the specifics of adolescence and youth as an important stage of the life cycle in modern society (Viner and others, 2012).

Most analyses of youth health suffer from two main limitations. On the one hand, health policies and programmes target either the adult population or children and adolescents. On the other hand, actions aimed at young people often focus on sexual and reproductive health. While it is true that teenage motherhood and sexually transmitted infections are extremely relevant issues for young people (especially among marginalized youth), this bias draws a cloak of invisibility over the issue of youth health from a broader and more holistic perspective. This invisibility leads to neglect not only of the health needs of young people but of their health rights as well.

In view of this, this chapter sets out to look at the health of young people in Latin America and the Caribbean, comparing it with the health of adults in the region and highlighting disparities within the youth population itself. Taking a social exclusion and inequality approach, this chapter begins with an overview of mortality and morbidity among young persons and then examines specific issues such as sexual and reproductive health, access to health insurance, licit and illicit drug abuse and mental health. It concludes with a review of health policies and recommendations for strengthening them.

A. Overview of youth health in Latin America and the Caribbean

1. What do young people in Latin America and the Caribbean die from?

Before answering this question, it should be noted that mortality rates among young people are lower than among adults and children (see figure II.1). In general, rates tend to fall during childhood and reach their lowest point at around 10 years of age. After that, the mortality rate gradually climbs until age 35 and then turns up more sharply. This pattern holds for both men and women, although men have higher mortality rates at all ages.

Figure II.1
Latin America and the Caribbean: specific mortality rates, by age and sex, 2010

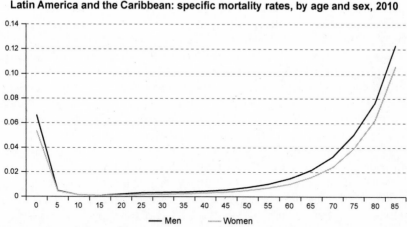

— Men   ⋯⋯ Women

Source: Latin American and Caribbean Demographic Centre (CELADE)-Population Division of ECLAC (2010), "Mortality", *Demographic Observatory*, No. 9 (LC/G.2490-P), Santiago.

In addition to having lower mortality rates than the adult population, this age range has specific causes of mortality that fall into particular patterns. As shown in figure II.2, injuries are the leading cause of death among young people (both men and women), meaning that most of them die from preventable causes. As people age, however, the proportion of deaths from injuries declines while the proportion due to non-communicable diseases rises, especially among women.

Figure II.2
**Latin America and the Caribbean (33 countries): cause-specific mortality,
by age group and sex, 2010**
(Percentages)

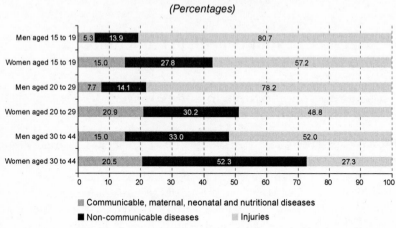

Source: Institute for Health Metrics and Evaluation [online] http://vizhub.healthdata.org/gbd-compare.

A look at deaths caused by injuries (see figure II.3) reveals differentiated patterns between men and women, and again between young people and adults. While violence is the leading cause of death due to injury for men, adults have a higher proportion of deaths from other types of injuries, such as unintentional injuries. By contrast, most deaths among women due to injuries are caused by exposure to the forces of nature, and this tendency increases with age. Lastly, road accidents are a major cause of death among both men and women of all ages. According to a Pan American Health Organization (PAHO) report, pedestrians, motorcyclists and cyclists are the most vulnerable and have the highest rate of fatal road injuries in most of the countries of Latin America (PAHO, 2015). Against this worrying backdrop, the PAHO Member States approved the *Road Safety Action Plan* to help the countries of the region achieve the goals for the Decade of Action for Road Safety —an initiative launched by the United Nations system in May 2011 to provide, among other things, advice and support on legislation, media campaigns, data collection and help for accident victims.

A significant new finding emerging from figure II.3 is the importance of the forces of nature as a cause of death. Hurricanes, floods and earthquakes occur frequently in Latin America and the Caribbean, with catastrophic impacts for persons living in countries with poor infrastructure —especially persons living in poverty and in precarious housing. The fact that men and women differ in terms of their vulnerability to the forces of nature has been documented worldwide (see, for example, Neumayer and Plümper, 2007; Nishikiori and others, 2006).

Figure II.3
**Latin America and the Caribbean (33 countries): deaths due to injuries,
by age group and sex, 2010**
(Percentages)

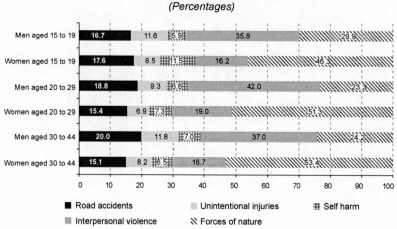

Source: Institute for Health Metrics and Evaluation [online] http://vizhub.healthdata.org/gbd-compare.

As Neumayer and Plümper (2007) note, biological and physiological differences between men and women may put the latter at a disadvantage in their immediate response to a disaster. Secondly, social norms may make women more vulnerable during natural disasters. For example, the traditional role of women as caregivers for children and older adults can limit their chances for escape. And in some countries it is more likely that women will be at home during natural disasters; if the housing is precarious (unlike men's workplaces), the impact of the disaster may be greater for women. Lastly, disasters may lead to a shortage of resources, making competition between individuals fiercer and exacerbating existing forms of gender discrimination.

2. Youth and morbidity: what diseases affect young people?

Although mortality is a reflection of the overall health status of young people in the region it is an incomplete metric, because it does not take into account diseases that limit life potential for persons in this stage of life but do not lead to death.

Another way to look at health is in terms of disability-adjusted life years (DALY). This metric has been the object of some strong, well-deserved criticism (see, for example, Anand and Hanson, 1997), especially with respect to its ethical and value-based underpinnings. Nonetheless, it is useful for synthetic conceptualization and measurement of the health of a given population and for identifying the causes that keep the population from enjoying full health. WHO defines a DALY as a year of healthy life lost; it reflects the impact of different risks on mortality and morbidity. The sum of DALYs in a population, that is, the disease burden, represents the gap between current health status and ideal health status for the population, where everyone lives into old age free of disease and disability.[2]

According to recent data (see table II.1), DALYs related to mental health account for much of the total burden of disease for the young. DALYs for women in the 15-19 age range show that mental health problems stand out among the diseases and conditions that contribute the most to the disease burden (unipolar depressive disorders, major depressive disorders and anxiety disorders). This pattern is slightly different for the 20-29 age group, but unipolar depressive disorders still rank first. For female adults aged 30 to 44, unipolar depressive disorders continue to account for a high proportion, but cardiovascular diseases, neoplasms and diabetes are the main contributors to the disease burden.

Table II.1
Latin America and the Caribbean (33 countries): main diseases and disorders contributing to the disease burden, by sex and age, 2010

Aged 15 to 19	
Men	Women
Violence	Unipolar depressive disorders
Exposure to forces of nature	Exposure to forces of nature
Road injuries	Major depressive disorders
Unintentional injuries	Anxiety disorders
Unipolar depressive disorders	Skin and subcutaneous diseases
Aged 20 to 29	
Men	Women
Violence	Unipolar depressive disorders
Exposure to forces of nature	Exposure to forces of nature
Road injuries	Major depressive disorders
Drug use disorders	Diabetes and urogenital and endocrine diseases
Unipolar depressive disorders	Anxiety disorders
Aged 30 to 44	
Men	Women
Violence	Cardiovascular and circulatory diseases
Exposure to forces of nature	Neoplasms
Road injuries	Diabetes and urogenital and endocrine diseases
HIV/AIDS and tuberculosis	Unipolar depressive disorders
Cardiovascular and circulatory diseases	Lower respiratory infections, meningitis and other common infectious diseases

Source: Institute for Health Metrics and Evaluation [online] http://vizhub.healthdata.org/gbd-compare.

---

[2]   For further information, see [online] http://www.who.int/healthinfo/global_burden_disease/metrics_daly/en.

In the case of men, violence, exposure to the forces of nature and road accidents are among the three major diseases and conditions that contribute to the DALY in all age brackets considered. These are followed by mental health disorders (unipolar depressive disorders, major depressive disorders and drug use disorders), which are found in a high proportion among youth. Meanwhile, major contributors to the disease burden among adult males are HIV/AIDS, tuberculosis and cardiovascular diseases.

Overall, injuries are the leading cause of death among young people in the region. Within this category, young men tend to die from violence, while young women are more likely to die from causes related to the forces of the nature. While injuries (violence in particular) are the leading cause of death in adult men, non-communicable diseases account for a third of the deaths in this group. For adult women, non-communicable diseases are the leading cause of death.

As for morbidity, non-communicable diseases (including mental health disorders) are what prevent the female youth of the region from enjoying full health. Mental health disorders contribute significantly to the burden of disease among young women; for adult women, the major causes are associated with chronic diseases. Injuries (specifically, those related to violence, exposure to the forces of nature and road accidents) are the leading contributors to the disease burden for men in the three age groups investigated. Violence is indeed a threat to the health of young people and adults in the region, as a cause of both death and morbidity, especially when it leads to permanent disability.

However, as will be seen below, there are substantial mortality and morbidity gaps according to socioeconomic level. Poverty, lack of education, overcrowding, poor nutrition, lack of water and sanitation and marginalization and discrimination not only influence the exposure of young people to pathogens —they also create a context of exclusion that may favour the development of or exacerbate mental health disorders or drug abuse. Moreover, social exclusion limits access to medical care, for both diagnosis and treatment of disease. In situations of exclusion, protective factors (such as a stable family life, strong links with school and positive role models) are particularly important for promoting healthy youth development and mitigating the impact of exclusion.

B.   Sexual and reproductive health inequalities among young women in the region

While an examination of mortality and morbidity provides an overview of the health status of youth in Latin America, health is not evenly distributed across the population. The region shows significant health disparities by area of residence (rural or urban), belonging to indigenous or Afro-descendent groups and socioeconomic status. Socioeconomic health gaps are clearly evident in sexual and reproductive health.

The reproductive risks faced by young people are cause for growing concern because of the consequences they entail for persons at this stage of life, for their future and for the future of their children. Adolescent pregnancy in particular has raised concerns at the regional level because of its substantial and wide-ranging negative impacts on the overall development of the women, men, children, families and societies involved. Even more troubling is the fact that, despite efforts to bring down teenage pregnancy rates, in many of the countries of the region this indicator has stagnated at high levels (Rodriguez, 2014). According to an Inter-American Development Bank (IDB) study (Näslund-Hadley and Binstock, 2011), the adolescent fertility rate in the region is higher than 80 per 1,000. This figure, surpassed only by Africa, is nearly 50% higher than the world average of 55 per 1,000 young women aged 15 to 19. Given the region's level of economic and social development and its stage in the demographic transition, these adolescent pregnancy rates are much higher than what would be expected (Guzmán and others, 2006).

Adolescent pregnancy is not only a demographic phenomenon, but a complex social one as well, with a negative impact on the region. ECLAC and the United Nations Children's Fund (UNICEF) have highlighted a number of social issues associated with early reproduction (ECLAC/UNICEF, 2007). For example, teenage motherhood can truncate educational attainment, change life plans and curtail the exercise of young mothers' rights. Moreover, it contributes to the intergenerational transmission of poverty through these and other channels.

If a young woman becomes pregnant because of lack of access to family planning methods, this is an attack on her sexual and reproductive rights. However, it is also problematic if a young woman becomes pregnant due to the lack of a life plan or because she has little or no opportunities to carry it out, since this reflects a number of inequities and structural challenges. Underlying this last point is the fact that "adolescent fertility" encompasses planned and unplanned pregnancies. Along these lines, Rodríguez (2012) identifies three groups that are vulnerable to early childbearing. The first is made up of young women in traditional groups, including indigenous peoples, where early childbearing is associated with early unions rooted in cultural practices. The second group comprises young women in low socioeconomic strata, particularly in urban areas, where high adolescent fertility rates are associated with the lack of alternatives and life projects, combined with the absence of public interventions aimed at preventing pregnancy. And, lastly, there are young women in higher socioeconomic strata who are aware of the risks of early motherhood but fail to prevent pregnancy because they lack access to or behaviour patterns for preventive methods.

There are different paths that can lead to adolescent pregnancy, but it occurs disproportionately among young women in lower socioeconomic strata, and adolescent fertility has historically been associated with poverty (Rodríguez, 2008). Regardless of the socioeconomic stratification measure used (place of residence, educational level or level of household wealth), there is an inverse relationship between adolescent fertility rates and socioeconomic status.

Figure II.4 shows the percentage of teenage mothers in seven countries in the region based on the most recent census rounds. Young women living in rural areas are consistently more likely to be teenage mothers than those living in urban areas. Within each zone, young women in the poorest income quintile have the highest percentages of teenage motherhood.

Figure II.4
Latin America (7 countries): women aged 15 to 19 who are mothers, according to socioeconomic quintile and area of residence
(Percentages)

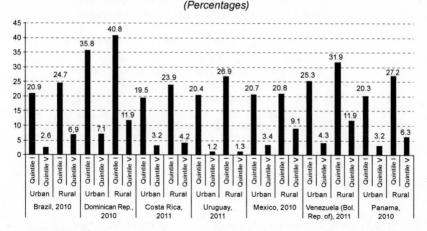

Source: Jorge Rodríguez, "La reproducción en la adolescencia y sus desigualdades en América Latina. Introducción al análisis demográfico, con énfasis en el uso de microdatos censales de la ronda de 2010", Santiago, Economic Commission for Latin America and the Caribbean (ECLAC).

One way to understand the relationship between socioeconomic status and adolescent pregnancy is by analysing the behaviours that affect the likelihood of becoming pregnant: differentiated behaviours lead to different risks of getting pregnant. The age of sexual initiation and contraceptive use are two variables that are directly related to the probability of getting pregnant; these behaviours vary widely according to socioeconomic level (measured here as wealth quintile).

Figure II.5 shows that age of sexual initiation is consistently earlier among young women in the lowest wealth quintile. Absent contraceptive use, this clearly puts them at risk of pregnancy. In some cases, the gap between young women in the lowest quintile and the highest quintile is as long as two years. The tendency of young women in higher socioeconomic strata to delay sexual initiation and avoid pregnancy could well be linked to life projects that include higher education or living in family environments that act as barriers to sexual initiation at younger ages (they are, for example, subject to greater parental supervision). Finally, research in the Caribbean has shown that having strong links with school is a factor that is closely associated with postponement of sexual initiation (Pilgrim and Blum, 2012).

Figure II.5
Latin America and the Caribbean (6 countries): age of sexual initiation among women aged 15 to 29, by wealth quintile

(Years)

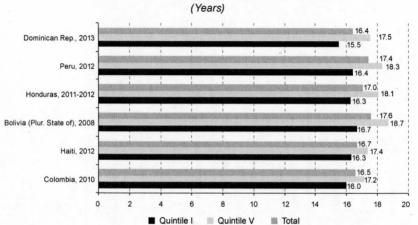

Source: Prepared by the author, on the basis of data from Demographic and Health Surveys of the respective countries.

There are also striking differences in condom use at last intercourse among young women by socioeconomic status (see figure II.6). In almost all cases, the percentage of young women in the wealthiest quintile who used a condom at last intercourse is at least twice the figure for poorer young women. This finding may be linked to lack of access to family planning methods such as condoms, power asymmetries between partners and, of course, differences in life plans. And, given that the use of condoms during last sexual intercourse is generally low, there are substantial differences between one country and another: 30.7% in Haiti versus 11.8% in Honduras. This clearly has implications not only for the likelihood of getting pregnant, but also for the risk of contracting a sexually transmitted infection, including HIV, which has a dynamic of its own related to the social exclusion of young people (see box II.1).

Figure II.6
Latin America and the Caribbean (5 countries): condom use at last intercourse
among sexually active women aged 15 to 29, by wealth quintile[a]
(Percentages)

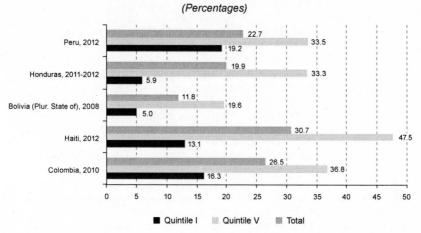

Source: Prepared by the author, on the basis of data from Demographic and Health Surveys of the respective countries.
[a] Sexually active is defined as having had sex in the four weeks prior to being surveyed.

Box II.1
Young people, HIV and social inclusion

One of the health goals set out in the 2030 Agenda for Sustainable Development is to end the human immunodeficiency virus (HIV) epidemic by 2030. Achieving this in Latin America requires focusing efforts on populations that have been on the sidelines of the response to HIV –specifically, young people.

Despite limited information about the HIV epidemic among young people, the available data paint an alarming picture. In Latin America, only 30% of young people correctly identify ways to prevent sexual transmission of HIV.[a] This shows the shortcomings of prevention services targeting this population as well as of comprehensive sexuality education programmes. And it is estimated that a third of new infections in Latin America occurs in young people aged 15 to 24, highlighting the vulnerability of this age group.[b]

Many unmet challenges remain for improving the response targeting young people. One of them has to do with the stigma and discrimination associated with HIV and the populations most at risk from the virus (men who have sex with men, transgender people, sex workers and drug users). A second challenge involves the need to overcome the lack of strategic information highlighting the impact of the HIV epidemic on young people. And young people participate very little in political decision-making concerning the response to HIV.

Making the issue even more serious are the social determinants of health that increase the risk and vulnerability of adolescents and young people to HIV. Poverty, social violence, ethnicity, age, gender (including sexual orientation and gender identity) and place of origin, among others, are factors determining the level of acceptance of and access to HIV prevention and care services.

Box II.1 (continued)

In Latin America and the Caribbean, population groups that are considered key to the epidemic and to the response are the ones most impacted by HIV. The youth segment of these populations is the most vulnerable to new infections. HIV prevalence among men aged under 25 who have sex with men is 7.3% in Chile, 8.8% in Ecuador, 4.1% in Honduras, 12.4% in Mexico, 13.1% in Paraguay and 10.5% in Peru.[c]

Under the Ministerial Declaration "Preventing through Education" adopted in Mexico City in August 2008, the Ministers of Health and Education of Latin America and the Caribbean pledged to achieve specific goals to respond to the HIV epidemic among young people and adolescents, by means of synergies between the ministries of health and education and civil society. By 2012 (four years after the declaration was adopted), the region's progress towards implementing the ministerial declaration stood at 58%.[d]

There are legal barriers to youth access to HIV and sexual and reproductive health services in the region. The age of consent for sexual relations is 14 in most of the countries, but in a number of countries minors need the consent of their parents or legal guardians for accessing certain sexual health services, including HIV testing. These regulations are contradictory because young people are more prone to unwanted pregnancies and to contracting sexually transmitted diseases, among other consequences.

As for gender gaps, about 70% of the young men who had more than one sexual partner in the last 12 months reported having used a condom during their last sexual intercourse. This figure drops to 43% among women aged 15 to 19 and 30% among women aged 20-24.[e] These data show how hard it is for young women to negotiate condom use, because of gender stereotypes and even because of violence. These low usage figures are compounded by the fact that only five of the countries of the region (Brazil, Colombia, Costa Rica, Ecuador and Mexico) provide for free distribution of the female condom.

To improve the social inclusion of young people living with HIV and those who belong to the population groups most affected by the epidemic in the national response to HIV, the following actions should be considered:

- increase the participation of adolescents and young people living with HIV and population groups most affected by the epidemic in political decision-making in response to HIV (this means regarding young people as partners and leaders rather than mere beneficiaries in formulating and implementing policies and programmes targeting HIV and sexual and reproductive health);

- boost investment in prevention and care programmes for young people, focusing on reaching adolescents and young people in key segments of the population;

- remove legal barriers that make it difficult for adolescents and young people to access HIV prevention and care and sexual and reproductive health services;

Box II.1 (concluded)

- expand existing social protection programmes to include adolescents and young people in the hardest-hit population groups and those living with HIV, so as to narrow the gap in access to prevention and care services (this includes promoting education and decent jobs for these population groups);
- enforce existing laws and policies against violence and discrimination based on HIV, sexual orientation and gender identity.

Source: Joint United Nations Programme on HIV/AIDS (UNAIDS).
[a] AIDSinfo Online Database, on the basis of Joint United Nations Programme on HIV/ AIDS (UNAIDS), *Global AIDS Response Progress Reporting 2013*, Geneva, 2013.
[b] Joint United Nations Programme on HIV/AIDS (UNAIDS), *The Gap Report 2014* [online] http://www.unaids.org/sites/default/files/en/media/unaids/contentassets/documents/ unaidspublication/2014/UNAIDS_Gap_report_en.pdf.
[c] Ibid., 1.
[d] International Planned Parenthood Federation (IPPF), *Evaluación de la Implementación de la Declaración Ministerial, Prevenir con Educación. Del acuerdo a la Acción: Avances en Latinoamérica y el Caribe*, 2012.
[e] Ibid., 1.

So, for two determining behaviours for adolescent pregnancy (sexual initiation and condom use), young women from lower socioeconomic strata consistently show behaviours that predispose them to pregnancy.

The differences in motherhood as an identity role for women provide another explanation for the childbearing gap among young women from different socioeconomic strata. From this perspective, adolescent pregnancy is the result of situations such as poverty, lack of motivation and school failure (often due to low-quality education), low expectations that completing education would lead to a well-paid job, little potential for social mobility and the absence of other life projects. In this context, motherhood is an avenue to activities, roles and responsibilities, and to inclusion and visibility in the young woman's family and community (Oviedo and García, 2011; Näslund-Hadley and Binstock, 2010).

Given the above, and as highlighted by Rico and Trucco (2014), the policy implications are different and should go beyond pregnancy prevention as a sexual and reproductive health education issue or one of contraceptive availability and use. While these are necessary for preventing early pregnancy, they are not sufficient: the situation calls for strategies that expand opportunities for young women and support them in achieving their goals.

Finally, as noted earlier in this section, traditional cultural practices of some groups, such as indigenous peoples, provide another take on teenage motherhood. As reported by ECLAC/PAHO (2011), indigenous women form a stable union and start reproduction at a stage of life that would be regarded as adolescence according to a Western timeline. Behaviours, experiences and the meaning of sexuality and pregnancy among indigenous youth are strongly determined by social and cultural norms. This cultural relativism adds complexity to the widespread notion that adolescent motherhood is a "problem".

C.   Access to health services

Another area of exclusion concerning youth health is limited access to health services. The fact that many young people in the region have no health insurance coverage (see figure II.7) may be linked to several factors. On the one hand, young people lose coverage under their parent's health insurance when they reach a certain age, and they underestimate their own need for medical care and health insurance because they perceive their risk of disease as low. In addition, young people's labour-market participation (in unstable, part-time jobs and in the informal market) does not provide access to health insurance. Although this pattern holds for the youth population overall, there are considerable gaps between young people from different economic strata. Because parental employment is a major route to health insurance coverage for young people, it is reasonable to think that young people in lower economic strata lack health insurance because their parents do as well. Besides the differences in health coverage, unequal access to the health care system may be due to a combination of barriers: economic, geographic, cultural and linguistic.

Young people who do have access may also feel alienated from the health system for a number of reasons. Health services might not provide the kind of care required because of a gap between supply of and demand for services or because services are not provided in an appropriate manner; because health workers might be prejudiced against young people or lack training for working with them; or because the lack of confidentiality may deter young people from seeking medical attention, especially where sexual and reproductive health and mental health are concerned.

Figure II.7
**Latin America and the Caribbean (4 countries): health coverage
among women aged 15 to 29, by wealth quintile**

(Percentages)

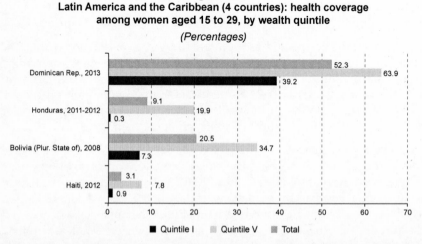

Source: Prepared by the author, on the basis of data from Demographic and Health Surveys of the respective countries.

Box II.2
Indigenous youth health in the region: a few figures

As noted throughout this chapter, exclusion, discrimination and marginalization create contexts that give rise to health problems. They also limit access to medical care, resulting in significant health gaps among young people according to socioeconomic status, race, ethnicity, sex, place of residence and sexual orientation. It is therefore crucial to shed light on these gaps and inequities.

Latin America has at least 10 million indigenous adolescents and young people aged 10 to 24, most of them in rural areas (ECLAC/PAHO, 2011)[a]. Indigenous young people in the region face inequalities linked to structural and proximal determinants of health. This makes them more vulnerable than non-indigenous youth (ECLAC/PAHO, 2011) —even more so for indigenous young women.

Chronic malnutrition (stunting) reflects the accumulation of consequences due to the lack of adequate food and nutrition during the most critical developmental years. It has significant short- and long-term consequences, such as impact on morbidity and mortality, as well as implications for educational achievement and productivity —the latter being one of the main mechanisms for the intergenerational transmission of poverty and inequality. For the age group of interest, presicely during their childbearing years, malnutrition may also have direct harmful effects on future generations. While this finding is not new, as Martínez and Palma (2014) have noted, there is a pressing need to develop more and better indicators to more clearly assess the relationship between ethnicity and malnutrition.

Chronic malnutrition among indigenous and non-indigenous women aged 15 to 29
(Percentages)

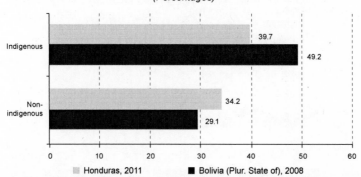

Source: Prepared by the author, on the basis of data from Demographic and Health Surveys of the respective countries.

As noted above, a strikingly high percentage of young people, indigenous or not, have no health insurance. Indigenous young women (even those with health insurance) face additional barriers to medical care: geographical inaccessibility (most of the supply of medical services, particularly specialties such as mental health, is centralized in urban areas) language barriers (when health workers do not speak their language) and cultural barriers (in view of the widespread underappreciation of traditional or non-Western health beliefs).

Box II.2 (continued)

**Lack of health coverage among indigenous and non-indigenous
women aged 15 to 29**
(Percentages)

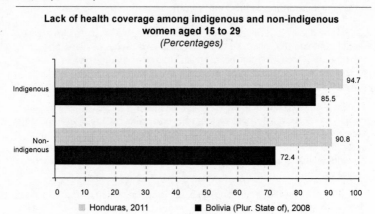

Source: Prepared by the author, on the basis of data from Demographic and Health Surveys of
the respective countries.

The sexual and reproductive health gaps between indigenous and non-indigenous young people have been well documented by numerous studies looking at different aspects of the issue. Patterns of sexual initiation, adolescent pregnancy, delivery care, maternal mortality and awareness of how HIV and other sexually transmitted infections are transmitted differ systematically between indigenous and non-indigenous young persons (ECLAC/ PAHO, 2011; Pasqualini and Llorens, 2010). For example, distorted or limited knowledge about HIV, added to the perception that it is a foreign disease having nothing to do with them, is particularly worrying in view of the increased migration of indigenous youth from the countryside to the city where HIV prevalence tends to be higher (ECLAC/ PAHO, 2011).

**Contraceptive use among indigenous and non-indigenous
women aged 15 to 29[a]**
(Percentages)

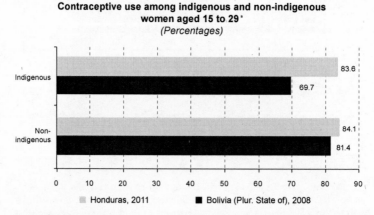

Source: Prepared by the author, on the basis of data from Demographic and Health Surveys of
the respective countries.
[a] Among non-pregnant women who have had sex in the past four weeks.

Box II.2 (concluded)

These figures confirm a tendency for health indicators among indigenous young women to be worse than among non-indigenous young women in terms of nutrition status, sexual and reproductive health and access to medical care. These gaps are far wider in the Plurinational State of Bolivia than in Honduras, pointing to differences between indigenous youth in the two countries and, possibly, between different indigenous peoples in each country. Understanding these nuances is crucial for designing better policies and programmes aimed at closing health gaps.

A major challenge in identifying health issues among indigenous youth is the lack of information and analyses. The aforementioned bias is even more pronounced in this population: although there are studies on sexual and reproductive health among indigenous youth, few take into consideration other health issues such as mental health (ECLAC/PAHO, 2011). As for statistics, although censuses include questions on ethnicity and race, they usually do not contain health questions. In the Demographic and Health Surveys that are the basis for the figures set out above, not all of the countries collect data on ethnicity, and those that do rely on language spoken instead of on self-identification.

Addressing these health gaps calls for health policies and programmes that (besides being tailored to the specific needs and realities of life of indigenous young people) value and respect the knowledge and contributions of traditional medicine (Rodríguez, 2012). However, because health is closely linked to other areas where indigenous young people are disadvantaged and excluded (such as education, housing and access to decent jobs), there is a need for coordinated action seeking social inclusion with a cross-cutting approach to ethnic and racial issues.

Source: Prepared by the author, on the basis of Economic Commission for Latin America and the Caribbean (ECLAC)/Pan American Health Organization (PAHO), "Salud de la población joven indígena en América Latina: un panorama general" (LC/R.2171), Santiago, 2011; R. Martínez and A. Palma, "Seguridad alimentaria y nutricional en cuatro países andinos: una propuesta de seguimiento y análisis", Políticas Sociales series, No. 187 (LC/L.3750), Santiago, ECLAC, 2014; D. Pasqualini and A. Llorens (comps.), Salud y bienestar de los adolescentes y jóvenes: una mirada integral, Buenos Aires, PAHO, 2010; and E. Rodríguez, "Salud pública, políticas sociales y desarrollo humano de adolescentes y jóvenes indígenas en América Latina: experiencias acumuladas y desafíos a encarar", 2012.

[a] This figure was calculated by adding the data available from the 2000 census round for 14 of the countries of the region: Argentina, Bolivarian Republic of Venezuela, Brazil, Chile, Costa Rica, Ecuador, Guatemala, Honduras, Mexico, Nicaragua, Panama, Paraguay, Peru and Plurinational State of Bolivia. The current count of indigenous young people surely exceeds this figure because, due to lack of data, it does not include indigenous youth in Colombia, the Dominican Republic or El Salvador.

D. Other youth health issues: drug use and mental health

As mentioned in section C, the approach to youth health is often a narrow one; this hinders a more holistic understanding of the issue and the design of policies and programmes that address these more complex realities. The nutritional status of young people (excess weight and other nutritional disorders), the problematic use of legal and illegal substances, mental health, chronic diseases (such as diabetes) and occupational health, among others, are issues about which comparatively little is known. This section provides an overview of mental health and the use of licit and illicit substances among young people. Both issues are part of the larger problem of social exclusion and inequality.

1.   Licit and illicit drug use

In the social imaginary, being young is associated with crisis: internal in trying to define and build an identity, and external in trying to find a place in the world. With regard to the latter, the notion of crisis in youth is also linked to differences between the young person's aspirations and the potential for achieving them offered by the society in which he or she lives (Pasqualini and Llorens, 2010).

In the health field, the tendency is to perceive youth as a time of risk and transgression (Krauskopf, 2000). This rather negative and limited view narrows the focus to specific problems that young people face. As a result, interventions target the individual and ignore the role of socioeconomic and sociocultural contexts in shaping these behaviours. Although this view has begun to change slightly, it persists in the area of licit and illicit drug use.

Although multiple factors (ranging from genetics to family and peer pressure to individual traits) can lead young people to substance abuse behaviours, this section puts forth that use of these substances is closely linked to sociocultural contexts and that use acquires meaning for users.[3]

Factors that trigger the onset of substance use are found at the individual level and in interpersonal relationships with peers. While drug addiction is regarded as psychopathological with strong organic roots in view of the level of dependence created in the body and the tension created on the will of the people involved (see Reith, 2004), prior to addiction come scenarios of exposure to use defined by culture and interpersonal relationships. In this context, identity construction processes play an important mediating role between young people and substance use. This influence is due, in part, to how the use of legal drugs is framed in the media, such as cinema, football and advertising.

Socially, precariousness and social exclusion have their own dynamic in the use and distribution of licit and illicit substances. Precarious and unstable conditions at home, life in the streets or bouncing back and forth between home, shelters, treatment and confinement centres and the street

---

[3]   Inappropriate or excessive consumption is understood to mean use involving potential harm to the health of the user or to his or her capacity for productive integration, self-esteem, family stability or defense of his or her community (Hopenhayn, de Rementería and Sunkel, 1999).

are especially risky scenarios for young people in terms of substance abuse and addiction. These sets of problems reinforce social exclusion (users are stigmatized as addicted, violent individuals on the margins of society) that is manifested not only in daily interactions but also in the health services that should care for them.

Legal and illegal drug abuse is a serious public health problem because of its extensive adverse effects at both a personal and a societal level. The use of legal drugs, such as tobacco and alcohol, has harmful organic health consequences that develop silently during youth but whose impacts become visible towards the end of this stage, at entry into adulthood or the onset of old age. The resulting organic problems may take many different forms but are often associated with liver disease in the case of alcohol and lung cancer and other respiratory diseases in the case of tobacco. The consequences of illicit drug abuse for the health of individuals are often linked with evolutionary psychology to drive a discourse pointing to the effects of illicit drug use on the neurological and cognitive development of children, adolescents and young people. Beyond the biological effects of illegal substances on the individual, another consequence of abusive consumption is that some young people with addictions are involved in substance distribution networks. They are thus exposed to scenarios of interpersonal violence and crime, adding another facet to the issue that will be addressed in chapter III. Substance abuse can also harm family and peer relationships.

Licit and illicit drug abuse among young people has significant direct and indirect costs for society as well. These can be summed up in years of productive life lost among young people with dependence, costs associated with the criminal justice system and health care and treatment costs. The cost of treatment for drug use is much lower than the health and social costs of dependence. According to estimates in the United States, every dollar invested in addiction treatment programmes yields a return of US$ 4 to US$ 7 just in reduced drug-related crimes, criminal justice costs and theft (National Institute on Drug Abuse, 2009). These "savings" come on top of significant savings for individuals as described in the preceding paragraph.

The lack of comparable data poses a major problem when discussing substance use among young people in Latin American and the Caribbean.[4] National youth surveys address the issue in detail and look at, for example, drug use by socioeconomic status and place of residence (urban or rural), but these surveys cannot be compared with each other. To provide an overview of what is happening at the regional level, this chapter uses data from the WHO Global School-Based Student Health Survey (2010a). This is a survey of middle- and high-school students using a standardized sampling process, a common

---

[4]   This problem arises not only in the analysis of drug use; overall, health data and statistics on this population group are scarce.

methodology and modules with standardized questions, thus facilitating comparisons across countries. The survey has the additional advantage of having been conducted in a number of countries in the region, including many in the Caribbean.[5] Although it does not allow for disaggregation by socioeconomic level, it is a useful source of information because substance use at these early ages can signal major problems with substances in the future that can, in turn, interfere with school or employment.

As seen in figure II.8, the data show that the prevalence of tobacco use varies across the countries of the region, from 4.9% in Anguilla to 25.5% in Argentina. Broadly speaking, prevalence tends to be higher in the four Latin American countries included in the study than in the Caribbean countries, although a significant percentage (24.6%) of students in Jamaica reported having smoked cigarettes recently. It is striking that cigarette initiation occurs at very early ages: most student smokers tried their first cigarette at age 14 or earlier (see figure II.9).

Figure II.8
Latin America and the Caribbean (15 countries): students who smoked cigarettes 1 or more days in the past 30 days
(Percentages)

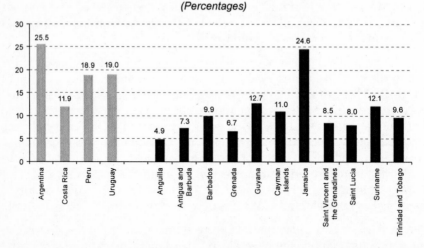

Source: World Health Organization (WHO), Global School-Based Student Health Survey, 2010 for Anguilla (2009), Antigua and Barbuda (2009), Argentina (2007), Barbados (2011), Cayman Islands (2007), Costa Rica (2009), Grenada (2008), Guyana (2010), Jamaica (2010), Peru (2010), Saint Lucia (2007), Saint Vincent and the Grenadines (2007), Suriname (2009), Trinidad and Tobago (2011), Uruguay (2006).

---

[5]   For more information about the survey see [online] http://www.who.int/chp/gshs/es/. The survey contains data from 18 countries in the region: Anguilla, Antigua and Barbuda, Argentina, Barbados, Cayman Islands, Costa Rica, Dominica, Grenada, Guatemala, Guyana, Jamaica, Montserrat, Peru, Saint Lucia, Saint Vincent and the Grenadines, Suriname, Trinidad and Tobago and Uruguay.

Figure II.9
**Latin America and the Caribbean (15 countries): student smokers
who tried their first cigarette at age 14 or earlier**

(Percentages)

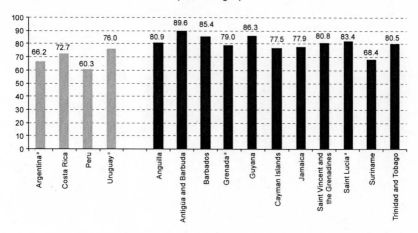

Source: World Health Organization (WHO), Global School-Based Student Health Survey, 2010 for Anguilla (2009), Antigua and Barbuda (2009), Argentina (2007), Barbados (2011), Cayman Islands (2007), Costa Rica (2009), Grenada (2008), Guyana (2010), Jamaica (2010), Peru (2010), Saint Lucia (2007), Saint Vincent and the Grenadines (2007), Suriname (2009), Trinidad and Tobago (2011), Uruguay (2006).
[a] Aged 13 or younger when tried cigarettes for the first time.

As with tobacco use, alcohol consumption varies among students across the region (see figure II.10). However, with few exceptions, the prevalence of alcohol consumption tops 30% —that is, 1 in 3 students reported having had at least 1 alcoholic drink in the last 30 days. This ranks alcohol as the substance most consumed by young people in this group of countries. As with cigarettes, alcohol initiation occurs at an early age (see figure II.11). Among students who have recently consumed alcohol, most had their first drink before age 14.

For cultural reasons, these data do not necessarily indicate a pattern of abuse, because many young people consume alcohol at an early age at home as part of a meal routine. However, when asked about consuming alcohol to the point of getting drunk, a high percentage of students respond in the affirmative (see figure II.12).

Figure II.13 shows the prevalence of illicit drug use among high-school students. The consumption of these substances tends to be higher among students in Caribbean countries than in Latin America.

Figure II.10
Latin America and the Caribbean (18 countries): students who have consumed at least 1 alcoholic drink 1 or more days in the last 30 days

(Percentages)

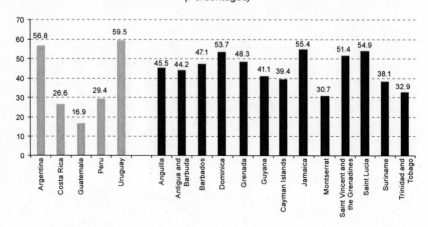

Source: World Health Organization (WHO), Global School-Based Student Health Survey, 2010 for Anguilla (2009), Antigua and Barbuda (2009), Argentina (2007), Barbados (2011), Cayman Islands (2007), Costa Rica (2009), Dominica (2009), Grenada (2008), Guatemala (2009), Guyana (2010), Jamaica (2010), Montserrat (2008), Peru (2010), Saint Lucia (2007), Saint Vincent and the Grenadines (2007), Suriname (2009), Trinidad and Tobago (2011), Uruguay (2006).

Figure II.11
Latin America and the Caribbean (11 countries): students who have consumed alcohol and had their first drink at age 14 or earlier

(Percentages)

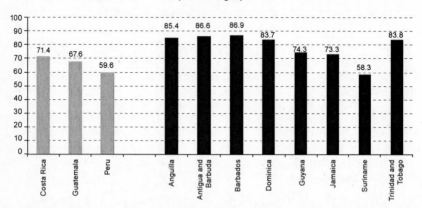

Source: World Health Organization (WHO), Global School-Based Student Health Survey, 2010 for Anguilla (2009), Antigua and Barbuda (2009), Barbados (2011), Costa Rica (2009), Dominica (2009), Guatemala (2009), Guyana (2010), Jamaica (2010), Peru (2010), Suriname (2009), Trinidad and Tobago (2011).

Figure II.12
Latin America and the Caribbean (18 countries): students who drank so much alcohol that they were drunk one or more times during their life

(Percentages)

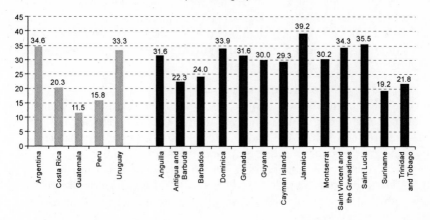

Source: World Health Organization (WHO), Global School-Based Student Health Survey, 2010 for Anguilla (2009), Antigua and Barbuda (2009), Argentina (2007), Barbados (2011), Cayman Islands (2007), Costa Rica (2009), Dominica (2009), Grenada (2008), Guatemala (2009), Guyana (2010), Jamaica (2010), Montserrat (2008), Peru (2010), Saint Lucia (2007), Saint Vincent and the Grenadines (2007), Suriname (2009), Trinidad and Tobago (2011), Uruguay (2006).

Figure II.13
Latin America and the Caribbean (15 countries): students who have used drugs such as marijuana, cocaine and ecstasy one or more times during their life

(Percentages)

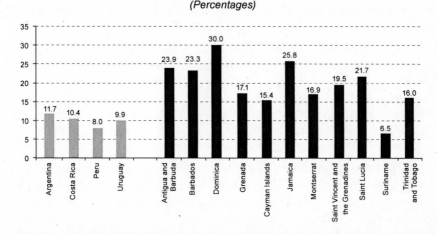

Source: World Health Organization (WHO), Global School-Based Student Health Survey, 2010 for Antigua and Barbuda (2009), Argentina (2007), Barbados (2011), Cayman Islands (2007), Costa Rica (2009), Dominica (2009), Grenada (2008), Jamaica (2010), Montserrat (2008), Peru (2010), Saint Lucia (2007), Saint Vincent and the Grenadines (2007), Suriname (2009), Trinidad and Tobago (2011), Uruguay (2006).

In short, both in Latin America and in the English-speaking Caribbean, alcohol consumption far exceeds tobacco and illicit drug use. In Latin America, tobacco use is more prevalent than illicit drug use; in the English-speaking Caribbean the opposite is true, with a higher percentage of students who report using drugs. Because the survey was conducted in schools and, by definition, does not include data on adolescents not attending school, it is reasonable to assume that the figures presented understate the prevalence of tobacco, alcohol and illicit drug use.

Young people who use tobacco or alcohol report having started at an early age, in most cases before turning 14. This suggests that prevention messages and public health initiatives against alcohol and tobacco use aimed at teens are coming too late. Finally, although these trends do not necessarily indicate abusive consumption, as already mentioned, many students admit to having drunk too much alcohol, which is worrying. The survey data do not allow for a more detailed analysis of the different kinds of illicit drug use: while it is true that all are harmful to some degree, their potential harmful effects do vary.

While the media and policy focus is on the problematic use of illicit substances among youth, particularly marijuana and cocaine (and their by-products, such as cocaine paste), the drugs most consumed by young people (and those that generate greater problems at this stage of life and for the future) are alcohol and tobacco. The fact that these are legal drugs does not make them less harmful; their victims include those whose own health is irreversibly affected and those who, under the influence of alcohol, are exposed to —and expose third parties to— risky situations such as unsafe sexual behaviour and driving under the influence of alcohol (ECLAC/OIJ, 2008).

Youth involvement in scenarios of violence (a subject that will be taken up in chapter III), overlaps with legal and illegal drug use. Alcohol consumption is linked to aggressive behaviour and violent crime (Parker and Auerhahn, 1998). Moreover, young people with illicit drug dependence may resort to theft and robbery to finance their addiction or engage in specific stages of production and distribution of illicit substances. This may expose them to violence as perpetrators or as victims.

The data used for this research cannot be disaggregated according to socioeconomic status. But the findings of national youth surveys conducted in the region yield data that provide an overview of some patterns. In countries as economically, socially and culturally diverse as Chile and Guatemala, young people from high strata are those who report greater illicit substances use (INJUV, 2013; SESC/CONJUVE/INE, 2011). This challenges the standard image of the poor and young drug addict and may be related to more income at the disposal of economically advantaged young people. However, youth drug use may be associated with different processes in different socioeconomic environments. In the case of young people from lower strata it may reflect a lack of opportunities, frustration with an education system that does not meet their needs or conflicts within the family. In addition, young people of low socioeconomic status with dependence on illicit substances have limited possibilities for access to treatment, making their addiction especially debilitating and problematic.

Substance abuse is both an effect and a cause of social exclusion. In the absence of protective factors, factors such as poverty, inequality, job opportunities relegated mainly to the informal market, the housing shortage, school models that do not always meet young people's needs and new family configurations can create contexts of vulnerability to substance abuse.

At the same time, young people with substance dependence are stigmatized and excluded, which has negative consequences for their health and for their chances of receiving appropriate treatment to overcome dependence. According to a number of studies in this field, there is a difference between interpersonal stigma and structural stigma (Hatzenbuehler and Link, 2014; Link and Phelan, 2014). Structural stigma is defined as "societal-level conditions, cultural norms and institutional policies that constrain opportunities, resources and wellbeing for stigmatized individuals or groups" (Hatzenbuehler and Link, 2014, p. 2). Stigmatization, then, is one factor that leads to social exclusion; its effects are legitimized by structural conditions.

2. Youth mental health: there is no health without mental health

Young people with mental health problems make up another group facing stigmatization. There is a strong relationship between mental health disorders and other health issues, and between mental health disorders and the more general problems related to youth development. Mental health problems are associated with school performance, substance use and abuse, violence and sexual and reproductive health. Therefore mental health has a significant impact on the development of young people and directly affects their ability to live a full life and achieve economic and social integration.

In Latin America and the Caribbean, there are few epidemiological studies of mental health among young people, and they are difficult to compare because of differences in measurement instruments, subject age range and periods covered. However, as shown by the disease burden analysis (see table II.1), mental health disorders are an important issue for young people, especially women in this age group.

Although women tend to have close relationships with more people than men do (Fuhrer and others, 1999), which is an important protective factor against mental health disorders, there is a differentiated pattern according to gender where these problems seem to affect women more than men. This finding is consistent with other international studies. For example, in a sample of 15 countries, Seedat and others (2009) report that women have a higher prevalence of internalizing disorders such as depression and anxiety, while men have more externalizing disorders such as substance abuse and antisocial behaviour.

The specific contributions of biological and psychosocial factors to mental health and the development of mental health problems in women and men are still unknown. Research on gender and mental health suggests that the experience of gender discrimination, concepts of masculinity and femininity, stressors and differentiated stress mitigation strategies, the social and economic vulnerability of women and the experience of gender violence have significant impact (Gaviria and Rondon, 2010). Bias in the diagnosis of mental health disorders can also be contributing to the greater prevalence of these problems among women.

Mental health disorders are also indirectly linked to other leading causes of the disease burden among young people. Some studies have shown, for example, that young people with mental health disorders are at greater risk of contracting HIV than those who do not have them (Donenberg and Pao, 2005). And there is a close link between mental health problems especially major depressive disorders and self-harm (Teti and others, 2014). Suicide is unquestionably the most serious manifestation of poor mental health.

Data on suicide rates should be interpreted with caution because such deaths may be attributed to other causes, either for cultural reasons or to avoid the stigma associated with suicide, among other reasons (WHO, 2002). Underreporting of suicides makes it more difficult to obtain reliable data on suicidal behaviours that do not have fatal outcomes. There is also a documented lack of data on suicide and mental health among certain subpopulations of young people, including indigenous youth and women (ECLAC/PAHO, 2011; Gaviria and Rondon, 2010). Despite these reporting difficulties, suicide does exist and is cause for concern among young Latin Americans because in some countries in the region it is trending up (Quinlan-Davidson and others, 2014).

Data from the Global School-Based Student Health Survey can be used to study how middle- and high-school students in the region think about and plan suicide. Young women report having considered suicide more often than men in all countries for which information is available (see figure II.14). While in some countries such as Montserrat and Peru the gap between men and women is striking, in others it is narrower (Jamaica and Saint Vincent and the Grenadines). Alarmingly, in nine countries in the region more than one in five young people reported having considered suicide; for six countries the figure rises to one in four.

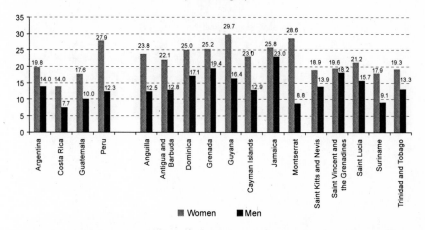

Figure II.14
Latin America and the Caribbean (17 countries): students who have considered suicide
(Percentages)

Source: World Health Organization (WHO) Global School-Based Student Health Survey, 2010 for Anguilla (2009), Antigua and Barbuda (2009), Argentina (2007), Barbados (2011), Cayman Islands (2007), Costa Rica (2009), Dominica (2009), Grenada (2008), Guyana (2010), Jamaica (2010), Montserrat (2008), Peru (2010), Saint Kitts and Nevis (2011), Saint Lucia (2007), Saint Vincent and the Grenadines (2007), Suriname (2009), Trinidad and Tobago (2011).

Even though the percentage of young people who report planning suicide tends to be slightly lower than the percentage of those who have considered carrying it out, the levels seen in many countries are still worrying (see figure II.15). Just like having suicidal thoughts, planning is, in most countries, higher among women than among men. These findings are consistent with studies showing that women attempt suicide and experience suicidal ideation more than men, even though suicide rates are higher for men (Teti and others, 2014).

Regardless of gender, mental health disorders have a significant impact on the potential for social inclusion of young people. As ECLAC notes (2014b), young people with mental illnesses may find it very challenging to complete their studies because of poor academic performance, discipline problems and poor attendance, which may ultimately result in their dropping out. This school trajectory leaves them ill-prepared to enter the labour market, with adverse effects for their employment situation later on. Mental health issues during adolescence and youth can also affect the development of sound and healthy relationships with peers, parents and others. It has been shown that mental health difficulties affect young people's self-esteem and social interaction and may even increase the chances of their injuring or harming themselves and others (Bradshaw, O'Brennan and McNeely, 2008).

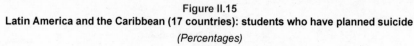

Figure II.15
Latin America and the Caribbean (17 countries): students who have planned suicide
(Percentages)

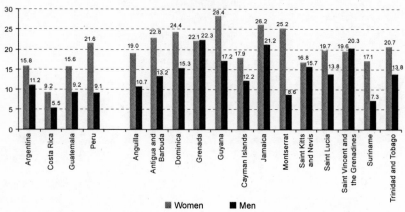

■ Women   ■ Men

Source: World Health Organization (WHO) Global School-Based Student Health Survey, 2010 for Anguilla (2009), Antigua and Barbuda (2009), Argentina (2007), Barbados (2011), Cayman Islands (2007), Costa Rica (2009), Dominica (2009), Grenada (2008), Guyana (2010), Jamaica (2010), Montserrat (2008), Peru (2010), Saint Kitts and Nevis (2011), Saint Lucia (2007), Saint Vincent and the Grenadines (2007), Suriname (2009), Trinidad and Tobago (2011).

The cause of mental health problems in youth is multifactorial. Poverty, working or living on the street and experiences such as bullying at school, traumatic events and conflict and post-conflict situations are major risk factors for the mental health of young people (UN, 2014). According to a WHO report on mental health and development (WHO, 2010b), there is a feedback relationship between vulnerability and mental health, which makes it more complex. And the relationship between poverty and mental health problems is a feedback loop as well: persons living in situations of poverty experience high levels of stress, trauma and social exclusion and have low levels of access to medical care. This exacerbates the risk and severity of mental health problems. It is also true that persons with mental health disorders may be more at risk of poverty due to poor education performance, poor labour-market participation, the high cost of medical care, stigma and social exclusion.

However, as highlighted by Patel and others (2007), most young people do not develop mental health disorders –not even those who face many adversities and multiple risk factors. This points to the importance of protective elements that mitigate the impact of risk factors and should be enhanced to promote mental health among young people. The sense of connection and belonging, social support and low levels of conflict are some of these protective elements (Patel and others, 2007). The family context is important too, because the support of parents is essential for building resilience in young people.

E. Policies and programmes: promoting a healthy life[6]

According to the most recent United Nations Population Fund (UNFPA) report, *State of World Population 2014*, the number of young people has reached a historical record (UNFPA, 2014). In Latin America and the Caribbean, young people account for more than 25% of the population (ECLAC/UNFPA, 2012). Enabling them to achieve their maximum potential to be the leaders of tomorrow calls for investing now in key areas for their development, such as health.

The region's young people are not a homogeneous group. As laid out in *Time for equality: closing gaps, opening trails* (ECLAC, 2010), the heterogeneity of situations, contexts and circumstances facing youth in Latin America must be acknowledged. Indeed, this chapter has identified very different health realities for young people from different socioeconomic strata.

As ECLAC has noted, democracy, development and exercise of rights all involve ensuring equal access to and resources for education, health, employment and social security, in order to address the immense social and economic inequalities that plague the region (ECLAC, 2010). Doing so calls for implementing policies aimed at reducing the vulnerability and social inequality that weigh on certain segments and social groups, such as young people. Ensuring equal access and resources will foster more proactive involvement in society and further the fulfilment of potentials and life projects (ECLAC, 2014c).

1. Health policies and programmes: an overview

Disease and death rates tend to be lower among young people than among persons in other stages of life, but their health risks associated with exogenous factors are higher. Their specific health needs are usually overlooked in conventional sector-based policies; many youth health policies do not target them specifically but rather lump young people and some segments of the young population together with other age groups.

Many health policies aimed at this population group are intersectoral because they are linked to schools. Providing preventive knowledge to stop or reduce unprotected sex and the use and abuse of legal and illegal drugs is the main axis for many social programmes, driven above all by education and health authorities. Such programmes focus especially on school-age young people who have not necessarily had sex or used any substance.

There are also more general policies promoted by health ministries that encompass the young population (see table II.2). Most of these policies take a comprehensive rights-based approach to health. Some explicitly target certain

---

[6] The review of health-related policies set out in this section is not an exhaustive compendium. It is based on a search of the websites of the ministries of health and education, as well as youth institutions, for countries with such policies in place.

health issues; some mention mental health, but none of them focus on it. These policies tend to refer to "health" generically. Many youth health programmes in the countries of the region are designed and implemented to promote universal access to health systems (see table II.2). They call for, among other things, respect for confidentiality, anonymity and proximity of services.

The fact that there are institutions more or less aimed at youth-related matters is no guarantee that they are putting in place comprehensive and inclusive policies to meet the needs of young people (ECLAC/UNFPA, 2012). There is no real access to public health system benefits. Contempt, inconvenient hours and burdensome requirements for obtaining medication or treatment are some of the obstacles to accessing medical services in the countries of the region (ECLAC/OIJ, 2008).

Regarding sexual and reproductive health (see table II.3), many of the programmes that seek to promote responsible sexuality among young people are informative in nature. They focus on conveying knowledge of the importance of condom use and the prevalence and modes of transmission of HIV and other sexually transmitted diseases and related issues. This kind of information is necessary, but knowledge alone will not lead to behaviours that can protect health. The use of contraceptives is a clear example: knowledge of contraceptive methods is almost universal in Latin America, but many young people neither access nor use them (ECLAC/OIJ, 2008). There is a need, then, for practical interventions providing access to contraception and to strategies for negotiating safer sex practices within couples.

As mentioned in another section, early motherhood is closely linked to young women's expectations, plans and opportunities. That is why pregnancy prevention policies need to be broader in scope, going beyond seeing it as a sexual and reproductive health education issue to address opportunities and social inclusion processes for young women so they can develop and carry out their life plans.

Along with prevention programmes, there is a need for programmes to help pregnant adolescents complete the education cycle. Pregnant adolescents and teenage mothers need a support network that encourages them to continue their studies, with comprehensive programmes that provide economic and care support, counseling and psychosocial care. And it is imperative to fight the discrimination faced by pregnant adolescents and teenage mothers in schools.

The factors that lead to problematic drug and alcohol use among young people are complex and interrelated, so preventing use requires a multidisciplinary approach that takes account of this complexity and encompasses the contexts and spaces where consumption begins. Overall, policies in the region (see table II.4) do not follow this approach but rather focus on the individual. They are mainly aimed at strengthening the capacity of young people to resist drug use, but not their environment.

Table II.2

Policies, programmes and projects: overall health and access

Country	Policy, programme, project	Responsible institution or agency	Status	Objective
Argentina	National Integral Adolescent Health Plan	Ministry of Health	Ongoing	Promote and disseminate the right of adolescents to have independent access to the health system, without requiring an accompanying parent or adult and in the framework of respect for confidentiality.
Argentina	Remediar programme (Cure)	Ministry of Health	Ongoing	Promote equity and ensure access to medicines for the population covered by the exclusive public health system.
Bolivia (Plurinational State of)	National Plan for Integrated Attention for Adolescents and Youth	Ministries of Health and Sports		Help to improve the health of adolescents and young people and promote the exercise of their rights by designing preventive and promotional cross-sector interventions in line with the guidelines of the National Development Plan and the Five-Year Plan for Youth; carry out comprehensive and differentiated actions targeting health care for adolescents and young people in the country, mobilizing public (national, department and local) and private resources under the Family Health and Intercultural Community Model (SAFCI).
Chile	National Programme for Comprehensive Care for Adolescents and Young People: Action Plan 2011-2020	Ministry of Health	Ongoing	Improve access to and the supply of services (differential, comprehensive or integrated) at the different levels of the health care system responding to the needs of young people.
Costa Rica	National Health Strategic Plan for Youth and Adolescents 2010-2018	Ministry of Health	Ongoing	Generate information on adolescent health; strengthen and consolidate the efforts of the National Health System to establish environments favourable to health and comprehensive development; implement comprehensive interinstitutional services with nationwide coverage; develop and strengthen programmes for training human resources in health and comprehensive care for adolescents; design social communication strategies that favour the construction of a social environment that is supportive of health.
Cuba	National Programme for the Integrated Health Care of Adolescents	Ministry of Public Health		Increase coverage and improve comprehensive care of adolescents with a gender approach, so as to help improve their quality of life, resizing the resources available in the National Health System with the active involvement of adolescents, families and the community as well as intersectoral cooperation.
Guatemala	Health Promotion and Education (PROEDUSA)	Ministry of Public Health and Social Assistance	Ongoing	Promote and develop health protection by means of community involvement and social mobilization, preventing disease through a healthy lifestyle.
Guatemala	Policy for Adolescent and Youth Health	Ministry of Public Health and Social Assistance	2003-2012	Appropriate and insert the health needs and demands of adolescents and young people within the framework of their culture, territory and capabilities, through human development and social capitalization aimed at self-managed sustainable development of their health and a culture of peace, democracy and poverty reduction with self-management capabilities.

Table II.2 (concluded)

Country	Policy, programme, project	Responsible institution or agency	Status	Objective
Honduras	National Programme for the Integral Care of Adolescents (PAIA)	Department of Health		Contribute to the comprehensive development of young people through interventions for health promotion, prevention, recovery and rehabilitation.
Mexico	*Jóvenes en Impulso* ("Youth in impetus") programme	Mexican Youth Institute (IMJUVE)	Ongoing	Involve young people in some kind of community practice or brigade with monthly financial support, for them to contribute to the development of, mainly, sports and recreational skills. There are four health-related brigades: one to encourage bicycle use, the sexual health brigade, the Move It and Lose It brigade and the health and first aid brigade.
Mexico	School and Health programme	Secretariat of Health; Under Secretary of Prevention and Health Promotion	2007-2012	Carry out intersectoral, proactive, integrated and effective interventions with elementary school children and young people in high school and higher education, teaching students how to control the causal determinants of and improve their health, and boost student achievement.
Panama	Comprehensive Child and Adolescent Health Programme	Ministry of Health	2008-2012	Monitor compliance with comprehensive care standards for children and adolescents in health facilities.
Peru	National Strategic Plan for Adolescent Health 2012-2021	Ministry of Health		Design and propose health policies and develop methodologies and tools that can facilitate monitoring and evaluation of health rights at the national, regional and local levels.
Dominican Republic	National Integrated Healthcare Programme for Adolescents (PRONAISA)	Ministry of Public Health	Ongoing	Provide comprehensive health care for young people in a timely, continuous and humane way, by promoting, protecting and maintaining physical, mental and social health to help reduce morbidity and mortality in this group.
Venezuela (Bolivarian Republic of)	National Integrated Care Programme for Children and Adolescents (PNANNA)	Ministry of People's Power for Health	Ongoing	Ensure universal access to quality health care for children and young people in an efficient, integrated and personalized manner by means of health promotion, prevention and recovery as appropriate for this age group; encourage active community participation in identifying priorities, allocating resources and promoting healthy lifestyles.
Uruguay	National Adolescent Health Programme	Ministry of Public Health	Ongoing	Promote the comprehensive health of adolescents and their families through integrated and coordinated promotion, protection, recovery and rehabilitation based on the principles of primary health care at the primary care level.

Source: Prepared by the author, on the basis of information from the respective countries and Ernesto Rodríguez, "Salud pública, políticas sociales y desarrollo humano de adolescentes y jóvenes indígenas en América Latina: Experiencias acumuladas y desafíos a encarar", 2012 [online], http://www.paho.org/derechoalaSSR/wp-content/uploads/Documentos/Salud-Publica-Politicas-Sociales-y-Desarrollo-Humano-de-Adolescentes-y-Jovenes-Indigenas-en-America-Latina.pdf.

Table II.3

Policies, programmes and projects: sexual and reproductive health

Country	Policy, programme, project	Responsible institution or agency	Status	Objective	Target population
Argentina	National Programme of Integral Sexual Education	Ministry of Education	Ongoing	Coordinate the design, implementation and evaluation of activities involving implementation, support and enhancement of the National Comprehensive Sex Education Programme in order to teach comprehensive sex education at all education levels.	Children and young people in the country's education system
Argentina	Plan for Reducing Maternal and Infant Mortality and Mortality in Women and Adolescents	Ministry of Health	Ongoing	Identify the main causes of death among women, adolescents and children, in order to take action; focus on management processes, human resources, inputs and infrastructure that may be an obstacle to timely, good service.	Women, young people and children in the public health system
Guatemala	National HIV/AIDS Programme	Ministry of Public Health and Social Assistance	Ongoing	Organize management, legalization, epidemiological research, training and planning processes to reduce the spread and slow the effects of acquired immunodeficiency syndrome (AIDS).	Sexually active young people and adults
Mexico	Sexual and Reproductive Health for Adolescents	Ministry of Health; Under Secretary for Prevention and Health Promotion	2007-2012	Contribute to the development and welfare of young people by improving their sexual and reproductive health and reducing unwanted pregnancies and sexually transmitted diseases. The strategy is based on the recognition of cultural and sexual diversity, gender relations, overcoming social inequality and promoting respect for and exercise of sexual and reproductive rights.	Children and young people attending schools registered by the program
Paraguay	National Programme on HIV/AIDS and Sexually-Transmitted Infections (STIs) (PRONASIDA)	Ministry of Public Health and Social Welfare		Guide the comprehensive, integrated and committed national response to HIV and sexually transmitted infections, and provide decentralized promotion, prevention and comprehensive care services in keeping with the principles of respect for human rights, fairness and universal access and the gender approach so as to slow the spread of the epidemic and improve the quality of life of people living with or affected by HIV and sexually transmitted infections.	Children, adolescents, young people and adults with HIV/AIDS

Source: Prepared by the author, on the basis of information from the respective countries.

Table II.4

Policies, programmes and projects: drugs

Country	Policy, programme, project	Responsible institution or agency	Status	Objective	Target population
Argentina	National Programme on Education and Prevention of Addiction and Drug Abuse	Ministry of Education	Ongoing	Promote the values and attitudes that strengthen the capacity of people to prevent addiction and drug abuse. Guide educational practices focused on discussion of the subject in schools.	Children and young people aged 13 to 17
Bolivia (Plurinational State of)	Prevention of Drug Abuse and Crime in the Department of Santa Cruz	United Nations Office on Drugs and Crime (UNODC), Autonomous Department of Santa Cruz-Department Secretariat of Education, Department Service of Education (SEDUCA) -Ministry of Education, Prefecture of the Department of Santa Cruz	2011-2013	Slow the growth of drug abuse and crime, promoting healthy lifestyles and enhancing protective factors in society through comprehensive, sustainable and broadly participatory intervention strategies in order to raise awareness and train and mobilize society against drug use.	Children and young people aged 10 to 24
Chile	Actitud, Activa tu Desarrollo ("Attitude, activate your development") programme	Chile Previene programme, National Service for Drug and Alcohol Consumption Prevention and Rehabilitation (SENDA)	2010	Promote the development of protective skills and competencies, creating a culture of prevention in school communities.	Children and young people aged 6 to 18
	Prevention, Detection and Early Intervention in Drug Use in Schools (PDEIT)	Institute on Alcohol and Drug Dependency (IAFA), Ministry of Health	Ongoing	Foster sustainable development of programmes and projects for prevention, detection and early intervention in schools, with an emphasis on promoting healthy lifestyles, preventing, resisting and discouraging the consumption of tobacco, alcohol and other drugs among children and young people.	Children and young people attending schools registered by the programme
Mexico	Action Programme for Addiction Prevention and Treatment	Ministry of Health; Undersecretary for Prevention and Health Promotion	2007-2012	Reduce use and abuse of and dependence on drugs and alcohol, as well as their impact in terms of disease and injury, not only among young people but also in their families and social environments. The goal is to reduce by 10% the prevalence of first consumption of illegal drugs among young people.	Young people aged 12 to 17 who are drug addicts or have ever tried drugs
Peru	"Promesa" Anti-Drug Brigades	Anti-Drug Directorate, Division for Preventing Illicit Drug Trafficking (DIVPTID), Ministry of the Interior and National Police of Peru		Foster active participation in the prevention of drug use and abuse, and expand knowledge in this regard.	Children and young people attending school

Source: Prepared by the author, on the basis of information from the respective countries.

Alcohol and tobacco are the substances most commonly used by young people, but few policies focus on their use, particularly in the case of cigarettes. In addition, because young people are an especially attractive target for the alcohol industry and tobacco companies, health policy must be combined with stringent regulation of these sectors.

As for young people who are already in a situation of drug dependence, some positions (driven above all by the media) take an alarmist approach, advocating a crusade against drugs and "drug addicts" (Hopenhayn and others, 2002). This approach is counterproductive. Young people who have an abusive relationship with drugs or alcohol are up against a difficult situation and need support, not stigmatization or discrimination. Again, there are few initiatives aimed at providing treatment for young people with dependence on these substances.

This reality is set in a context where policies for controlling illicit drugs are increasingly questioned and where the debate as to the need for more effective drug policy, focused on health and safety, is growing more intense by the day. This would require changing the approach and redirecting policies and resources to promote social and health interventions in order to reduce demand and seek alternatives to incarceration for drug-dependent offenders, casting aside punitive laws that have not been effective (OAS, 2014). According to recent data from the Organisation of American States (OAS, 2013), 12 countries in the region have decriminalized personal consumption or eased penalties for drug possession regarding marijuana. These initiatives have not increased consumption, and they have eased the burden on consumers and the court system.

2. Health policies and programmes: what could be improved?

This health policy summary reveals some gaps. The fact that many health programmes are linked to schools, although intuitive, is problematic because doing so excludes young people who are outside the education system, presicely the youth who face multiple challenges to achieving good health. Few policies include the population over 19 years of age —and even fewer encompass persons over 24. As Rodriguez (2011) points out, it would be ideal to implement public policies with a generational perspective that follow people throughout their life cycle. This is especially relevant for health, because health develops throughout life and each stage influences the next. This is obvious in the case of mental health: the problems young women face in this area continue into adulthood, when the prevalence of mental health disorders is also higher among women.

There is a shortage of programmes targeting mental health. Some research in the region has identified major shortfalls in the supply of mental health services and resources, both in terms of funding and in terms of skilled personnel for providing treatment (PAHO, 2009; Rodríguez, 2007 and 2010). In addition, the distribution of the few services that do exist is highly concentrated in urban areas. All this creates a gap in the treatment of mental health problems between those who need it and those who receive it; the gap is more acute among young people than among adults (Rodriguez, 2010). Moreover, some research has shown that the structure of mental health services does not meet the needs of young people with these problems, because the services offered are focused on serious but rare disorders (Belfer and Rohde, 2005).

As ECLAC (2014b) has noted, dealing with the needs of young people suffering from mental illnesses requires prevention and treatment strategies that reflect their true situation. Prevention needs to aim at universality to promote mental health in the youth population, with programmes targeted on populations at higher risk of developing these disorders. Initiatives that set out to promote capabilities such as emotional regulation, social skills and conflict resolution could be very helpful. Some prevention models are oriented specifically towards the family, school, the workplace or the community, while others target different levels simultaneously.

Another general observation regarding health policy aimed at young people is that the focus is on primary prevention (to reduce or eliminate the possibility that young people will adopt behaviours that can harm their health), with little in the way of secondary and tertiary prevention.[7] Even when there are treatment and rehabilitation programmes, economic and geographical accessibility and the fear of exclusion and stigmatization act as barriers to the use of these services by young people. Failure of young people themselves to recognize mental health or addiction problems also works against the use of mental health services and highlights the need to identify, destigmatize and raise awareness of this issue.

Finally, given the interrelationship between health issues (sexual and reproductive health, mental health and drug and alcohol abuse), policy proposals need to be more integrated. In addition to substantive content, the way in which information is transmitted must also fit the realities of young people. For example, social networks should be used to reinforce prevention messages and facilitate access to treatment and subsequent follow-up. Another strategy that some of the programmes use (and that can be effective) is the peer education model, where peers act as educators in sessions on health.

---

[7]   Primary prevention seeks to avoid the acquisition of a disease or disorder. Secondary prevention aims to detect a disease or disorder early on so as to prevent its progression, with a focus on vulnerable populations. Tertiary prevention includes measures aimed at treatment and rehabilitation of a disease or health issue.

This more holistic approach should also seek to strengthen protective factors in the lives of young people (especially those facing other conditions of exclusion) instead of just focusing on risk reduction. The idea is not to prefer one strategy to another; implemented as a whole they are more likely to result in a substantial decrease in behaviours that pose risks to the health of young people.

In order to create environments that promote good health status and facilitate social inclusion, it is important to provide knowledge and strategies that enable young people to make good decisions about their health. The emphasis is on the need to act on the risks and protective factors that arise where young people develop (family, school and community context).

3.   Recommendations

The observations set out above are summarized in the following recommendations geared towards enhancing policy responses so as to contribute to improving the health of young people in Latin America and the Caribbean.

Improve data and information on youth health in Latin America, in order to design evidence-based policies

As stressed throughout this chapter, data related to the health of young people are scarce, not only from the point of view of epidemiology, but also on use of and satisfaction with health care services. Without this information it is difficult to develop policies that respond to the health needs of youth, much less monitor and assess whether these policies have been successful. Although a number of countries in the region have conducted national youth surveys, if they are isolated instances that are not repeated over time it will be difficult to understand the evolving health of young people or monitor the impact of policies and programmes implemented to improve their health.[8]

Strengthen services targeting young people that are sensitive to cultural differences and stress confidentiality

Prevention, care and treatment services for young people should be tailored to their actual situation (their stage of psychoemotional development and their social, economic, cultural and family environment). And the focus should, obviously, be on the health issues that are most relevant for this population group. In providing these services, it is essential to respect the decision-making autonomy of young people and ensure confidentiality.

---

[8]   For further information, see [online] http://www.celaju.net/herramientas-de-trabajo/encuestas-nacionales-de-juventud/.

Make policies more intersectoral

Despite the close links between the health and education sectors, other sectors can also be involved in promoting youth health. Closer institutional coordination at the national and local level between authorities responsible for youth and those who develop programmes and projects that directly or indirectly concern the youth sector (such as education, health, safety and employment) should be fostered. This way, "youth policies" would reinforce each other instead of being just a list of sector-based policies.

Boost resources for promoting youth health

As the region's population ages, public resources will be allocated to meet the needs of the older population to the detriment of other age groups, especially in the health sector (Rossel, 2013). This, and the fact that there will be proportionately fewer young people in the future, calls for investments that enable young people to fully contribute to the economic and social development of their communities and countries. This does not just mean investing financial resources, but also ensuring that health personnel are trained to work with young people.

Bibliography

Anand, Sudhir and Kara Hanson (1997), "Disability-adjusted life years: a critical perspective", *Journal of Health Economics*, vol. 16, No. 6, Amsterdam, Elsevier.

Belfer, Myron Lowell and Luis Augusto Rohde (2005), "Child and adolescent mental health in Latin America and the Caribbean: problems, progress, and policy research", *Pan American Journal of Public Health*, vol. 18, No. 4/5.

Bradshaw, Catherine P., Lindsey M. O'Brennan and Clea A. McNeely (2008), "Core competencies and the prevention of school failure and early school leaving", *New Directions for Child and Adolescent Development*, vol. 2008, No. 122, Wiley.

Donenberg, Geri R. and Maryland Pao (2005), "Youths and HIV/AIDS: psychiatry's role in a changing epidemic", *Journal of the American Academy of Child & Adolescent Psychiatry*, vol. 44, No. 8.

ECLAC (Economic Commission for Latin America and the Caribbean) (2014a), *Preliminary Reflections on Latin America and the Caribbean in the Post-2015 Development Agenda Based on the Trilogy of Equality* (LC/L.3843), Santiago.

___(2014b), *Social Panorama of Latin America 2014* (LC/G.2635-P), Santiago.

___(2014c), *Compacts for Equality: Towards a Sustainable Future* (LC/G.2586(SES.35/3)), Santiago.

___(2010), *Time for equality: closing gaps, opening trails* (LC/G.2432(SES.33/3)), Santiago.

ECLAC/CELADE (Economic Commission for Latin America and the Caribbean/ Latin American and Caribbean Demographic Centre-Population Division) (2010), "Mortality", *Demographic Observatory*, No. 9 (LC/G.2490-P), Santiago.

ECLAC/OIJ (Economic Commission for Latin America and the Caribbean/Ibero-American Youth Organization) (2008), *Juventud y cohesión social en Iberoamérica. Un modelo para armar* (LC/G.2391), Santiago.

ECLAC/PAHO (Economic Commission for Latin America and the Caribbean/Pan American Health Organization) (2011), "Salud de la población joven indígena en América Latina: un panorama general" (LC/R.2171), Santiago.

ECLAC/UNFPA (Economic Commission for Latin America and the Caribbean/United Nations Population Fund) (2012), *Informe regional de población en América Latina y el Caribe 2011: Invertir en Juventud* (LC/G.2391), Santiago.

ECLAC/UNICEF (Economic Commission for Latin America and the Caribbean/United Nations Children's Fund) (2007), "Teenage motherhood in Latin America and the Caribbean: trends, problems and challenges", *Challenges. Newsletter on Progress towards the Millennium Development Goals*, No. 4 [online] http://repositorio.cepal.org/bitstream/handle/11362/36002/desafios_4_eng_Final_en.pdf?sequence=1.

Fuhrer, Rebecca and others (1999), "Gender, social relations and mental health: prospective findings from an occupational cohort (Whitehall II study)", *Social Science & Medicine*, vol. 48, No. 1, Amsterdam, Elsevier.

Gaviria, Silvia and Marta B. Rondon (2010), "Some considerations on women's mental health in Latin America and the Caribbean", *International Review of Psychiatry*, vol. 22, No. 4.

Guzmán, José Miguel and others (2006), "The demography of Latin America and the Caribbean since 1950", *Population*, vol. 61.

Hatzenbuehler, Mark L. and Bruce G. Link (2014), "Introduction to the special issue on structural stigma and health", *Social Science & Medicine*, vol. 10 [online], http://dx.doi.org/10.1016/j.socscimed.2013.12.017.

Hopenhayn, Martin, Iban de Rementería and Guillermo Sunkel (1999), "Criterios básicos para una política de prevención y tratamiento de drogas en Chile", *Políticas Sociales series*, No. 34 (LC/L.1247-P), Santiago, Economic Commission for Latin America and the Caribbean (ECLAC).

Hopenhayn, Martín and others (2002), "Prevenir en drogas: enfoques integrales y contextos culturales para alimentar buenas prácticas", *Políticas Sociales series*, No. 61 (LC/L.1789-P) Santiago, Economic Commission for Latin America and the Caribbean (ECLAC).

INJUV (National Institute for Youth) (2013), *7ma Encuesta Nacional de Juventud 2012*, Santiago.

Institute for Health Metrics and Evaluation [online] http://vizhub.healthdata.org/gbd-compare.

Krauskopf, Dina (2000), *Participación social y desarrollo en la adolescencia*, San Jose, United Nations Population Fund (UNFPA).

Link, Bruce G. and Jo Phelan (2014) "Stigma power", *Social Science & Medicine*, vol. 103 [online] http://dx.doi.org/10.1016/j.socscimed.2013.07.035.

___(1995), "Social conditions as fundamental causes of disease", *Journal of Health and Social Behavior*, vol. 35, American Sociological Association.

Maddaleno, Matilde, Paola Morello and Francisca Infante-Espínola (2003), "Salud y desarrollo de adolescentes y jóvenes en Latinoamérica y el Caribe: desafíos para la próxima década", *Salud Pública de México*, vol. 45, Cuernavaca, National Public Health Institute.

Marmot, Michael and Richard G. Wilkinson (2006), *Social Determinants of Health*, New York, Oxford University Press.

Martínez, Rodrigo and Amalia Palma (2014), "Seguridad alimentaria y nutricional en cuatro países andinos: una propuesta de seguimiento y análisis", *Políticas Sociales series*, No. 187 (LC/L.3750), Santiago, Economic Commission for Latin America and the Caribbean (ECLAC).

Näslund-Hadley, Emma and Georgina Binstock (2011), "El fracaso educativo: embarazos para no ir a clases", *Technical Notes*, No. IDB-TN-281, Washington, D.C., Inter-American Development Bank (IDB).

____(2010), "The miseducation of Latin American girls: poor schooling makes pregnancy a rational choice", *Technical Notes*, No. IDB-TN-204, Washington, D.C., Inter-American Development Bank (IDB).

National Institute on Drug Abuse (2009), *Principles of Drug Addiction Treatment: A Research-Based Guide*, second edition.

Neumayer, Eric and Thomas Plümper (2007), "The gendered nature of natural disasters: the impact of catastrophic events on the gender gap in life expectancy, 1981-2002", *Annals of the Association of American Geographers*, vol. 97, No. 3.

Nishikiori, Nobuyuki and others (2006), "Who died as a result of the tsunami? Risk factors of mortality among internally displaced persons in Sri Lanka: a retrospective cohort analysis", *BMC Public Health*, vol. No. 6.

OAS (Organization of American States) (2014), *The OAS Drug Report: 16 Months of Debates and Consensus*, Washington, D.C.

____(2013), *The Drug Problems in the Americas*, Washington, D.C.

Oviedo, Myriam and María Cristina García (2011), "El embarazo en situación de adolescencia: Una impostura en la subjetividad femenina", *Revista Latinoamericana de Ciencias Sociales, Niñez y Juventud*, vol. 9, No. 2.

PAHO (Pan American Health Organization) (2015), *Global Status Report on Road Safety 2015*, Washington, D.C. [online] file:///C:/Users/Andrea/Downloads/9789241565066_eng.pdf.

____(2010), *Salud sexual y reproductiva y VIH de los jóvenes y adolescentes indígenas en Bolivia, Ecuador, Guatemala, Nicaragua y Perú*, Washington, D.C.

____(2009), "WHO-AIMS Country Reports" [online] http://new.paho.org/hq/index.php?option=com_content&task=view&id=445&Itemid=1106&lang=en y http://www.who.int/mental_health/who_aims_country_reports/en/index.html.

Parker, Robert Nash and Kathleen Auerhahn (1998), "Alcohol, drugs, and violence", *Annual Review of Sociology*, vol. 24.

Pasqualini, Diana and Alfredo Llorens (comps.) (2010), *Salud y bienestar de los adolescentes y jóvenes: una mirada integral*, Buenos Aires, Pan American Health Organization (PAHO).

Patel, Vikram and others (2007), "Mental health of young people: a global public-health challenge", *The Lancet*, vol. 369, No. 9569 [online] http://search.proquest.com/docview/199076575?accountid=41816.

Pilgrim, Nanlesta and Robert Blum (2012), "Protective and risk factors associated with adolescent sexual and reproductive health in the English-speaking Caribbean: a literature review", *Journal of Adolescent Health*, vol. 50, No. 1.

Quinlan-Davidson, M. and others (2014), "Suicide among young people in the Americas", *Journal of Adolescent Health*, vol. 54, No. 3.

Reith, Gerda (2004), "Consumption and its discontents: addiction, identity and the problems of freedom", *The British Journal of Sociology*, vol. 55, No. 2, Wiley.

Rico, Maria Nieves and Daniela Trucco (2014), "Adolescentes: derecho a la educación y al bienestar futuro", *Políticas Sociales series*, No. 190 (LC/L.3791), Santiago, Economic Commission for Latin America and the Caribbean (ECLAC) [online] http://www.unicef.org/lac/Adolescentes_derecho_educacion_bienestar_futuro.pdf.

Rodríguez, Jorge (2012), "Salud pública, políticas sociales y desarrollo humano de adolescentes y jóvenes indígenas en América Latina: experiencias acumuladas y desafíos a encarar" [online] http://www.paho.org/derechoalaSSR/wp-content/uploads/Documentos/Salud-Publica-Politicas-Sociales-y-Desarrollo-Humano-de-Adolescentes-y-Jovenes-Indigenas-en-America-Latina.pdf.

____(2011), "Políticas de juventud y desarrollo social en América Latina: bases para la construcción de respuestas integradas", *Documento de Trabajo*, San Salvador.

Rodríguez V., Jorge (2014), "La reproducción en la adolescencia y sus desigualdades en América Latina. Introducción al análisis demográfico, con énfasis en el uso de microdatos censales de la ronda de 2010", *Projects Document* (LC/W.605) Santiago, Economic Commission for Latin America and the Caribbean (ECLAC).

____(2012), "La reproducción en la adolescencia en América Latina: viejas y nuevas vulnerabilidades", *Realidad Datos y Espacio. Revista Internacional de Estadística y Geografía*, vol. 3, No. 2, National Institute of Statistics and Geography.

____(2008), *Reproducción adolescente y desigualdades en América Latina y el Caribe: un llamado a la reflexión y a la acción*, Santiago, Economic Commission for Latin America and the Caribbean (ECLAC).

Rodríguez, Jorge J. (2010), "Mental health care systems in Latin America and the Caribbean", *International Review of Psychiatry*, vol. 22, No. 4.

____(2007), *La reforma de los servicios de salud mental: 15 años después de la Declaración de Caracas*, Washington, D.C., Pan American Health Organization (PAHO) [online] http://www.ops-oms.org.pa/Lz_HAA/Doc/Agenda.pdf.

Rossel, Cecilia (2013), "Desbalance etario del bienestar. El lugar de la infancia en la protección social en América Latina", *Políticas Sociales series*, No. 176 (LC/L.3574), Santiago, Economic Commission for Latin America and the Caribbean (ECLAC).

Seedat, Soraya and others (2009), "Cross-national associations between gender and mental disorders in the World Health Organization World Mental Health Surveys", *Archives of General Psychiatry*, vol. 66, No. 7.

SESC/CONJUVE/INE (Executive Secretariat for Civic Service/National Youth Council/ National Institute of Statistics) (2011), *Primera Encuesta Nacional de Juventud en Guatemala (ENJU 2011)*, Guatemala City.

Teti, Germán and others (2014), "Systematic review of risk factors for suicide and suicide attempt among psychiatric patients in Latin America and Caribbean", *Pan American Journal of Public Health*, vol. 36, No. 2.

UNFPA (United Nations Population Fund) (2014), *State of World Population 2014. The Power of 1.8 Billion: Adolescents, Youth and the Transformation of the Future*, New York, United Nations.

United Nations (2014), *Mental Health Matters: Social Inclusion of Youth with Mental Health Conditions*, New York.

Viner, R.M. and others (2012), "Adolescence and the social determinants of health", *The Lancet*, vol. 379, No. 9826 [online] http://search.proquest.com/docview/1015610268?accountid=41816.

WHO (World Health Organization) (2010a), Global School-Based Student Health
    Survey 2010.
___(2010b), "Mental Health and Development: Targeting People with Mental
    Health Conditions as a Vulnerable Group", Geneva [online] http://www.
    who.int/mental_health/policy/mhtargeting/en/.
___(2002), *World Report on Violence and Health*, Geneva.
___(1948), "Constitution of the World Health Organization" [online] http://apps.
    who.int/gb/bd/PDF/bd47/EN/constitution-en.pdf.

Chapter III

Inclusion and contexts of violence

Humberto Soto
Daniela Trucco[1]

A. Violence and youth[2]

The countries of Latin America and the Caribbean will not be able to tackle the challenges they must overcome to progress towards equality and improve youth inclusion in poverty reduction and in education, employment or health unless they take an integrated approach to all elements of the prevailing context in the region. The demographic transition, urbanization processes, technological progress and food insecurity are just a few of these elements; other important ones are human insecurity and violence.

In the past few years, major development strides by the region's countries, including some that have been highly positive for young people, have paradoxically coexisted with high indices of violence and insecurity. Unlike the situation in other regions of the world, in Latin America and the Caribbean the countries are at peace, but there are extreme levels of violence

[1] The authors are grateful for conceptual and statistical contributions received from the consultants Sebastián Möller, Carlos Mario Perea and Matías Salces. They also appreciate the comments and suggestions made by Néstor López of the International Institute for Educational Planning (IIEP) of the United Nations Educational, Scientific and Cultural Organization (UNESCO), Buenos Aires.

[2] Much of this conceptual review was developed in *Social Panorama of Latin America 2014* (ECLAC, 2014).

within society, to the point that the region has the world's highest homicide rate (UNODC, 2014, p. 22).

Violence (intentional or not) is the leading cause of death among the population aged between 15 and 50 in Latin America and the Caribbean. Seven of the 14 most violent countries in the world are in this region: Belize, the Bolivarian Republic of Venezuela, Colombia, El Salvador, Guatemala, Honduras and Jamaica. Between 2000 and 2010, the region's homicide rate rose 11%, whereas in most other world regions it came down or stood still. Countries with information available report that thefts have almost tripled over the past 25 years. Moreover, on a typical day in Latin America, 460 individuals, mostly women, are victims of sexual violence (UNDP, 2013).

The youth population is particularly affected by this context of violence and insecurity. As described in chapter II, violence is the leading cause of death among young people. This chapter discusses how that fact is merely the most visible face of a problem that affects young people in different ways, inasmuch as they are frequently caught up in violent situations, whether as victims or perpetrators, in spheres ranging from the family to the collective arena, with very diverse causes and consequences, most of them very particular to this stage of life.

The seemingly greater prevalence of manifestations of violence among youth has made this phenomenon into a stigma, which presents the young —just because of their life stage— as criminals and perpetrators of violence, distorting the approach to the problem and to possible solutions.

1.   Multidimensional nature of violence: manifestations in youth

The concept of violence is multidimensional, since it presents in diverse spheres and arenas, and affects those involved in different ways with a range of different types of consequences. Given this complexity, analysis of the context of violence in the youth environment requires a framework to structure it. The framework used in this chapter is based on two of the typologies most commonly employed in research on the topic in recent years, which are complementary: the proposal by Galtung (1990) and that derived from the ecological model developed by Bronfenbrenner in 1979 and adopted by the World Health Organization (WHO) in 2002.

Galtung's typology facilitates identification of the parties (perpetrators and victims) and the ways in which violence is perpetrated, by defining types: direct (perpetrated personally between individuals), structural (perpetrated against groups as a result of inequality within society) and cultural or symbolic (perpetrated against individuals and groups through the imposition of systems of thought or perception).

Box III.1
Typology of violence proposed by Galtung, 1990

Galtung's typology distinguishes the dynamics in processes of violence, and proposes the following types:

- Direct violence: this is the most visible kind and is realized through acts of violence (physical, verbal or psychological) with the intention of harming a person or a group. It may be directed at people, at groups or at nature.

- Structural violence: this refers to the inequalities embedded in the structure of society, which exclude or even gradually eliminate certain groups by denying them food, housing, health, employment, security and recreation, among others. Structural violence is manifested through social exclusion, socioeconomic inequality, racism, inequality on the basis of sex or any other form of discrimination that detracts from human well-being.

- Cultural or symbolic violence: this is the imposition and reproduction of a system of thought and perception that legitimizes an unequal social order, such as that described above. According to Galtung, this may be manifested in two ways: by subverting the criteria of moral judgement regarding violent practices or by making them invisible so that no judgement is incurred (Galtung, 1990).

Source: Johan Galtung, "Cultural violence", *Journal of Peace Research*, vol. 27, No. 3, SAGE, 1990.

Box III.2
Typology based on the ecological model (WHO, 2002)

The "ecological model", developed by Bronfenbrenner in 1979 and later adopted by WHO in the *World Report on Violence and Health* (2002) is useful for grasping the phenomenon of violence, which is construed as something highly complex arising from the correlation of many individual and specific contextual factors acting upon young people's surroundings. The model is used to analyse factors that influence behaviour (or that increase the risk of perpetrating or suffering violence), classifying them in a four-level system that is then used to define three types of violence. The levels are:

- Biological and personal history factors that influence the behaviour of individuals and increase their likelihood of being victims or perpetrators of violence. The factors that may be traced or measured include demographic characteristics (age, education and income), psychological or personality disorders, addictions and prior history of aggression and abuse.

- Proximal social relationships —for example, relations with peers, intimate partners and family members— and how these increase the risk of becoming a victim or perpetrator of violence. In the case of youth violence, having friends who encourage or commit acts of violence can raise the risk of becoming a victim or perpetrator of violence.

- Community contexts in which social relations are embedded, such as schools, workplaces and neighbourhoods, seeking to identify the characteristics of these settings that increase the risk of acts of violence. This risk may be influenced by factors such as residential mobility (whether people stay for a long time in a particular neighbourhood or move frequently), population density, high levels of unemployment or problems such as drug trafficking in the area.

Box III.2 (concluded)

- Broader societal factors that contribute to creating a climate that encourages or inhibits violence, such as the availability of weapons and societal and cultural norms. Such norms include those that give priority to parental rights over child welfare, regard suicide as a matter of individual choice instead of a preventable act of violence, entrench male dominance over women and children, support the use of excessive force by police against citizens or support political conflict. Other more general factors at this level are health, economic, education and social policies that contribute to maintaining economic or social inequalities between groups within society.

Source: World Health Organization (WHO), *World Report on Violence and Health*, Washington, D.C., 2002.

The typology used by WHO on the basis of the ecological model complements that of Galtung, since it more clearly identifies the spheres in which violence is perpetrated, as well as its possible consequences, by the types it establishes: self-inflicted (suicidal behaviour and self-harm), interpersonal (within the family, towards children, a partner or the elderly, and in the community, between acquaintances or strangers) and collective (social, political or economic).[3]

The two typologies complement each other through combinations of their respective classifications of violence. Table III.1 shows manifestations of youth violence arranged in schematic form according to these combined frameworks.

Direct self-inflicted violence, in which the individual is both victim and perpetrator, is a very significant behavioural problem among adolescents and young people. It usually occurs within the household family setting, with sometimes extreme consequences, as in the case of suicide (see further details on mental health statistics and suicidal behaviours in chapter II).

Young people may be victims or perpetrators of direct interpersonal violence when it is committed within the family by parents against children or by a partner. This sort of violence can also be committed in other spheres by other young people or adults, whether known or not, and has diverse physical or psychological consequences for youth development and often shapes their behaviour in other areas.

---

[3]   This classification is used particularly by the secretariat of the Central American Social Integration Secretariat (SISCA) and the Democratic Security Directorate of the Central American Integration System (SICA) in their Strategic Framework for the Prevention of Violence.

Table III.1
**Manifestations of violence in youth classified by complementarity
between the Galtung and ecological model typologies**

		Ecological model typology		
		Self-inflicted	Interpersonal	Collective
Galtung typology	Direct	Self-harm and suicide	Physical or psychological aggression within the family, or by or towards a partner or close friends	Physical or psychological aggression towards schoolmates (school bullying or harassment and cyberbullying), neighbours, authorities or gangs
	Structural	Self-exclusion	Discrimination within or around the family on the basis of ascribed characteristics (for example, belonging to a minority group)	Social exclusion
	Cultural/symbolic	Low self-esteem	Exclusion associated with culturally embedded concepts (for example, traditional gender roles)	Stigmatization

Source: Prepared by the authors.

Young people may also be victims or perpetrators of direct collective violence when it arises in school or community environments, directed either by youth groups towards individuals (who may be young or not) or by neighbourhood groups or authorities towards young individuals or groups. Two particular cases of this type of violence have become significant in the youth setting: (i) violent confrontation between groups of young people, which can have serious social impacts —in the case of gangs, for example, and (ii) school bullying perpetrated through social networks— cyberbullying. These examples will be explored in more depth later in this chapter.

The concept of structural violence enables identification of mechanisms of inclusion or exclusion and how they develop. These often include norms or laws that sanction the exclusion of certain groups, something that is particularly significant among young people. Although self-inflicted structural violence in the form of self-exclusion is significant, it is generally preceded and caused by a process of exclusion. Structural violence is thus particularly important among young people when it is interpersonal (chiefly in the immediate setting) or collective, because it leads to a scenario of discrimination and social exclusion of youth. Although young people tend to be victims more than perpetrators, often processes of discrimination and social exclusion occur among young people themselves, with some individuals acting as perpetrators of different kinds of violence, such as acts of youth delinquency or vandalism.

Symbolic violence, which usually transcends particular manifestations and can lead to the legitimization of violence in social relationships, as in the previous case, becomes very significant in youth populations. It can take an interpersonal form within the family (such as in the normalization of traditional gender roles and the acceptance of domestic violence) or a collective form, leading to discrimination against certain groups because they belong to a particular social class, an ethnic, sexual or other minority or a certain kind of youth organization (gang), exacerbating the stigma attached to young people, as mentioned earlier.

Ordering the manifestations of violence in this way allows us to lay the groundwork for a more detailed analysis of the expressions that are most significant from the point of view of youth inclusion. Since the intention here is not merely to analyse manifestations of violence among young people, but rather to seek ways to redress it, it is essential to look more deeply into two very important aspects. The first is to review the possible causes of manifestations of violence, seeking to understand why they occur and which are the best means of prevention. The second is to look in more detail at the spheres or domains in which these manifestations occur, in order to help design initiatives to prevent violence.

2.   Multicausality of violence: enablers[4]

Because of its multidimensional nature, violence is a ubiquitous phenomenon with many associated risk factors (at different levels) that are operationalized in relation both to the perpetrator of the violent act and the subjects affected (ECLAC/OIJ, 2008; WHO, 2002). In particular, violence affecting youth, be it as victims or perpetrators, is the result of a complex web of risk factors that arise at a given moment. Those risk factors may also be considered facilitators of attitudes that encourage violence.

There follows a review of some of the risk factors (or enablers) more often mentioned in the international literature, which are general in nature and can encourage different manifestations of violence in youth.[5]

(a) Growing inequality and exclusion

Several studies agree that although poverty appears to aggravate all types of violence, inequality and growing economic and social polarization are much more systematically correlated with violence, especially among the young. It has been found that the most violent communities are those that the State has somehow "abandoned" or neglected, as shown, for example,

---

[4]   This section is based on the work of Teresita Escotto (Escotto, 2015).
[5]   This section refers only to the risk factors most widely recognized by experts in the subject. There may be various types of risk factor —social, economic, cultural, political, situational, structural and institutional— operating at different levels.

by infrastructure in poor repair or lack of public services (such as a lack of public lighting, of paved streets or of health centres). It may therefore be more appropriate to talk about a social or community setting of poverty rather than household poverty.

One example is the case of gangs that (as will be analysed later) arise as an organized form of collective violence in those neighbourhoods that are most neglected by the State, and whose members may or may not be drawn from the poorest families (Cruz 2004, p. 287, cited in Escotto, 2015). One study conducted in El Salvador found that the communities worst affected by gang violence were not those with the lowest-income individuals, or "the poorest of the poor", but those in which resources were lacking relative to other communities (Cruz 2004, p. 286, cited in Escotto, 2015).

This is closely related to the tension between the expansion of symbolic consumption and constraints on material consumption. Some authors speak of a dramatic mismatch between aspirations for a better life and the real opportunities that large groups of the population have to achieve it (Briceño and Zubillaga, 2001, p. 171, cited in Escotto, 2015). In an increasingly globalized society, the new generations have growing aspirations to consumption and instant well-being, partly encouraged by widespread access to the media and to information. Despite having achieved levels of education and well-being unimagined by their parents, much of the youth population are disappointed by the labour options available (see chapter II). This frustration of expectations can be a trigger for violent behaviours.

(b) The after-effects of civil conflict

A number of Latin American and Caribbean countries have had violence embedded in the cultural matrix and in people's practices by socio-historical processes. This refers in particular to periods of post-war and post-dictatorship transition, where the idea of political violence begins to be associated with other types of violence. A recent World Bank study put forward two main hypotheses about the way in which civil conflicts could have contributed to the alarming levels of violence in Central America. One possibility is that war may have created a culture of violence among the population, breeding a tendency to rely on violence to fix problems, which has permeated the youth population. Beyond this, it may be that victims tend to retaliate in kind or take justice into their own hands. The second hypothesis is that recent armed conflict may contribute to higher violence levels through the transfer of firearms and munitions into the subregion (World Bank, 2011, p. 21, cited in Escotto, 2015).

According to this same source, independent studies indicate that some 4.5 million small arms were in circulation in Central America in 2007, most of them illegal. This report indicated that imports of arms were still increasing in the six countries of the Central American subregion many years after the end of the latest civil wars.

(c) Drugs trafficking

Drugs trafficking stokes violence in several ways, "including fighting between and within trafficking organizations, and fighting between traffickers and law enforcement officials, adding to the availability of firearms and weakening the criminal justice system by diverting judicial resources or corrupting the criminal justice system itself" (World Bank, 2011, p. 11). Score-settling through contract killing has become common, with young people frequently involved. Cocaine trafficking is particularly significant in this subregion, because of the large volume of money associated, which generates a series of distortions that will be discussed in more detail later.

(d) Process of migration and deportation

The case of migration to the United States is particularly important because it is the main destination for emigrants from the countries of Latin America and the Caribbean. According to the 2010 census, 21.2 million people born in some country of the region were resident in the United States, of whom 55.2% were of Mexican origin, 14.3% Central American, 12.8% South American and 17.5% Caribbean. If the population of a certain nationality resident in the United States is compared with the population of the respective country of origin, the ratio is highest for the Central American countries. For example, 1 in 5 Salvadorans, 1 in 10 Mexicans and 1 in 15 Hondurans reside in the United States. A fifth of these emigrants are young people aged between 15 and 29 years (ECLAC, 2014). Migration from Central America to the United States began in the 1960s and became more intense during periods of conflict in countries such as El Salvador, Guatemala and Honduras.

In the early years of this migratory process, young Central American migrants were socially rejected and segregated upon their arrival in the United States by youth of other nationalities. This led Central American migrants to establish gangs as a violent response to the social exclusion they encountered. The United States Immigration and Naturalization Service began to deport young gang members at the end of the 1980s, and stepped up these efforts in the 1990s with the establishment of the Violent Gang Task Force. Upon deportation, many of the young people who had been involved in these gangs replicated the same models of violent organization in their countries of origin. This was the origin of most of the most violent gangs now operating in Central America (Savanije, 2007, p.12, in Murcia, 2015).

Although migration has lessened, it nevertheless continues, with young people forming one of the population segments most likely to migrate, which exposes them to violence, discrimination and health risks. In extreme cases, young women can become victims of trafficking for prostitution (SEGIB/OIJ, 2008, p. 31, cited in Escotto, 2015). The adverse effects of migration, especially of the cross-border variety, can be critical for the lives of young migrants, since their journey may bring them into situations of danger and violence. Upon arrival they may find their rights limited and be exposed to abuses by employers, as well as experiencing poor access to services and situations of discrimination and marginalization (ECLAC, 2014).

(e) Intrafamily violence

Experts have found that a factor associated with violent behaviours is the intergenerational transmission of mistreatment within the family: children who witness violent responses by their parents are more likely to follow those response models, as well as the gender role stereotypes in that interaction. Violent forms of upbringing and parental abuse or neglect not only contribute to the development of antisocial and self-harming behaviours, as well as low self-esteem and despair, but also limit children's possibilities of internalizing patterns of control and self-control, which translates into an inability to manage aggressive impulses (Larraín, 2002, p. 15, cited in Escotto, 2015).

(f) Lack of sense of belonging among youth

Lack of a sense of belonging —understood as non-adherence to shared values or recognized forms of participation, unwillingness to acknowledge others in relation to perceptions of discrimination or new communicative practices, and lack of trust in social structures and of confidence in the future— is a major cause of certain manifestations of violence. It has been noted, for example, that "lack of identity" has led many young people "to join gangs due to the absence of positive role models both at home and in their communities, and to being socially excluded (from education and employment opportunities)" (World Bank, 2011, p. 19, cited in Escotto, 2015).

This lack of a sense of belonging can also be an outcome, and not only a cause, of violence, leading to a vicious cycle that needs to be broken. From a sociological point of view, violence may be seen as the cause and effect of social disintegration within a human group. A cause, because violence creates and entrenches division and distrust between people, leading to forms of coexistence in which human interaction is restricted by mechanisms of discrimination and marginalization; and effect, because it is a symptom of an unfair combination of material and immaterial factors that gradually erode people's sense of belonging to a society (Universidad Centroamericana José Simeón Cañas, 2011, cited in Escotto, 2015).

One of the cultural features embedded in the countries of the region, in some more than others, is a tendency towards violent means for conflict resolution. This occurs from the private sphere through to community and collective spaces and shapes practices from childhood. In many countries, the media reinforce this image and reward violent behaviour, which viewers learn and later imitate. Violent actions are presented as acceptable alternatives for dispute settlement, and can thus shape day-to-day behaviour (Krauskopf, 2002, p. 12, cited in Escotto, 2015). The media sometimes portray gang members as examples worthy of imitation and groups of supporters of sports teams who are violent and destructive in stadiums are sometimes held up as models of youthful and manly behavior.

(g) The stigmatization of youth

Certain youth groups, such as gang members or youth from vulnerable urban areas, tend to be stigmatized. In the collective imaginary and in the media, young males from poor urban areas tend to be stigmatized as a potential threat and sign of violence (ECLAC, 2008a, p. 23). These expressions of symbolic violence can reinforce processes of exclusion and ultimately become self-fulfilling prophecies: the fact of being born and growing up in certain neighbourhoods deprives young people of opportunities to participate in a society that discriminates against them, and so their route towards integration arises through violent groups and behaviours.

(h) Alienation from institutions

Adolescents and young people drop out of school for many reasons, including family financial pressures. Being expelled by a system that does not offer suitable conditions to remain in education can increase the risk factors for young people. This is particularly significant when it is associated with a violent setting, inadequate management of conflict among young people or between young people and the staff of educational establishments, failure to address the special needs of students with learning or behavioural difficulties, and the use of violent means by school authorities against the student body. The school setting will be examined in more depth later, as a specific context of violence faced by young people and adolescents.

This, added to the frustration of young people seeking to enter a labour market that fails to offer decent, worthwhile work, heightens their risk of becoming perpetrators of violence. These are young people who see little hope of gaining a good foothold in the labour market. Of the few jobs they find, most do not meet the conditions necessary to qualify as decent work, and the reality of many young workers remains far removed from respect for basic labour rights.

The situation of the hard core of youth exclusion (those young people not in education or employment, nor engaged in any other activity) speaks of a rupture of the linkages that support capacity-building and participation in social capital. Insofar as the labour market and education system are the main spheres of inclusion, this is a risk factor that increases youth propensity to become involved in different types of violence. Young people's acceptance of their own marginalization leaves them vulnerable and conditions them to reproduce poverty and exclusion, exposes them to reproductive health risks and, in some cases, makes them potential participants in illicit activities (SEGIB/OIJ, 2008, p. 33, cited in Escotto, 2015).[6]

It must be recalled that the enablers of violence described are general in nature, and each manifestation of violence can be associated in turn with other more specific causal factors. It is likewise acknowledged that none of the youth violence enablers mentioned acts alone or is a sure explanation of violence per se, so that tackling one factor in isolation from the others is highly unlikely to have the desired effect of reducing violence. On the contrary, it could be counterproductive and ultimately escalate violence.

Since the issue involves a combination of national-level factors, such as general economic and social conditions (levels of inequality, drugs trafficking, population dynamics, access to education and employment and even a history of civil conflict), and more particular aspects, such as the family and cultural setting and sense of belonging of individuals, it must be addressed from different standpoints under an integrated approach.

In this regard, it is necessary to counter risk factors with "protection factors" to diminish (or eliminate) their worst effects and thus help to reduce violence. Protection factors need to be carefully identified and developed to create the right conditions to promote a context of peaceful family, community and social coexistence. This point merits a more detailed analysis of the spheres and spaces in which violence affecting youth arises, and is the subject of the next section.

3. Ubiquity of violence: youth spaces or spheres

In recent years, Latin America and the Caribbean has gone from a situation of collective violence (in a context of dictatorships and civil wars) to one in which interpersonal violence appears to have been garnering greater prominence in the media and greater attention as a subject of study (Imbusch, Misse and Carrión, 2011, p. 98). Essentially, this attention has focused on the concept of crime, which is hard to define, and the stigmatization of people living in sectors beset by violence. In the first place, crime is a phenomenon

---

[6]   See chapter II.

delineated by the criminal law, meaning that behaviour which is treated as a crime in one context may be considered reprehensible but not criminal in another. Young people are immersed in various spaces or spheres of violence that are not limited to serious public offences but which affect their development opportunities.

The enablers described above, which have helped shape today's situations of violence, mean there is a need for youth-focused multidimensional analysis of violence, to look into the existence of a close relationship with social exclusion processes for both victims and perpetrators, where violence and context feed upon and into each other, so that social, territorial and family settings can end up encouraging the young to seek violent solutions (ECLAC/OIJ, 2008).

Based on the proposed complementarity of typologies (Galtung and the systemic approach), the spaces in which the different types of violence can manifest in youth are vast. Virtually nowhere is free of violence, since it may occur in closed, private spaces, such as the household, school or place of work, and in public spaces, such as institutions and in the media (including the Internet). It is important to analyse the specific features of each of those spaces as places prone to violence.

Comparative analysis of information on domestic and school violence is difficult to do at the regional level, but the data generated by case studies or surveys specifically designed for this purpose reveal high levels of violence in school and family settings, but also in public spaces. In fact, according to the Latinobarómetro Survey for 2008, between 25% and 29% of young people —in the average figures for 18 countries of the region— perceived themselves as living in situations of violence at school, in the family, between gangs and in the neighbourhood. Brazil is a particular case in point, with over half the young people surveyed stating that they lived in contexts of violence in such immediate environments as school (see table III.2).

As described here, young people in the region face contexts and manifestations of violence in different spheres, originating in turn in a multiplicity of factors. The following sections analyse in more detail some of the spheres and manifestations of violence found to have a great impact on young people, and which have moreover been made notorious by media coverage. In particular, the relationship between gender and violence in youth will be examined, looking at different spheres and manifestations and examining the gang environment. Then, at a more community level, manifestations of direct interpersonal and collective violence at school are reviewed, as a key sphere of socialization for adolescent and youth generations. Lastly, the manifestations of collective violence that beset many of the regions' cities in the form of organized violence (especially the issue of gangs and violent youth organizations) are analysed.

Table III.2
Latin America (18 countries): perceptions of violence in different settings among the population aged 16 to 29 years, 2008
(Percentages)

	At school	In the family	In the neighbourhood	Between gangs
Argentina	29	20	16	20
Bolivia (Plurinational State of)	28	32	23	28
Brazil	52	40	42	38
Chile	26	27	15	29
Colombia	33	32	25	21
Costa Rica	24	25	23	19
Dominican Republic	35	28	32	28
Ecuador	19	19	17	18
El Salvador	25	17	19	26
Guatemala	33	35	34	34
Honduras	32	28	25	24
Mexico	33	34	27	26
Nicaragua	29	22	28	30
Panama	29	32	34	28
Paraguay	20	18	18	18
Peru	28	27	20	32
Uruguay	29	21	14	21
Venezuela (Bolivarian Republic of)	29	32	31	34
Latin America [a]	**29**	**27**	**25**	**26**

Source: Economic Commission for Latin America and the Caribbean (ECLAC), on the basis of special tabulations of data from the 2088 Latinobarómetro Survey.
[a] Simple average of the results for the 18 countries included in the measurement.

B. Gender and violence in youth

There is a wealth of information globally and within the region on the prevalence of manifestations of violence against women in all age groups. Given its importance, and the fact that many manifestations of violence have particular consequences among the youth population, it is worth examining the relationship between gender and violence in youth, since violence against women occurs in all spheres and across all the types and dimensions of violence considered (see table III.1).

Generally speaking, the convergence between gender, youth and violence has been little analysed, and few studies attempt to establish whether the fact of gender influences the risk of being a victim or perpetrator of a particular type of violence among young people. Still fewer studies seek to identify whether youth is a factor differentiating the risk of perpetrating acts of gender-based violence.[7]

This section attempts to examine whether gender is an enabling factor in violence; in other words, whether gender establishes per se a differential level of risk of being a victim or perpetrator of violence. It also examines whether the fact of being young is an enabler of gender violence and, especially, whether young men are more likely to engage in acts of violence against women. Lastly, a close examination will be conducted of the particular case of violence against women in the gang setting, where those factors are considerably heightened.

1. Gender as a risk factor in becoming a victim or perpetrator of violence in youth

Violence against women is defined as "any act of gender-based violence that results in, or is likely to result in, physical, sexual or psychological harm or suffering to women, including threats of such acts, coercion or arbitrary deprivation of liberty, whether occurring in public or in private life" (United Nations, 1993).[8] Because it encompasses multiple sociological aspects, including long-embedded family and cultural factors, the gender-based type is one of the most complex manifestations of violence to analyse and is considered a scourge that must be eradicated from our societies.

There is statistical information that can yield some partial conclusions on the hypothesis that young people's sex can be considered a differential risk factor for the likelihood of falling victim to some type of violence. For example, for the ultimate consequence of violence —loss of life— figures estimated from administrative records held by the Global Health Observatory for 2012 show that mortality from intentional injuries in Latin America and the Caribbean is 8.5 times higher among young men (aged 15 to 29) than among women in the same age range (WHO, 2013). This reflects a higher likelihood among young men of suffering the consequences of violence in this particular manifestation, a conclusion shared by the great majority of studies on youth violence.

More detailed analysis shows that 17% of deaths from intentional injury among young men are self-inflicted (suicide), while among young women the percentage rises to 37.8%. Although this does not mean that young women commit suicide more than young men (the suicide rate shows a ratio of three to one between males and females), it does show evidence that supports qualitative analysis of the reason for the difference in the relative level of

---

[7] The *World Report on Violence and Health* produced in 2002 by the World Health Organization (WHO, 2002) is an example of the few studies on the issue and is thus an essential reference.

[8] This is the definition adopted in article 1 of the United Nations Declaration on the Elimination of Violence against Women [online] http://www.un.org/documents/ga/res/48/a48r104.htm.

self-inflicted violence among young women, after taking into account the differential level of risk of death from intentional injury.

In the case of direct violence associated with criminal acts, information from the Americas Barometer 2012 produced by the Latin American Public Opinion Project (LAPOP) shows that in the Latin American countries where the survey was carried out, young women are more likely to be victims of rape or sexual assault than women of other ages or young men. The data from this source also indicate that young women are twice as likely to be abducted as young men (see table III.3). The reference is to indications, because the information shows a low report rate of sexual assault and abduction. In this regard, it is important to recall that one of the problems is underreporting and underrecording in the various instruments of data collection on this type of violence in the region, because chauvinist cultural patterns remain whereby blame tends to be apportioned to the victim herself, as if she had caused or sought the assault.

Table III.3
Latin America (18 countries): individuals reporting having been the victim of crime in the 12 months preceding the survey, by sex and age, 2012[a]

(Percentages)

	Total	Young people (15-29)			Other ages		
		Men	Women	Total	Men	Women	Total
Robbery without a weapon, aggression or physical threat	4.7	4.9	6.1	5.5	4.4	4.3	4.4
Robbery without a weapon, with aggression or physical threat	2.3	3.4	2.9	3.1	2.0	1.8	1.9
Armed robbery	4.6	8.0	5.0	6.5	4.6	2.8	3.7
Physical aggression without robbery	0.8	1.3	0.7	1.0	0.8	0.6	0.7
Rape or sexual assault	0.1	0.0	0.3	0.2	0.0	0.1	0.1
Abduction	0.1	0.0	0.1	0.1	0.1	0.1	0.1
Damage to property	0.7	0.6	0.4	0.5	0.8	0.7	0.7
Home burglary	1.9	1.4	1.7	1.6	2.0	2.3	2.1
Extortion	0.7	0.7	0.6	0.6	0.8	0.6	0.7
Other	1.0	1.0	1.0	1.0	1.0	0.9	1.0
Total	16.8	21.4	18.9	20.2	16.6	14.2	15.3

Source: Latin American Public Opinion Project (LAPOP), Americas Barometer, 2012.
[a] Argentina, Bolivarian Republic of Venezuela, Brazil, Chile, Colombia, Costa Rica, Dominican Republic, Ecuador, El Salvador, Guatemala, Honduras, Mexico, Nicaragua, Panama, Paraguay, Peru, Plurinational State of Bolivia and Uruguay.

Where manifestations of violence associated with direct victimization of women are concerned, information from the demographic and health surveys of Latin America countries that have included questions on the topic shows that between 10% and 30% of young women report having been pushed or struck by their partners, although there is no clear evidence that this percentage is higher than for women of other ages.[9] In the case of sexual assault, especially forced sex, young women are more likely than those of other ages to be victims, especially at the hands of their partners, with prevalence rates of between 5% and 11%. Notably, in the case of attack by people other than a partner —which is a much lower percentage (in turn showing the significance of intimate partner violence)— there is evidence that young women are more likely to be victims.

Generally speaking, the information available is too limited to analyse other manifestations of violence, such as violence associated with human trafficking (including sexual and psychological violence), ill-treatment of children by their parents, school violence or community violence, among other types, to identify whether young women and men are at significantly greater risk than other age groups. In most cases, it is clear from intuitive sources or qualitative studies that the difference exists. However, the data to corroborate this quantitatively have yet to be produced.[10]

Although, for most types of violence, the information sources do not help to identify whether sex is a determining factor in commission propensity, data from the *Global Study on Homicide* show that in this specific case, some 95% of homicide perpetrators at the global level are male (UNODC, 2014).[11]

This tendency is confirmed by analysis of information from surveys of female victims of violence and the great majority of qualitative studies on gender violence. These sources support the general conclusion that in most cases and regardless of age group, violence against women is perpetrated by men, which speaks to the need for more comprehensive analyses mainstreaming gender in the approach to youth violence.

2.   Youth as a factor in the perpetration of gender violence

A clear differentiation has been identified between the sex of perpetrators and victims of gender violence, strongly slanted towards males as perpetrators and females as victims. Because of this, the hope is that the indices of gender violence can be brought down by a generational cultural shift whereby men become aware that violence against women is unacceptable and women cease to view this type of violence as normal.

---

[9]   Information is available for the Colombia (2010), Dominican Republic (2007), Haiti (2012), Honduras (2012), Peru (2012) and Plurinational State of Bolivia (2008).

[10]   This challenge is even greater when it comes to the most extreme manifestation of gender violence —femicide— because of the lack of records available, reflecting, in turn, difficulties with typification.

[11]   The analysis of youth violence carried out for El Salvador found the same figure: 95% of murderers in the country were men (Youth Regional Alliance, 2010).

However, there seems to be no evidence that gender violence is less prevalent among younger groups, which suggests that the intergenerational transmission of the message calling for respect for the right to a life free from violence is not being achieved among the region's youth . The data in demographic and health surveys for some countries of the region show that between 15% and 40% of young women saw their father strike their mother as children, implying that these women may consider it normal for their partners to strike or abuse them as they grow up. However, the proportion of women aged over 29 who have witnessed this situation is considerably higher than for younger women, which is a positive indicator for the process of reduction of violence against women.

The information from these same surveys shows that most of those who have suffered violence at the hands of a partner do not seek help, with little difference in this regard between younger and older women. Again, this reflects the twofold victimization of women whereby social convention can lead them to be stigmatized if they seek help after suffering abuse. One important aspect reflected in these data is that in situations of abuse, young women tend to seek help from their parents more than older women did, showing the importance of intergenerational awareness-building and family support in this area.

3.   Violence against women in gangs

Generally speaking, information on the role of women in gangs is limited to the results of certain case studies. Some of these studies, carried out in 2006 in El Salvador, Guatemala and Honduras, documented that the majority of gang members were men and even that active participation by women in gangs had declined sharply (Aguilar, 2006; Ranum, 2006 and Andino, 2006, cited in Aguilar and Carranza, 2008). One of these studies indicated that women generally represent less than a quarter of gang members (Demoscopía, 2007, cited in Bravo, 2013).

With only a few exceptions, women do not play the same roles as men in gang activities. Women involved in gangs usually play traditional gender roles in activities ranging from provision of food to cover-up and protection, arms concealment and tending to injuries. They are not generally consulted in decision-making, they are punished for infidelity and are obliged to seek their partner within the gang. They sometimes play a submissive sexual role in a context in which, in most cases, male gang members do not seek stable relationships with women, or do so outside the gang (Lacayo, 2015).

Some studies that have explored the role of women in gangs have documented that one of the ways in which gangs attempt to attract young men is the lure of ready access to money, power and sex. The sex is provided by bringing women, mainly adolescents, into the gang. These are usually young women coming from backgrounds of limited opportunities and bleak family settings (and often with a history of partner or intrafamily abuse). Young women seeking independence are attracted by a scenario of promiscuity which is anything but liberating. These women become gang property and gang members exercise overt sexual violence against them through rape or collective abuse (Rubio, 2008).

Although this theme calls for further exploration in terms of its most tangible manifestation, the few case studies that address it show conclusively how gender inequality is magnified within gangs and reveal the need to analyse the theme of sexual violence against women, mainly adolescents, who become involved with gangs.

C.   School violence

A high proportion of young people spend much of their daily life in an educational establishment. As shown in table III.2, some 30% of young people state that they have experienced situations of violence at school. A number of studies conducted from the 1970s to the present have analysed school violence as a theme of great importance in relation to the formation of new generations. In particular, because violent behaviours run counter to what is expected from school: a safe, protected domain in which new generations are supposed to be taught citizenship-building and democratic conduct (Román and Murillo, 2011). One of the conclusions of the studies is that it is important to distinguish between violence that enters school from external social spheres and violence generated within the establishment itself.

In a broad sense, violence at school, like violence in other spheres, is rooted in the social transformations taking place within society as a whole. The changes occurring in the past few decades, driven by processes of globalization that define spaces and territories, the globalization of centres of power and decision-making, and the growing prevalence of the market and of consumption in people's day-to-day lives, have been highly significant. Added to the penetration of new information and communications technologies (ICTs), this has had a particular impact on the lives of adolescents and young people (López, 2011). In addition, the expansion of access to education in the region has made the school population much more diverse. Educational establishments, by nature conservative, have been unable to fully take in some of these changes.

Although the enablers of violence vary according to the particularities of each territory, the countries of the region share certain cultural factors. The first has to do with a type of symbolic violence associated with a generalized culture that accepts violence as a means to resolve conflict. One of the roles that the education system should play is precisely to promote a change of attitudes and values within younger generations, to accept the existence of conflict but to address it through non-violent means (IIHR, 2011).

The second factor common to countries of the region is also symbolic and has to do with discrimination and limited tolerance for difference in societies that are highly unequal. School, especially at the secondary level, was once optional and selective, geared towards the formation of elites. The opening of the educational space to broad socio cultural diversities has generated a tension with the cultural tradition of competition and discrimination, which impedes the tolerance of difference and coexistence within educational establishments. López (2011, p. 236) argues that there is a value mismatch between the students schools would wish to have, and the students actually in the classroom. Not only are the new students different, but it is evident that the difference creates unease and, moreover, is seen and treated as something negative. Low tolerance of difference is also expressed among the students themselves, who imitate the discriminatory and violent behavior of their parents and of settings around the school, as direct or symbolic interpersonal violence within the school space (see table III.1).

Manifestations of violence within the educational sphere are diverse and must be understood within the set of interpersonal relations in which they occur and the differing degree of intensity or seriousness of the actions involved. In this regard, it is necessary to differentiate between acts of violence perpetrated by adults (the school authorities) against students, those perpetrated by students (and their parents) against school teachers and authorities, and violence between peers. Peer violence —school bullying— has become more significant in recent times because of the attention it has received in the media, and this is the type examined in depth in this section.

The concept of school bullying refers to different sorts of intimidation, harassment, abuse and victimization occurring repeatedly between school pupils. It consists of physical or psychological aggression that is repeated over lengthy periods of time and it has different consequences, all equally worrying, for all the students involved in these behaviours. Three types of actors are involved in these situations: victim, perpetrator and witnesses (Román and Murillo, 2011). Bullying is common in adolescence, during the process of identity construction, where the perpetrator needs witnesses for the aggression to contribute to his or her own process of identity reaffirmation.

According to a report on school violence by Plan International and the United Nations Children's Fund (UNICEF) (Eljach, 2011), peer violence in childhood is common and even normal at the stage of development and socialization. These processes must be accompanied by adult support to guide and impose behavioural boundaries. The use of violence in adolescence is different because it is a conscious act. It can often be interpreted as an act of self-recognition and self-validation, based on confrontation and disparagement of another. That is why it needs witnesses. Adolescents who choose this way to affirm their identity tend not to have received the recognition they need in their own environment (familiar or school) or did not have suitable guidance or boundaries that would have contained this sort of behaviour while growing up.

In order to design effective strategies to tackle the problem of bullying, it is important to consider the perpetrator and not, as is common, to work only with the victim, as if he or she were responsible for the violent treatment through failure to adapt socially. The actions of the perpetrator must also be considered as a response to a series of problematic factors in his or her own development. Discriminatory attitudes that often end up as violent adolescent behaviour come from imitation and what they have learned from the adult world immediately around them (Eljach, 2011). For that reason, as well as sanctions, it is necessary to provide support and work on the personal resources of conflict management and tolerance. Educating the school group in their role as protectors of the victim when witnessing violence can also be a highly effective strategy for controlling this type of behaviour at school.

1.   Peer violence at school: some figures

Some studies on the subject suggest that physical violence in schools has lessened, but emotional or psychological violence has increased. This type of bullying can be highly damaging because it is hidden and often goes unnoticed as it leaves no physical trace (Eljach, 2011). As in other spheres of violence, it is hard to find comparable statistics for the countries of the region. One of the few statistics available in the specific area of peer violence at school is compiled by the Global School-Based Student Health Survey, in which 23 Latin American and Caribbean countries took part in the decade of the 2000. These data show that, on average, 28% of school pupils participating in the study reported having suffered school bullying during the preceding month. In other words, about a third of students report facing this problem on a relatively day-to-day basis in their school life (see figure III.1).

An indirect measurement based on a compilation of national studies on violence at school, carried out by Plan International and UNICEF (Eljach, 2011), finds that between 50% and 70% of the school population reports having been a victim or a witness to peer aggression during their school life. Although the questions in table III.4 are not comparable, the information compiled from national youth surveys bears out this trend, especially in the case of adolescents between 15 and 19, a large proportion of whom are in the school system. The figures are similar for the cases of Guatemala (69%)

and Peru (51%) because, unlike the Chilean survey, the questions included having been a witness or a victim. In the Chilean survey, the values coincide with the victimization trends shown in figure III.1.

Figure III.1
Latin America and the Caribbean (23 countries): population aged between 11 and 17 reporting having suffered bullying in the past month
(Percentages)

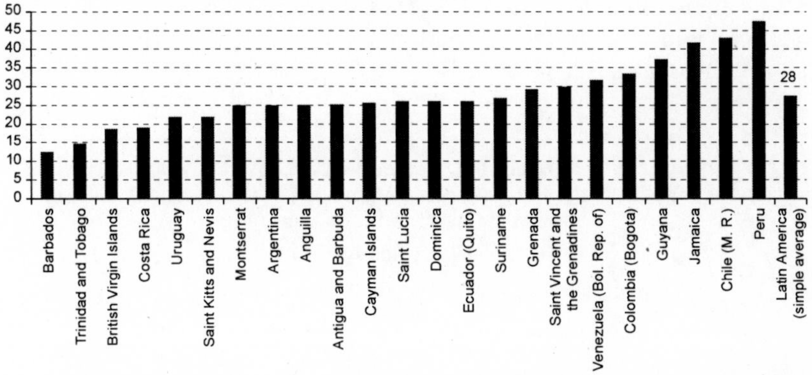

Source: Economic Commission for Latin America and the Caribbean (ECLAC), on the basis of special tabulations of data from the Global School-based Student Health Survey (GSHS) of the World Health Organization.

Note: For the Bolivarian Republic of Venezuela, Chile, Colombia and Ecuador the information covers only the metropolitan regions of Barinas, Santiago, Bogota and Quito, respectively. The actual years for each country are: 2003 for Bolivarian Republic of Venezuela; 2005 for Chile; 2006 for Uruguay; 2007 for Argentina, the Cayman Islands, Colombia, Ecuador, Saint Lucia and Saint Vincent and the Grenadines; 2008 for Grenada and Montserrat; 2009 for Anguilla, Antigua and Barbuda, the British Virgin Islands, Costa Rica, Dominica, and Suriname; 2010 for Guyana, Jamaica and Peru; and 2011 for Barbados, Saint Kitts and Nevis and Trinidad and Tobago.

Table III.4
Chile, Guatemala and Peru: young people aged 15-29 stating that physical violence occurs at their school or place of study, by age group
(Percentages)

Age group	Chile: Have you been a victim of physical violence in any of these situations? At school or place of study	Guatemala: Has physical violence occurred between students at your school or institute during the past year?	Peru: What problems most often occur or have occurred at your educational establishment? Physical violence between students
15-19 years	39	69	51
20-24 years	36	21	27
25-29 years	26	9	22

Source: Economic Commission for Latin America and the Caribbean (ECLAC), on the basis of special tabulations of data from the seventh National Youth Survey of Chile, 2012; the first National Youth Survey of Guatemala (ENJU), 2011; and the first National Youth Survey of Peru (ENAJUV), 2011.

Several of these national studies conclude that violence is not limited to the poorer schools, but occurs at all socioeconomic levels and in similar proportions in public and private schools. There is even evidence of greater prevalence of certain types of violent conduct in schools associated with high purchasing power groups (Eljach, 2011). The types of violence occurring are varied and not necessarily the same for males as for females. The information available shows that physical aggression is the dominant type of male violence, mentioned in 20.9% of cases, while for young women teasing over physical appearance arises in 23.5% of cases. These are types of violence that reflect behaviours and discrimination associated with traditional gender roles and inequalities.

Figure III.2
Latin America and the Caribbean (23 countries): types of bullying experienced by the population aged 11 to 17 reporting having been a victim of bullying in the past month, by sex
(Percentages)

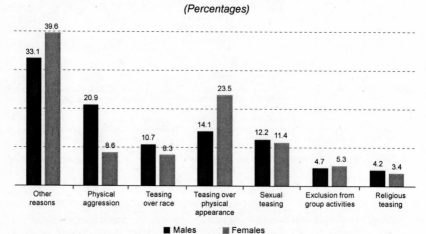

Source: Economic Commission for Latin America and the Caribbean (ECLAC), on the basis of special tabulations from the Global School-based Student Health Survey (GSHS) of the World Health Organization.
Note: For the Bolivarian Republic of Venezuela, Chile, Colombia and Ecuador the information covers only the metropolitan regions of Barinas, Santiago, Bogota and Quito, respectively. The actual years for each country are: 2003 for Bolivarian Republic of Venezuela; 2005 for Chile; 2006 for Uruguay; 2007 for Argentina, the Cayman Islands, Colombia, Ecuador, Saint Lucia and Saint Vincent and the Grenadines; 2008 for Grenada and Montserrat; 2009 for Anguilla, Antigua and Barbuda, the British Virgin Islands, Costa Rica, Dominica, and Suriname; 2010 for Guyana, Jamaica and Peru; and 2011 for Barbados, Saint Kitts and Nevis and Trinidad and Tobago. The category "other reasons" covers diverse causes of violence which cannot be classified in any particular type.

This information bears out the findings of various studies carried out internationally: that school violence is a fairly widespread phenomenon in all countries and at all social levels and is not limited to isolated events in certain countries or types of school (Román and Murillo, 2011). The different studies, especially those carried out in developed countries, but also in Latin America, have demonstrated the negative effects that peer violence has on victims in the school setting. These include poor academic performance, lack of motivation, low self-esteem and psycho-social development issues (Román and Murillo, 2011).

Box III.3
**Some considerations on homophobic school bullying
in Latin America**

One of the many facets of school bullying has to do with sexual orientation or gender identity. What is termed homophobic bullying often originates in suppositions associated with different labels used to discriminate against men and women on the basis of real or perceived sexual orientation or gender identity (UNESCO, 2013). Labels based on real or perceived sexual orientation or gender identity can also become cross-cutting ways of insulting many students. This sort of bullying can occur in the classroom and over social networks. Although systems of electronic communication have improved, cyberbullying often allows aggressors to use the anonymity to dissociate themselves from the responsibility and the consequences of facing the object of their aggression directly.

Homophobic school bullying is not simply an attack between peers. In several countries, in fact, teachers are the ones who isolate a student who has a different sexual orientation or gender identity to the rest. School and the education imparted allow students to develop the knowledge and skills to improve their future. But they are also the main stage for homophobic school bullying. It is thus a key sphere in which bullying can permeate students' social and psychological development.

School bullying is damaging for students' health and well-being. Teasing, provocation, hurtful nicknames, psychological manipulation, physical violence and social exclusion are all forms of school bullying. What is more, it is not suffered only by students with a sexual orientation or gender identity different to the rest, but also often by young people who are not lesbian, gay, bisexual, transgender or intersexual (LGTBI).

The aggression caused by homophobic school bullying impacts directly on the mental and physical health of victims. Young people who have suffered this sort of aggression often end up committing self-harm or even suicide.

Good practices for tackling homophobic bullying in Latin America

- Brazil: Brazil without Homophobia (2004) is a programme included under the Schools without Homophobia scheme, which adopts an interdisciplinary and large-scale approach to combating homophobia in educational establishments, conducting qualitative research on homophobia in schools and creating training material for students and teachers.

- Chile: The Movement for Sexual Diversity (MUMS) is sponsored by several municipalities. It involves workshops conducted in different educational establishments in Santiago, with the aim of tacking school bullying and violence in contexts of respect for sexual diversity.

Box III.3 (concluded)

- El Salvador: An initiative carried out by the Secretariat for Social Inclusion jointly with the Ministry of Education is aimed at raising awareness of school bullying and encouraging school principals to take action in cases of discrimination and homophobic school bullying.

- Mexico: The Foundation FUNSEVIDA is a support group for parents, family and friends, and created a video entitled "Homophobia and HIV: Fathers and Mothers Speak" in which they present their experiences. The Foundation also developed a project in six schools in the city of Jalapa, aimed at recognizing cases of homophobic school bullying and taking measures to tackle it. Over 50 workshops were held for secondary school educators, parents and students.

Thus the bullying begins to be reproduced from within the gender-related structures in which young people have been raised. The discrimination is embedded in the activities that each student carries out that are not conventionally associated with the gender attributed to the person by his or her companions.

The challenge for schools thus consists of establishing clear, strict rules of behaviour, supporting their students socially and pedagogically, welcoming gender difference and making it explicit, creating a setting in which fair complaints and judgements may be made, helping students who are victims or perpetrators, and ensuring that each anti-discrimination initiative introduced by students or teachers is well received.

It is essential for an educational environment to be safe, respectful and free of discrimination. Creating space for cooperation, both within and outside the classroom, is the responsibility of all those studying, teaching, working or managing the school. These scenarios of solidarity should be designed to eliminate insults, sexism, pejorative language, and negative terms and models of behaviour that impede the free right of all young people to receive an education.

Source: Economic Commission for Latin America and the Caribbean (ECLAC), on the basis of United Nations Educational, Scientific and Cultural Organization (UNESCO), "Respuestas del sector de educación frente al bullying homofóbico", *Buenas políticas y prácticas para la educación en VIH y salud*, Cuadernillo, No. 8, Santiago, 2013.

2.   The technology factor in the equation

As will be discussed in greater detail in chapter V, the digital age and the use of Internet, especially social networks, are increasingly part of the daily life of people in the region, especially young people. The Internet is a platform that opens a broad array of possibilities and opportunities that depend on the place of access, the quality of the connection and the skills of the users. Despite large gaps, it is hard to deny that adolescents and young people now function within a notably technological environment, which is reinforced in school and often at home as well.

Inevitably, this context has transformed some key elements affecting young people's development process, in both positive and negative ways. The greater quantity and availability of information challenges and transforms ways of learning, as well as the skills that must be developed in order to learn better. Ways of relating to each other also change, since technology allows, for example, anonymous interactions with others, accessibility to large numbers of people, immediate communication, the establishment of virtual communities and automatic filing of the interaction (Pavez, 2014). It also opens channels of communication that did not exist before: Internet and the social networks have played an important role in many social, student and youth movements in the region and beyond (see chapter V).

These transformations generate opportunities and risks for the experiences of adolescents and young people. It is important to consider the limits and risks involved in using the Internet, especially for the younger population, given their limited capacity for self-regulation and their susceptibility to social pressure (O'Keefe and Clarke-Pearson, 2011, cited Pavez, 2013). Some of the better known risks and those most reported in the media are sexual grooming, adult stalking of minors for sexual purposes and cyberbullying. Cyberbullying occurs in the form of repeated harassment, persecution, denigration, violation of intimacy, exclusion or impersonation over the Internet or over other electronic media, by a group or an individual against a person who cannot defend him or herself (Smith and others, 2008, cited in Pavez, 2014). Although, as reviewed in earlier sections, violence and abuse of all types are not new in the school context, the form they are acquiring is, especially thanks to the Internet. This is because of the speed with which the message spreads, the breadth of the audience and its dissemination form part of an unprecedented phenomenon that can jeopardize educational systems not prepared to face them, and can make online platforms into instruments of emotional destruction (UNICEF, 2011, cited in Pavez, 2014).

Cyberbullying has features that make it not only more lasting over time, but also more damaging than bullying in person. For example, aggressors can hide their identity, which increases their impunity and makes the victim more defenseless. They can also multiply in number and take the humiliation to much broader audiences. It is a phenomenon that spreads at high speed and, though there is no direct physical aggression, it makes the injury public and thereby makes the victim more vulnerable (Cerezo-Ramírez, 2012, cited in Pavez, 2013).

Because it is an emerging phenomenon, few studies have tackled the issue of school bullying over the Internet in Latin America. Brazil is a pioneer in measuring this type of behaviour, and estimates that 33% of a total of 5,827 students surveyed reported that a friend had been a victim of cyberbullying in 2009, and that 30% had suffered mistreatment over the Internet, including disparagement over social networks, circulating embarrassing photos of them or their families, stealing passwords and impersonating them in social networks (Eljach, 2011). In Argentina, a study carried out jointly by Microsoft and the National Institute to Combat Discrimination, Xenophobia and Racism (INADI) concluded that 16% of school pupils surveyed had been intimidated or threatened at some point, and that 15% had experienced some sort of discrimination over a social network (UNICEF, 2011).

Cases are increasing in Chile, as well. The National Survey on School Violence, for which 49,637 students between the ages of 12 and 17 were interviewed in 2009, found that 8% had suffered Internet bullying at school. A worrying situation is the vicious cycle that arises between victims and perpetrators, since 48.3% of those who acknowledged having bullied other children over the Internet were also victims of serious school violence. This situation is even worse among girls, since 61.4% female perpetrators of online bullying of schoolmates had also been victims of bullying in person or over the Internet (Sepúlveda, 2012, cited in Pavez, 2013).

In a context in which the right to privacy, decency and reputation are vulnerable, without a normative framework to protect them in the digital world and where practices such as cyberbullying are on the rise, positions become polarized on the subject, with some of the arguments revolving around the ideas of protecting against empowerment and restricting capacity-building. However, children, adolescents and young people are bearers of rights, who are owed comprehensive economic, social and cultural protection, so visions of victimization should be set aside with regard to use of the Internet. Efforts should be directed towards redeeming opportunities and the advantages of being part of the digital world, while taking steps to protect against risk. This is little explored ground, but there seems to be a consensus in seeking the answer in the education system, not only to promote access to ICTs, but also to develop digital skills (Pavez, 2014, p. 5). Schools face the challenge of becoming places in which guidance is provided on behaviours, tools and capacities that can lessen risks and leverage the advantages of ICT use for future generations.

D.   Collective violence in the city[12]

Given the great tensions and difficulties involved for some countries, the urban dimension of violence, with enablers associated with criminality and drug trafficking, is among the most visible and worrying types for the region. It has a massive influence over young people's alternatives for development and social inclusion, because it creates a scenario that can involve them as victims or perpetrators in criminal manifestations of violence (see table III.1). According to the latest report by the United Nations Office on Drugs and

---

[12]   Much of this section was prepared for Social Panorama of Latin America 2014 (ECLAC, 2014) and includes inputs prepared by the consultant Carlos Mario Perea.

Crime (UNODC, 2014), an average of 30% of all homicides on the American continent are linked to organized crime or gangs, as compared to less than 1% in Asia, Europe and Oceania (ECLAC, 2014).

Fear, the immediate expression of insecurity and weakened social cohesion, permeates contemporary society, which is less and less able to generate cohesion. Throughout history, every society has at some point made a particular group the repository for its deep-seated fears, usually a population that is stigmatized and thus rejected and excluded. Young people are now that population, especially those living in the extensive areas of poverty found in Latin American cities.

The stigma has arisen on the basis of a symbolism that is very easily transferred from poor youth to criminal youth, closing yet more doors to inclusion. The marero (Central American gang member), tattooed up to the face and with an extremely aggressive attitude, is the ultimate embodiment of the archetype that provokes urban panic. His figure and the use the global media has made of it are revealing of the stigma now attached to this population, on to which today's society projects its fear of insecurity. This judgement is not necessarily based on the real evidence of the facts.

This stigmatization of youth in the context of insecurity and violence is paradoxically, in itself, yet another manifestation of collective structural violence. It must therefore be asked what is holding up the stigma that the society of insecurity has attributed to young people?

1. Homicide as the ultimate expression of direct violence

Little is known about the perpetrators of violence and their age distribution. Statistics are few and hard to find, and record-keeping is deficient, partly because so much crime goes unpunished in many of the region's countries. For example, in Mexico, according to the published data, the conviction rate for homicide in 2008 was fairly similar for young people aged 16 to 29 (10.7 per 100,000 inhabitants) and adults aged between 30 and 44 (9.6 per 100,000 inhabitants), dropping substantially for the group of adults aged 45 to 59 (5.2 per 100,000 inhabitants).[13] A more general approach to gauging participation in acts of violence are the figures for victims of extreme violence, such as homicide, the assumption being that the risk of falling victim to them rises with the degree of participation in violent organizations.

A comparative view of youth participation in homicides, compared with those aged between 30 and 44 and those aged between 45 and 59, does not support the stigma associated with the young. In the case of death rates from interpersonal violence involving assaults with firearms, blades and

---

[13] Legal statistics on criminal matters available on the Internet site of the National Institute of Statistics and Geography (INEGI), see [online] http://www.inegi.org.mx/.

other weapons, for example, the data for Latin America and the Caribbean between 1990 and 2010 do not suggest that violent deaths among those aged 15 to 29 are significantly different in nature to those among people aged 30 to 44 (see figure III.3). The two curves are roughly equal, and while the proportion of adults fell between 1995 and 2005, the differences were not enough to be statistically significant.

Figure III.3
Latin America and the Caribbean: rate of mortality from interpersonal violence, by age group, 1990-2010
(Deaths per 100,000 inhabitants)

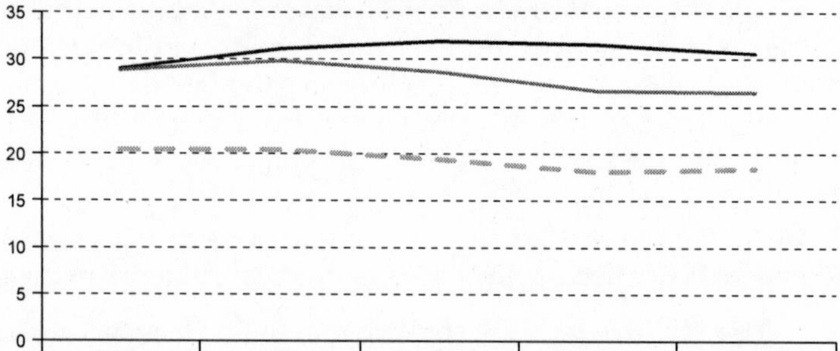

	1990	1995	2000	2005	2010
— Aged 15-29	29	31	32	32	31
— Aged 30-44	29	30	29	27	27
— Aged 45-59	20	20	19	18	18

Source: Institute for Health Metrics and Evaluation [online] http://vizhub.healthdata.org/gbd-compare/ and Economic Commission for Latin America and the Caribbean (ECLAC), *Social Panorama of Latin America 2014* (LC/G.2635-P), Santiago, 2014.

If this same information is analysed at the national level, taking the countries' worst affected by waves of violence in recent years (with rates in excess of 27 homicides per 100,000 inhabitants), it can be seen that the behaviour of the youth population is variable. There is no general rule that young people are the main victims of homicide; rather, the situation depends on the country, the time period and the general context of violence facing each society. For example, the rate of mortality from homicide by age group in the Bolivarian Republic of Venezuela, Brazil and Colombia (the three countries in the South American subcontinent with a higher level of violence) shows that the bulk of those affected in the last two decades were young (see figure III.4).

Figure III.4
Bolivarian Republic of Venezuela, Brazil and Colombia: rate of mortality
from interpersonal violence, by age group, 1990-2010 [a]

(Deaths per 100,000 inhabitants)

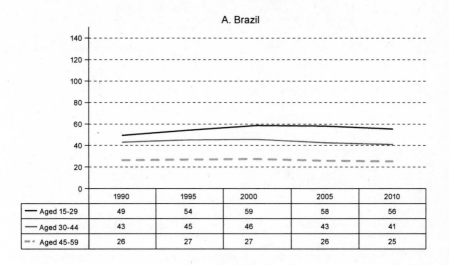

A. Brazil

	1990	1995	2000	2005	2010
Aged 15-29	49	54	59	58	56
Aged 30-44	43	45	46	43	41
Aged 45-59	26	27	27	26	25

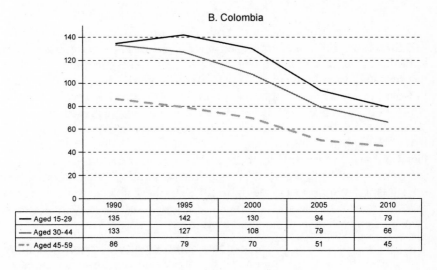

B. Colombia

	1990	1995	2000	2005	2010
Aged 15-29	135	142	130	94	79
Aged 30-44	133	127	108	79	66
Aged 45-59	86	79	70	51	45

Figure III.4 (concluded)

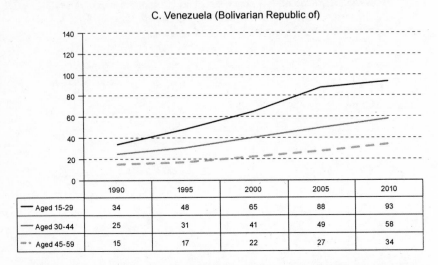

C. Venezuela (Bolivarian Republic of)

	1990	1995	2000	2005	2010
Aged 15-29	34	48	65	88	93
Aged 30-44	25	31	41	49	58
Aged 45-59	15	17	22	27	34

Source: Institute for Health Metrics and Evaluation [online] http://vizhub.healthdata.org/gbd-compare/ and Economic Commission for Latin America and the Caribbean (ECLAC), *Social Panorama of Latin America 2014* (LC/G.2635-P), Santiago, 2014.
[a] The differences between age groups are statistically significant except for the difference between the 15 to 29 and 30 to 44 groups in Colombia.

Even when the social context of these countries is taken into account, in terms of the presence of organized and powerful violent actors associated with the dynamics of drug trafficking and criminal organizations, violent territorial fiefdoms (drug traffickers in Rio de Janeiro in Brazil, or guerrillas in Colombia) are not enough to explain the situation. The case of Central America bears this out. Increased violence linked to the presence of these actors does not imply a higher level of youth involvement in homicide, as would be expected from the stigma. The cases of El Salvador, Guatemala, Honduras and Mexico confirm this: up until 2000, young adults (aged 30 to 44) displayed a slightly higher level of participation, although the difference was not statistically significant (see figure III.5). In the last decade, a time when general violence has been on the increase, segments of the youth population have participated on a more equal footing.

Thus, while more young people die from violent causes in the more violent countries of South America, in the nations with the same characteristics in the centre of the continent it is adults who are most affected or the impact is the same on both age groups. It should be stressed that there is a considerable difference in homicide rates between the two subcontinents, with a figure of 37 per 100,000 inhabitants for Central America and 16 per 100,000 inhabitants for South America (UNODC, 2012). Thus, the theory that the young are disproportionately involved in acts of violence is unsupported, as the victims are essentially in the 15-44 age group. Nonetheless, the context for youth integration is clearly a very difficult one in some of the region's cities. There is no doubt that young people form part of the context of violence, but this violence is a generalized phenomenon involving the whole of society, including the mature adult population.

Figure III.5
El Salvador, Guatemala, Honduras and Mexico: rate of mortality from interpersonal violence, by age group, 1990-2010 [a]
(Deaths per 100,000 inhabitants)

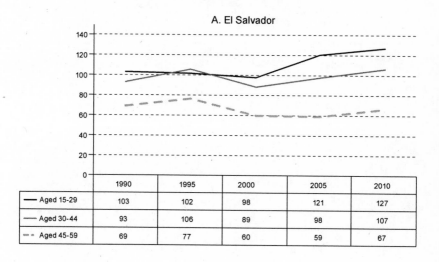

A. El Salvador

	1990	1995	2000	2005	2010
—— Aged 15-29	103	102	98	121	127
~~ Aged 30-44	93	106	89	98	107
⁓ Aged 45-59	69	77	60	59	67

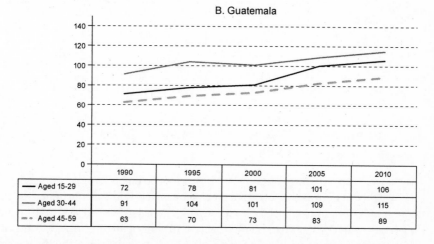

B. Guatemala

	1990	1995	2000	2005	2010
—— Aged 15-29	72	78	81	101	106
~~ Aged 30-44	91	104	101	109	115
⁓ Aged 45-59	63	70	73	83	89

Figure III.5 (concluded)

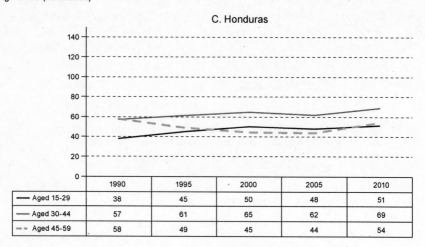

C. Honduras

	1990	1995	2000	2005	2010
—— Aged 15-29	38	45	50	48	51
~~ Aged 30-44	57	61	65	62	69
~~ ~ Aged 45-59	58	49	45	44	54

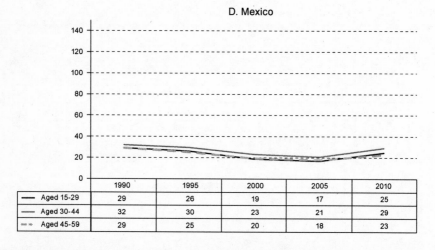

D. Mexico

	1990	1995	2000	2005	2010
—— Aged 15-29	29	26	19	17	25
~~ Aged 30-44	32	30	23	21	29
~~ ~ Aged 45-59	29	25	20	18	23

Source: Institute for Health Metrics and Evaluation [online] http://vizhub.healthdata.org/gbd-compare/.
[a] Differences in young people's mortality rates are not statistically different from those of other age groups in any of the countries.

2.   Organized participation in violence: gangs and drug trafficking

The statistical approach to gauging the extent of involvement in violent behaviour based on victim figures indicates that the stigma attached to violent youth derives not so much from the scale of their participation in acts of violence as in the way they participate. What the mass media most highlight are organized forms of urban violence among the young (usually males) in gangs going by the name of *pandillas, maras, clicas* or *combos,* depending on the country. Young people of this type are categorized in the collective imaginary as "deviants" or "misfits".

The *Social Panorama of Latin America 2008* (ECLAC, 2008b) noted that research findings indicated that the vast majority of those responsible for violence against young people in urban settings are of the same age and sex as their victims. In most cases, the perpetrators are males acting in groups. This type of organized violence arises as a consequence of the formation of local groups in the context of situations of marginalization and disruptive behaviours: gangs. These are bands that develop their own subcultures and fight among themselves for territorial control of neighbourhoods or districts. In some cities, large groups of youths commit a variety of crimes in their immediate surroundings but also engage in acts of intimidation and coercion (ECLAC, 2008b).

The information collected in the LAPOP 2012 study shows that around a third of the population perceive their local area as being affected by organizations of this kind (see table III.5), with the proportion being somewhat higher among the young (an average of 35%, compared to 31% for adults). It should be pointed out that citizens of the countries of northern triangle of Central America (El Salvador, Guatemala and Honduras), where *maras* have a strong presence in the main cities, are not the ones where gangs are considered most prevalent. There is greater awareness of them in other countries in the area, such as Panama and particularly the Dominican Republic, where this perception has been growing in recent years.

Youth involvement in different forms of organized urban violence in the region is undeniable. The territorial role of gangs within cities is one of the things that do most to create a feeling of insecurity among the population at large, as it directly affects community life. The figure of a gang member standing on the corner, alienated from the institutions he should be participating in at his stage of the life cycle (traditionally school or work) feeds the stigma of the violent youth. It represents a threat to civic order and the city as a cultural project because its sovereignty is based on the local district or *barrio* (Perea, 2008). The territorialization of organized criminal power is associated with the high levels of segregation and "ghettoization" in many Latin American cities.

Gangs have emerged as a direct effect of what has been described as structural violence, exclusion and marginalization from the development of society. Specialists in youth issues have been arguing for decades that gangs are organizations that provide some Latin American youths with a form of social inclusion: when all there is are poverty, very limited employment options and a near-absence of the State and institutions in general, then the only thing left to give a sense of future to many young people's lives is their peer group in the barrio. Gangs give them power, a cash income, a space and a feeling of belonging that no other social institution provides. As ECLAC (2008b) described it, belonging to a gang operates as a form of "inclusion within exclusion"; many gangs act as microsystems of social integration that reflect, compensate for and reinforce lack of integration into society. However, Reguillo notes that organizations of this type have changed in recent years from a core space of belonging to one of survival: "Youth groupings in contexts of exclusion and poverty seem to operate for many of their members as a setting that provides a minimum of security and trust, however precarious" (Perea, 2008, p.9).

Table III.5

Latin America and the Caribbean (18 countries): residents' perception of the incidence of gangs or *maras* in their local area, by country and age group, 2012

(Percentages)

Country	Age 16-29 years	Age 30 years and over
Guyana	19	14
Haiti	20	19
Jamaica	25	20
Belize	28	27
Nicaragua	28	24
Paraguay	30	24
Honduras	31	26
Mexico	33	35
Guatemala	36	31
Uruguay	37	35
Brazil	37	40
El Salvador	38	32
Costa Rica	39	32
Peru	40	35
Ecuador	41	38
Colombia	42	33
Panama	43	45
Dominican Republic	55	48
Latin America and the Caribbean[a]	**35**	**31**

Source: Economic Commission for Latin America and the Caribbean (ECLAC), on the basis of special tabulations of data from the biannual survey of the Latin American Public Opinion Project (LAPOP), 2012.

[a] Simple averages of the results from the 18 countries included in the measurement.

This phenomenon cannot be grasped without understanding the sociopolitical and cultural history of each territory in which these organizations emerge. These parameters influence the way they organize, the power criminal organizations have to recruit young people and the type of territorial dominance they exercise. It is important to analyse membership of these groups and the levels of violence that some of their efforts to assert this dominance result in, set as they are within a multiplicity of social processes that facilitate this kind of alternative social inclusion for some of the region's young people. The literature has identified many risk factors associated with the incorporation of certain sections of youth into violent territorial groups. They include the weakening of the social fabric, the aftermath of a history of civil violence, the availability of firearms, increasing inequality and marginalization, the alienation of some groups of young people from institutions, and education systems that reject and discriminate against them, among other things.

However, there is one thing that it is important to highlight, as it is common to a number of the region's countries (particularly those that have suffered from alarming cycles of violence) and is also particularly characteristic of the region: cocaine trafficking, which in the past few decades has become the dominant illegal market in cities marked by violence, such as Medellín in Colombia, Rio de Janeiro in Brazil, Ciudad Juárez in Mexico and, recently, cities in the northern triangle of Central America comprising El Salvador, Guatemala and Honduras. It is a market which provides large profit margins and around which another set of illegal activities is organized (Perea, 2014). In many of these cities, there is no prospect whatever of the legal market, much less the State, creating economically competitive forms of employment for young people from marginalized populations. In some countries, such as Mexico and those of Central America, the cartels are increasingly tending to use gangs to "outsource" abduction and contract killing activities, particularly when they come into conflict with one another and have to find more recruits quickly and at lower cost. Cocaine trafficking in the region has played a key role as a driver of conflict and a multiplier of violence.

Although Perea (2014) argues that drug trafficking does not account for all crime in Latin America and the Caribbean, nor can it be treated as just another form of organized crime. By multiplying violence, cocaine trafficking has raised conflict levels in the region.

Perea's analysis clearly shows that the more cash builds up in drug trafficking networks, the higher the levels of social violence. Cocaine trafficking is the most profitable in this category in the region, which has become the global centre of production of this substance.

One of the main factors in understanding the levels of violence facing marginalized youth in the region's cities has to do with the location of their country and city in the links of the drug trafficking chain. Perea (2014) describes four main links in this chain: production, processing, commerce and consumption. The further up the chain, the higher the profits. The *campesinos* growing the cocaine crops (mostly in Colombia, Peru and the Plurinational state of Bolivia) receive barely 1% of the total amount garnered in sales. Margins rise steeply towards the end of the business chain and the greatest profits are generated at the final link. Those making up the middle link, who transport the cocaine from where it is produced to middle countries, receive around 9% of the profits, while those taking the drug to the largest areas of consumption (the final link) receive about 25%. The retail sale in markets in which the drug is actually consumed accounts for 65% of the profit from trafficking, but it is distributed among a larger number of individuals, not organizations or cartels (Perea, 2014). The final wholesale trade is thus the stage that puts most profits in fewest hands (in the 1990s this stage was concentrated in Colombia; now most of it is within the Mexican cartels).

The fact that the activity is illegal and thus has no established regulations to mediate conflict, leads to the use of violence. The higher the profits, the greater the conflict and, thus, the worse the violence involved in marking out power relations between organizations. As Perea points out (2014), the large, organized incidents of violence occurring in the drug trade have taken place at the final link of the chain, where the most cash accumulates; this was the case of Colombia and now of Mexico. The crisis being experienced by countries with more fragile States, such as those of the northern triangle of Central America, is plain to see. They have been most affected by changes in cocaine trafficking routes into the United States since Colombia ceased to be the epicentre. Today, 95% of the cocaine entering the United States moves through Mexico or its territorial waters, and it is estimated that between 60% and 90% of it passes through Central America first (World Bank, 2011, cited in Escotto, 2015).

The way these organizations embed themselves in each city and each country depends greatly on institutions and the social fabric, and on the power structures of the criminal organizations themselves. These same factors determine the way they interact with society on the ground and the extent to which local youths are involved. Nonetheless, drug trafficking is one of the central factors in the crises of violence, and the Latin America and Caribbean region needs to respond as a bloc vis-à-vis the world and vis-à-vis consumption (most of which takes place in countries outside the region). As Perea says, this billion-dollar activity privatizes power and further undermines the justice system in many countries. It also heightens inequality and segregation and serves to increase the stigmatization of poor young people and citizen insecurity (Perea, 2014).

Understanding youth from the perspective of the stigma of violence distorts appreciations of the roots of the problem and opens the way to alarmist and exaggerated proposals for preventing and solving it. The stigma constrains our understanding of the different situations and contexts experienced by most young people and is used to justify policies that treat aggressive behaviour by some groups of individuals as part of growing up. As has been seen throughout this chapter, the causes are manifold, and those underlying the most extreme urban violence are associated with types of behaviour that are often directed from the adult world and form part of a context of large-scale law-breaking and crime. What is taking place reveals a society that is proving incapable of including its new generations.

E.   Alternatives for moving towards peaceful coexistence

The alternatives for reverting the current context of violence and its harmful consequences for youth must be approached from a comprehensive standpoint that takes into account the complexity described in this chapter and reflects the multiplicity of enablers of each of the manifestations of violence. Some of these enablers are general in nature, such as those associated with socioeconomic contexts or social transformations, and others are more symbolic. The latter include some of the region's cultural hallmarks, such as traditional gender roles and the acceptance of violence and violent means to resolve conflict.

This complexity also involves a diverse array of actors and scenarios in situations of violence, and thus calls for actions in different spheres, such as efforts to close inclusion gaps and to design policies to support the population with less access to the benefits of economic growth, to break away from culturally embedded visions that sanction discrimination and exclusion, to open up inclusive spaces (education and employment) and many other routes to discouraging violence. It must also be recognized that many expressions of violence already occurring need prevention and control strategies, with particular attention afforded to groups at risk of suffering violence and those at risk of perpetrating it, and even those who have already done so.

There is much that can and should be done, and in a context of limited resources, it is important to prioritize actions and identify what is most urgent. It is also important to examine what has been done before and continue it, if it has proven effective. It is even worth replicating measures taken elsewhere in the world if they have been successful, with the caveat that action must always be coordinated within an integrated approach and consider the specific features of the territory in question since, as mentioned earlier, isolated initiatives could be counterproductive.

In terms of identifying priorities, it is important to ascertain what young people themselves want, as the main stakeholders in this task. As argued in *Social Panorama of Latin America 2014* (ECLAC, 2014), it is important to ensure that adolescents and young people are present and involved in the formulation, implementation, oversight and validation of multisectoral public policies at all levels, with sustainable budgets and an awareness of particular contexts and situations. Policies that are inappropriate for the young have significant costs for all, both because they worsen the problems described in the earlier sections and because of the consequences of failing to include this population properly in economic development efforts and thereby sacrificing their creativity and energy. In other words, a virtuous circle is foregone and a vicious circle is entrenched.

1.   A youth vision of settings free of violence

In recent years, different youth participation forums have been held in connection with the worldwide debate on the new development goals, with a view to identifying the main challenges they face in the region. Their priorities are as diverse as the groups represented, although they have come together on certain issues regarded as essential and critical to the full development of youth in the region. One of these common issues is, precisely, the opportunity to live in settings free of violence (ECLAC, 2014).

It has been argued in diverse forums that public policies are needed to raise youth awareness of the culture of peace and to eliminate all forms of violence against women via prevention and education programmes and processes aimed at men and women at every stage of their lives. Femicide should be recognized as the ultimate manifestation of violence against women and as a crime that should be specifically classified in legislation (United Nations, 2014a). What young women have mainly called for are increased fiscal spending to prevent and combat gender violence, easier access to health-care and security systems in the event of assault, reparation programmes and laws on discrimination and racism, among other things.

Another important issue for many young people is protection against violence in virtual spaces, such as bullying and harassment on the Internet and social networks. Some forums have also advocated that States should move towards a security paradigm that protects young people rather than acting repressively against them, which means avoiding institutional violence of any kind and fully guaranteeing their rights.

The global consensus is that young people recognize the importance of their own role in conflict prevention and resolution, appreciating that this is an indispensable condition for the development of peaceful, inclusive and safe societies. The recognition of the importance of their role has been reflected in the formation of youth groups specifically aimed at violence prevention (for example, youth groups against violence in Central America).

In short, young people propose to opt for awareness-raising strategies, seeking to shift the cultural vision towards a culture of peace, and focus efforts on preventing gender violence and school violence, without disregarding the rest of the elements that make up the current context of violence.

2.   Policies and programmes addressing youth violence

With respect to action already under way, the latest *Global Status Report on Violence Prevention* (WHO/UNODC/UNDP, 2014) compiled information on general initiatives in terms of legislation, policies and programmes put in place in the countries of the region in this sphere (see table III.6). The results support the following considerations with respect to developing policies and strategies on violence and youth in the region.

Table III.6
Latin America and the Caribbean (19 countries): plans, laws and programmes relating to different types of violence

Country	National action plan	Youth violence laws		Youth violence prevention programmes	Intimate partner violence prevention programmes	Sexual violence prevention programmes	National prevalence surveys for non-fatal violence
	Youth violence	Against weapons on school premises	Against gang or criminal membership	School anti-bullying	Dating violence prevention in schools	In schools and universities	Youth violence
Belize	Yes	Yes	Yes	No	Yes	Yes	No
Bolivia (Plurinational State of)	Yes (subnational)	No	Yes	Yes	No	No	No information
Brazil	Yes	Yes	No	Yes	Yes	Yes	Yes
Colombia	Yes	Yes	Yes	Yes	Yes	Yes	No information
Costa Rica	No	Yes	Yes	Yes	Yes	Yes	Yes
Cuba	Yes	Yes	Yes	No	Yes	Yes	No
Dominica	No	Yes	No	Yes	No	Yes	No
Dominican Republic	Yes	Yes	Yes	Yes	No	Yes	No
Ecuador	Yes	No	Yes	No	No	Yes	No
El Salvador	Yes	Yes	Yes	Yes	Yes	Yes	No
Guatemala	Yes	Yes	Yes	Yes	No	Yes	No
Guyana	No	No	Yes	No	No	No	No
Honduras	Yes	No	Yes	Yes	Yes	No	No
Jamaica	Yes	Yes	No	Yes	Yes	Yes	Yes
Mexico	Yes	Yes	Yes	Yes	Yes	Yes	Yes
Nicaragua	Yes	Yes	Yes	Yes	No	Yes	No
Panama	Yes	Yes	Yes	Yes	Yes	Yes	No
Peru	Yes (subnational)	No	No	Yes	Yes	Yes	No
Trinidad and Tobago	Yes	No	Yes	Yes	Yes	Yes	No information

Source: Prepared by the authors, on the basis of World Health Organization/United Nations Office on Drugs and Crime/United Nations Development Programme, *Global Status Report on Violence Prevention 2014*, Geneva, 2014.

(a) Availability of information

The report mentioned found that most of the countries in the region have no information system available that could help to create accurate diagnoses of violence prevalence. Only 4 of 19 countries analysed had national surveys that compiled information on non-lethal violence.

In this regard, homicides, on which there is a great deal of information, are just one indicator of violence, but there are non-fatal expressions of violence experienced within the family, at school, in the city or in other spheres of daily life, that need to be addressed comprehensively. It is essential to have information on those non-lethal forms of violence in order to address youth violence properly and develop relevant policies and programmes.

(b) National action plans and normative frameworks

Developing a national-level action plan is a key step towards effective violence prevention. It is a means of coordinating everything that various public policy sectors can do to tackle the roots of the problem in an integrated manner. The report found that over 80% of the region's countries had made progress in creating national action plans on youth violence, despite lacking detailed statistical information on the subject (this was higher than the international average of 53%).

Most of the countries have also passed framework legislation and specific laws against violence, an important step in establishing accepted rules of conduct and building safe societies. Most of these laws have focused on preventing the possession of weapons in educational establishments, and on membership of gangs or organized violent groups. The report finds that many of these laws are not actually enforced, however, which draws attention to the importance of focusing national efforts on real enforcement of existing laws, and creating institutional mechanisms and resources to create safer environments (WHO/UNODC/UNDP, 2014).

The review conducted by the by Pan American Health Organization (PAHO, 2006) found that many national youth plans included concern for violence issues affecting young people. However, this was presented from a generic point of view, but not centralized or organized. These plans thus provide few tools for addressing youth violence in a timely and relevant manner (PAHO, 2006).

(c) Violence prevention programmes

With respect to youth violence prevention programmes, the findings of the report indicate that the strategies put in place at the international level tend to aim at building life skills and preventing intimidation. Most of the countries are implementing some type of school bullying prevention scheme (see table III.6) and, in the case of violence against women, the main strategy is to change social and cultural norms.

Many of the region's countries are also combating school and gender violence from the standpoint of new generations. Most of the approaches are based on citizenship building and the promotion of democratic values among young people and in their community settings. Many programmes focus on or are approached from within school settings, and some use peer mediation as an effective tool for education and conflict resolution.

School violence prevention programmes fall into three main categories: those aimed at generating information, those aimed at promoting peaceful coexistence in schools, and those aimed at promotion of rights, including the right to a violence-free setting. In the first case, actions have been taken over the past 10 years to examine the issues of school violence in depth, with programmes such as the Argentine Observatory of Violence in Schools and the Observatory on Violence and Coexistence in Schools in Peru.

In the case of measures aimed at making schools safe, violence-free places through promotion of peaceful coexistence and internal prevention, programmes identified include the National School Mediation Programme in Argentina; the policy on School Coexistence for Quality Education for All in Chile; the Programme for Conflict Management at School and the Peace Alliance, Education for Peace in Colombia; School in our Hands and the Student Arts Festival in Costa Rica; the Learn Without Fear campaign, the School Safety Plan and the School Violence Prevention Plan in El Salvador; the National Safe Schools Programme, the National Programme to Abolish and Eliminate School Violence and the Opening Schools for Equity project in Mexico; the From Violence to Coexistence Programme, the League against School Bullying and the School Prosecutors programme in Peru; and the Bicentennial Security Deployment in the Bolivarian Republic of Venezuela.

Some of the most successful school-based strategies are those that promote the opening of schools to the community (Open Schools in Guatemala and Brazil). The PAHO study (2006) identified the following elements as crucial to the effectiveness of these programmes: getting young people and local communities to take ownership of the school space, and thus protect it instead of attacking it; making school a friendlier place for the community overall, which makes it more attractive for dropouts to return; and generate more empathy in the educational process by offering (non-exclusive) life learning tools.

A number of programmes focus on ensuring youth rights in contexts of school violence, including: the National Programme for the Rights of Children and Adolescents in Argentina; the Building Citizenship Project in Chile; the Decennial National Plan of Education - Education in and for Peace, Coexistence and Citizenship in Colombia; and the School Defenders programme in the Bolivarian Republic of Venezuela.

Measures have also been taken in the area of gender violence and child abuse. In this case, examples are the Training and Treatment Programme for Family Violence, Child Battering and Sexual Abuse in Argentina; the District Plan for Comprehensive Care of Victims of Violence and Sexual Abuse in Colombia; and the Programme to Prevent and Combat Youth and Gender Violence based on education and human rights protection in El Salvador.

Another category of violence prevention programmes touching on youth are those that operate through "community policies". A number of countries have developed programmes at the city level (Bogota, Sao Paulo, Belo Horizonte), and others, such as Nicaragua, have major programmes in place at the national level. Nicaragua's violence prevention model coordinates all the ministries involved in prevention and treatment of violence within the framework of a shared responsibility model. It also includes grass-roots support through what are known as "family, community and life cabinets" comprising the inhabitants of the communities involved. Under this modality, the police coordinate a preventive, proactive and community-based model that includes ongoing professionalization of the police force and coordination with voluntary police and two further entities—the Women's and Children's Police Station and the Youth Affairs Directorate—that deal in particular with youth violence. The remit of the Youth Affairs Directorate includes working closely with violent youth and young people involved with gangs or in trouble with the law. The idea is to deal with these young people by means of a peaceful strategy applying a six-step protocol (truce, diagnosis, care, armistice, demobilization and social reintegration), aimed at gaining commitment from the young people themselves, their families and the community.

As indicated by PAHO (2006), the experiences of those community police that have been evaluated in Latin America suggest that they increase public trust in the police and bring the community closer. They do not necessarily reduce rates of police abuse, which would require parallel retraining strategies as well as surveillance and early warning systems to detect reiterated breaches by certain police. The evidence is less clear in relation to the reduction of violence and criminality. Some countries have also developed programmes to build routes back into society for young people who are in marginalized situations, have committed violence or are at risk of doing so. This is the case of the prevention programme for children and adolescents at risk of entering crime in Chile; the Open School Programme in Brazil; the Programme to strengthen protection measures for adolescent offenders in Ecuador; and Young Protagonists, Open Schools and the Youth Athletic League in Guatemala. Through such activities as art workshops and sports, these programmes foster coexistence to prevent youth delinquency or drugs consumption.

Lastly, several youth violence prevention programmes implemented over the past 10 years have been identified, which do not focus on any particular subject. This is the case of the Youth Development and Violence Prevention Project in the Dominican Republic. There are also programmes of a general nature, but that permeate the youth group, such as the citizen skills-development project to prevent violence and build democracy in Colombia, the Integral Security Programme in Panama, the Violence, No Thanks! programme in the Dominican Republic, and the programme promoting the right to be well treated in the Bolivarian Republic of Venezuela.

Some of these programmes are no longer current. This may be because of budgetary constraints or because they were associated with political cycles in the countries (government terms). Some have been more successful, such as the open schools and peace culture schemes, while others have not produced the desired outcomes, such as those promoting specific youth participation. In this last regard, initiatives promoting labour market integration and citizen participation appear to be more effective (Rodríguez, 2006).

(d) The influence of the stigma associated with youth

The stigma of violence attached to youth warrants particular mention in relation to its impact on policymaking. This stigma arose in the 1980s and persists in the collective and cultural imaginary, reinforced in large part by the messages conveyed by the media, something that has led to a debate in many countries about lowering the age of criminal responsibility. Concern over the age of criminal responsibility forms part of the unease arising in a context of insecurity that breeds angst among the citizenry, leading public opinion to call for strong punishment for adolescents, on the basis that they are aware of their actions and cannot be exonerated of the responsibility for embarking upon a life of crime. In this regard, it is important to recall that State policies or strategies of over-criminalization, repression, non-compliance with the law, criminal responsibility for adolescents and others that were vigorously pursued in the 2000s proved counterproductive, as levels of violence continued to rise.

The alternative is to implement youth inclusion policies with mechanisms of communication and shared reflection on the causes of youth victimization and violence. The first step in forging a culture of peace is to internalize the basic idea that conflict is not to be denied, but can always be resolved without violence.

Peaceful negotiation and resolution should be part of formal and non-formal education, as this would give the new generations tools for relating, understanding the other and resolving disagreements without resorting to violence. The State needs to be capable of transmitting models of a culture of peace through policies, judicial systems, transparency, support for the community, and its institutions in general (ECLAC, 2014).

3.   Recommendations for youth inclusion in contexts of violence

In order to start to resolve the current context of violence, the range of approaches taken must reflect the various dimensions of violence discussed in this chapter. This means designing comprehensive policies that focus on the multiple causes, with a solid State presence, through strategies coordinated at different levels and considering the territorial perspective. Policies must also include long-term strategies to improve aspects of the general social context, such as a culture of non-violent conflict resolution in which violence decreases precisely because perpetrators of violence wish to stop. All the social stakeholders must recognize their shared responsibility and foster trust in institutions, especially in institutions such as the police.

Some general recommendations may be made in this regard. The first is that any approaches taken must clearly establish how each dimension of the issue will be tackled in order to avoid duplication of measures and target efforts better. As PAHO has argued (2006), violence must be treated as a structural and highly complex phenomenon: it is time to discard the over-simplistic policy approaches that are all too common in the region, with exclusively repressive responses or moralistic campaigns that often automatically associate poverty with violence.

The second general recommendation is the coordination of the various public departments working on violence and youth issues. They must work in a complementary manner to forge a comprehensive national policy approach to the problem. Accordingly, some sort of forum for inter-agency coordination is crucial.

These two initial recommendations form the basis for designing responses with comprehensive, integrated approaches that, as Rodríguez has stated, have been the most successful because they work on the citizen culture itself, and aim to achieve sustainability over time and space, while limiting the use of short-term responses (Rodríguez, 2006, p. 3). Priorities should be established among long-term responses, fostering the values of peace, tolerance and peaceful conflict resolution. The security agenda should complement this perspective and work for pacification in the framework of respect for human rights (Alvarado, Rodríguez and Vommaro, 2013).

A third recommendation is to develop national information systems capable of portraying the real magnitude of the problem and identifying the worst affected population groups, in order to target measures better and monitor their progress.

A fourth important consideration is the need to build up the capacities of institutions responsible for designing, implementing and coordinating, in terms of the knowledge to develop appropriate methods for designing, monitoring and evaluating useful strategies. Part of this may be achieved by raising the youth agenda to a level at which resources can be properly allocated to capacity-building to enable State institutions to implement the agenda in a sustainable and relevant manner, as well as clearly tackling youth violence in national youth and public safety programmes, with well defined functions for different institutions.

The fifth general recommendation is to achieve more and better coordination to avoid duplication of efforts between all the parties involved in conducting youth and violence prevention programmes and projects. These include national bodies, local authorities, civil society organizations and international cooperation agencies (whether bilateral or multilateral). In this regard, it is worth recalling that civil society organizations and international cooperation agencies have played a very important role in violence prevention, albeit on a small scale. It is thus recommended that these integrated responses draw support from community social capital. The design of local strategies benefits from synergies and complementarities between State institutions and community-level social networks (PAHO, 2006).

As a sixth general recommendation, it is important to acknowledge young people as the main actors in the measures taken, and have them play decisive roles in design and implementation so that they take ownership of those actions. This is the model recognized to be most successful in the treatment of violence in youth (Rodríguez, 2006).

When it comes to approaches to violence specifically —and on the basis that prevention is generally more efficient than control— Buvinic, Morrison and Orlando list a set of recommendations for violence prevention, ordered by type, as set forth below.[14]

(a) Primary prevention strategies

It is important to reduce the risk factors that raise the likelihood of an individual or group suffering or being a perpetrator of violence, through strategies for the short, medium, and long terms. Short- and medium-term measures recommended for consideration include:

- Strategies to reduce risks in the immediate surroundings, such as alcohol or drugs consumption, or possession of weapons.

- Awareness-raising and education campaigns for the population at large, with particular emphasis on youth, aimed at promoting a culture of peace from within different spheres, including practice modelling: in the education system and in the media, at work and within the family (awareness-raising for parents should be seen as extremely important).

---

[14]   For more information, see Buvinic, Morrison and Orlando (2005).

- School is a key institution in these processes. Studies of successful experiences have identified certain important variables in making programmes more effective. Recommended measures are those which democratize school management and establish positive relations between students and teachers; prepare the community to deal with conflict in a suitable manner, proactively and avoiding impunity; and involve the family and the educational community in general (PAHO, 2006).

- The media can also play a key role in awareness-raising. There is a tendency to focus on the negative impact the media can have on efforts to promote violence prevention, by dwelling on acts of violence and stigmatizing young people in crime reporting (PAHO, 2006). Efforts are needed to work with the media in the opposite direction.

- Legislation on violence should be assessed in terms of how it treats youth violence, with a view to guiding or governing the way institutions proceed in the event of violence in school and non-school settings, always from a rights-based perspective and with clear rules and implications for youth offenders.

Recommended long-term measures include:

- Support for initiatives at different levels (government, civil society or international cooperation) that promote youth social inclusion in education, employment and political participation, by opening opportunities for such inclusion with strategies such as school grants and support for first-time job-seekers, among other measures discussed in greater depth in previous chapters.

(b) Secondary prevention strategies

Secondary prevention focuses on more vulnerable groups that have already been affected by violence, such as individuals involved in gangs, living on the street or suffering from addiction.

- Better design and implementation of initiatives focusing on activities such as psycho-social assistance, care for young people with drugs or alcohol addiction, and demobilization of young gang members.

- Stronger strategies to address youth violence in school with protocols establishing roadmaps that take into account the rights of children and adolescents and the best interests of minors under the age of 18.

- Police institutions also play an essential role and much work is needed to change the predominant approach in the region, inasmuch as these institutions' trustworthiness and legitimacy in the eyes of neighbourhoods and communities are badly eroded by the imaginary of the poor youth as a potential criminal who needs to be controlled and punished. Work must be done to ensure that the police are an institution that can be turned to for protection (PAHO, 2006).

(c) Tertiary prevention strategies

Tertiary prevention is restorative in nature. It consists of the rehabilitation and social reintegration of individuals who have been in trouble with the law or have already been involved in violence, as well as reparations to victims.

- Design and implementation of a social policy that promotes criminal responsibility (sanction), but also social reintegration through mechanisms to include young people in the spheres of education or work, viewing violence as a significant enough phenomenon to trigger formal inclusion mechanisms in the event of law-breaking.

- Prosecution of violence with stronger justice systems, making forums available for complaints and proper follow-up of processes, for both victims and perpetrators. This includes stronger police capacities for report handling, use of investigative tools and processing and procedures relating to suspects.

- Promotion of initiatives directed towards the youth population in conflict with the law. This encompasses all young people who are imprisoned or detained and lack opportunities to reintegrate into the country's social, economic and political life upon completion of their sentence. They must be acknowledged as individuals with the right to be treated with dignity and to be given the tools to develop the capacities and skills they need to lead a decent and productive life once they regain their freedom.

Lastly, it is well worth identifying and "replicating" successful experiences or good practices on youth social inclusion in other countries of the region. South-South cooperation is also a valuable source of such experiences, and good use can be made of studies or analyses carried out by universities or non-governmental organizations (NGOs) that contribute to a better understanding of the issue, especially in the following areas: school dropout; organized crime, drug trafficking and rising drug consumption; suicide in childhood or adolescence; precarious conditions of youth employment; intrafamily violence; cross-border youth migration; return of young deportees; and rehabilitation and reintegration of young people in conflict with the law. These studies can help to identify useful elements for public policy actions plans aimed at reducing youth involvement in the multiple dimensions of violence described in this chapter, by promoting a broader concept of social inclusion conducive to development with equality, and particularly to the right of all the young people in the region to develop in a setting free of violence.

Bibliography

Aguilar, Jeanette and Marlon Carranza (2008), "Las maras y pandillas como actores ilegales de la región", San Salvador.

Alvarado, Sara Victoria, Ernesto Rodríguez and Pablo Vommaro (2013), *Informe CLACSO-UNESCO: políticas de inclusión social de jóvenes en América Latina. Situación, desafíos y recomendaciones para la acción* [online] http://www.celaju.net/informe-unesco-clacso-politicas-publicas-de-juventud-e-inclusion-social-en-america-latina-y-el-caribe/.

Bravo, Rebeca G. (2013), *Maras en Centroamérica y México (Costa Rica, Guatemala, Honduras, Nicaragua, Panamá, El Salvador)*, Madrid, Spanish Commission for Refugee Assistance.

Buvinic, Mayra, Andrew Morrison and María Beatriz Orlando (2005), "Violencia, crimen y desarrollo social en América Latina y el Caribe", *Papeles de Población*, No. 43, Autonomous University of the State of Mexico.

Dammert, Lucía and others (2010), *Crimen e inseguridad: indicadores para las Américas*, Santiago, FLACSO Chile/Inter-American Development Bank (IDB).

ECLAC (Economic Commission for Latin America and the Caribbean) (2014), *Social Panorama of Latin America 2014* (LC/G.2635-P), Santiago.

___(2008a), "Situación y desafíos de la juventud en Iberoamérica", paper prepared for the XVIII Ibero-American Summit of Heads of State and Government, San Salvador.

___(2008b), *Social Panorama of Latin America 2008* (LC/G.2402-P), Santiago.

ECLAC/OIJ (Economic Commission for Latin America and the Caribbean/Ibero-American Youth Organization) (2008), *Juventud y cohesión social en Iberoamérica. Un modelo para armar* (LC/G.2391), Santiago.

Eljach, Sonia (2011), *Violencia escolar en América Latina y el Caribe: superficie y fondo*, Panama City, Plan International/United Nation Children's Fund (UNICEF).

Escotto, Teresita (2015), "Juventudes en Centroamérica en contextos de inseguridad y violencia: realidades y retos para su inclusión social", forthcoming.

Fleitas Ortiz de Rozas, Diego M., Germán Lodola and Hernán Flom (2014), *Delito y violencia en América Latina y el Caribe: perfil de los países de la región*, Buenos Aires, Public Policies Association.

Galtung, Johan (1990), "Cultural violence", *Journal of Peace Research*, vol. 27, No. 3, SAGE.

IIHR (Inter-American Institute of Human Rights) (2011), *Informe interamericano de la educación en derechos humanos: Un estudio en 19 países. Desarrollo en las políticas de convivencia y seguridad escolar con enfoque de derechos*, San Jose.

Imbusch, Peter, Michel Misse and Fernando Carrión (2011), "Violence research in Latin America and the Caribbean: a literature review", *International Journal of Conflict and Violence*, vol. 5, No. 1.

INJUV (National Institute for Youth) (2012), *Séptima Encuesta Nacional de Juventud*, Santiago.

Lacayo, Nadine (2015), "Inclusión social juvenil en contextos de violencia. Estudio de caso Nicaragua", unpublished.

LAPOP (Latin American Public Opinion Project) (2012), "Base de datos del Barómetro de las Américas" [online] http://lapop.ccp.ucr.ac.cr/Lapop_English.html.

LLECE (Latin American Laboratory for Assessment of the Quality of Education) (2013), *Análisis del clima escolar: ¿Poderoso factor que explica el aprendizaje en América Latina y el Caribe?*, Regional Office for Education in Latin America and the Caribbean (OREALC).

López, Néstor (2011), "El desprecio por ese alumno", *Escuela, identidad y discriminación*, Néstor López (coord.), Buenos Aires, International Institute for Educational Planning (IIEP) of the United Nations Educational, Scientific and Cultural Organization (UNESCO), Buenos Aires.

Murcia, Walter (2015), "Pandillas en El Salvador: propuestas y desafíos para la inclusión social juvenil en contextos de violencia urbana", *Project Document* (LC/W.672), Santiago.

Ortega, Daniel and others (2014), *Por una América Latina más segura: Una nueva perspectiva para prevenir y controlar el delito*, Bogota, Development Bank of Latin America.

PAHO (Pan American Health Organization) (2006), *Políticas públicas y marcos legales para la prevención de la violencia relacionada con adolescentes y jóvenes. Estado del arte en América Latina 1995-2004*, Washington, D.C.

Pavez, María Isabel (2014), "Los derechos de la infancia en la era de Internet: América Latina y las nuevas tecnologías", *Políticas Sociales series*, No. 210 (LC/L.3894), Santiago, Economic Commission for Latin America and the Caribbean (ECLAC).

___(2013), "Juventud latinoamericana y el uso y apropiación de redes sociales: desafíos e interrogantes", Santiago, unpublished.

Perea Restrepo, Carlos (2014), "La muerte próxima. Vida y dominación en Río de Janeiro y Medellín", *Análisis Político*, vol. 27, No. 80.

___(2008), *¿Qué nos une? Jóvenes, cultura y ciudadanía*, Medellín, La Carreta.

PLAN (2008), *Learn without Fear: The Global Campaign to End Violence in Schools*.

PLAN International/UNICEF (United Nations Children's Fund) (2013), *Toolkit and Analysis of Legislation and Public Policies to Protect Children and Adolescents from All Forms of Violence in Schools*, Panama City.

Regional Youth Alliance (2010), "Diagnóstico de la violencia juvenil en El Salvador", San Salvador.

Rodino, Ana María (2013), "Safety and peaceful coexistence policies in Latin American schools: human rights perspective", *Sociología, Problemas e Práticas*, No. 71.

Rodríguez, Ernesto (2006), *Jóvenes, violencias y cultura de paz en América Central: enfoques, dilemas y respuestas a desplegar en el futuro*.

Román, Marcela and Francisco Javier Murillo (2011), "Latin America: school bullying and academic achievement", *CEPAL Review*, No. 104 (LC/G.2498-P), Santiago, Economic Commission for Latin America and the Caribbean (ECLAC).

Rubio, Mauricio (2008), "La pandilla proxeneta, violencia y prostitución juvenil en Centroamérica", *URVIO. Revista Latinoamericana de Seguridad Ciudadana*, No. 4, Quito, FLACSO Ecuador.

SENAJU (National Youth Secretariat) (2011), *Primera Encuesta Nacional de la Juventud Peruana (ENAJUV 2011)*, Lima.

SESC/CONJUVE/INE (Executive Secretariat for Civic Service/National Youth Council/National Institute of Statistics) (2011), *Primera Encuesta Nacional de Juventud en Guatemala (ENJU 2011)*, Guatemala City.

UNDP (United Nations Development Programme) (2013), *Informe regional de desarrollo humano 2013–2014. Seguridad ciudadana con rostro humano: diagnóstico y propuestas para América Latina*, New York.

UNESCO (United Nations Educational, Scientific and Cultural Organization) (2013), "Respuestas del sector de educación frente al bullying homofóbico", *Buenas políticas y prácticas para la educación en VIH y salud*, Cuadernillo, No. 8, Santiago.

UNICEF (United Nations Children's Fund) (2014), *Hidden in Plain Sight: a Statistical Analysis of Violence against Children*, New York.

___(2011), "Internet segura. Sin riesgo ni discriminación" [online] http://internet. inadi.gob.ar/wp-content/uploads/2011/12/internet-segura.pdf.

United Nations (2014), "ECOSOC Forum on Youth 2014. #Youth2015: Realizing the Future They Want" [online] http://www.un.org/en/ecosoc/youth2014/pdf/ background_note.pdf.

___(1993), "Declaration on the Elimination of Violence against Women" [online] http://www.un.org/documents/ga/res/48/a48r104.htm.

UNODC (United Nations Office on Drugs and Crime) (2014), *Global Study on Homicide 2013: Trends, Contexts, Data*, Vienna.

___(2012), *Global Study on Homicide 2011: Trends, Contexts, Data*, Vienna.

WHO (World Health Organization) (2013), "Global Health Observatory Data Repository" [online] http://apps.who.int/gho/data/node.main#.

___(2002), *World Report on Violence and Health*, Washington, D.C.

WHO/UNODC/UNDP (World Health Organization/United Nations Office on Drugs and Crime/United Nations Development Programme) (2014), *Global Status Report on Violence Prevention 2014*, Geneva.

World Bank (2011), *Crime and Violence in Central America: A Development Challenge* [online] https://siteresources.worldbank.org/INTLAC/Resources/FINAL_ VOLUME_I_ENGLISH_CrimeAndViolence.pdf.

Zurita Rivera, Úrsula (2012), "Las escuelas mexicanas y la legislación sobre la convivencia, la seguridad y la violencia escolar", *Educación y Territorio*, vol. 2, No. 1, June.

Chapter IV

Young people's access to culture in the digital era in Latin America

Guillermo Sunkel[1]

Introduction

In the past few decades much evidence has been gathered about the role that culture plays in development (UNESCO, 2010). The international community has recognized that culture makes a genuine contribution to policies, strategies and programmes designed to achieve inclusive economic and social development, environmental sustainability, harmony, peace and security. Culture has therefore come to be viewed as a driver and a facilitator of sustainable development. The value culture enshrines for development has also recently been recognized by the United Nations System Task Team on the Post-2015 United Nations Development Agenda (UNESCO, 2012).

Increasing awareness of the role played by culture includes a recognition of its links with various aspects of development, such as social inclusion. As noted by the Economic Commission for Latin America and the Caribbean (ECLAC), social inclusion requires the progressive compliance and fulfilment of rights critical to attain many of the aspirations of a safe,

---

[1] The author wishes to thank Andrés Espejo for having processed the statistical data used in this chapter and Matías Salcés for having compiled the information on cultural programmes used here.

healthy and prosperous society throughout the world (ECLAC, 2014b, p. 6). Culture, like education and health, is a realm in which the exercise of human rights is subject to processes of social exclusion. Therefore, young people must have access to culture —one of the most fundamental of cultural rights— if they are to have opportunities to express themselves in ways that will enable them to develop fully as people and become active participants in society.

Ensuring the cultural inclusion of socially excluded or vulnerable young people means providing them with the opportunity to access and consume culture so that they can express themselves, continue developing as persons, change their social situation and influence the society around them. Exercising the right to access and participate in the cultural sphere contributes to human development and to young people's well-being. Participation in cultural activities and the exercise of freedom of artistic expression are essential to forge inclusive, egalitarian societies (Bizkaia Observatory, 2012, p. 6).

Establishing a single definition of "culture" is no easy task. It is one of the more complex concepts in the social sciences and remains the subject of debate to this day. By trying to reconstruct the history of the concept, it becomes clear how the term is approached by the different fields of knowledge and schools of thought (ECLAC/OEI, 2014, p. 28). Currently, there is a tension between the anthropological notion of culture and the cultural notion of the State: while for the State culture is a specific sector, from an anthropological perspective, culture is the constituent element of all human actions and public policies (ECLAC/OEI, 2014, p. 15).

For the purposes of this chapter, the concept of culture refers to a specific sector that includes a broad spectrum of activities ranging from artistic activities —such as the visual arts— entailing both material and non-material forms of cultural heritage to cultural or creative industries (film, literature, music and so forth). Today, the cultural sector also includes new digital technologies or communications technologies that are having a profound impact on the ways in which human society produces, shares and utilizes cultural goods. But what distinguishes the activities carried out in the cultural sector and gives them a certain specificity is that their symbolic value prevails over their exchange value.

In view of the growing importance that digital technologies have acquired in young generations' daily lives, especially in the last few decades, it is important to include them in the concept of culture used here. In fact, while technological changes have had an impact on the whole of society, their impact has been especially strong on the younger generations, transforming the way that they live, the way that they experience time and space, and the way that they relate to others.

The main aim of this chapter is to undertake an examination of young people's access to culture in the digital era in Latin America. The notion of "access" is used here to refer specifically to users of culture (that is, the public), as distinct from cultural creators or producers. This approach is directly linked to cultural rights: when young people lack access to culture —as a result, for example, of socioeconomic or educational barriers— it is a violation of that right. The analysis here will therefore focus on determining whether there is equity in access to culture or, in other words, whether young people are able to exercise that right. This approach also relates to the concept of "cultural consumption", whereby culture is explored from the standpoint of the audience rather than taking the traditional approach, which is based on cultural products or the "production" of cultural objects. As will be explained later in this chapter, cultural consumption is not a matter of individual preference but rather has to do with class structure.

The main source of information used in this chapter is the Latinobarómetro 2013 culture module, which was designed at the request of the Organization of Ibero-American States for Education, Science and Culture (OEI) and includes a series of specific questions about culture and cultural consumption.[2] These questions deal with such matters as reading books and newspapers, going to the cinema and the theatre, watching videos, listening to music CDs or online, computer use, the use of e-mail and the Internet, online social networking, Internet connection sites, the activities people engage in when they are online, visits to heritage sites, participation in community celebrations, attendance at concerts, time spent watching television and time spent listening to the radio.

While the OEI culture module does make it possible to analyse young people's current cultural consumption patterns, it is important to stress the shortcomings of the available cultural statistics. Since these data are not part of a time series, it is not possible to identify trends. Nor can the data be disaggregated by the type of sociodemographic variables that would make it possible to distinguish adolescents from young people and consumption patterns in urban areas from those in rural zones. What is more, surveys on cultural consumption and youth surveys in the countries of the region suffer from problems in terms of their comparability and they are therefore of limited usefulness in putting together a picture of the situation in the region as a whole.

Section A of this chapter examines intergenerational changes in cultural consumption patterns and intragenerational gaps in access to cultural goods. Section B analyses whether young people in the region have equitable access to digital media or if there are gaps in access and use that prevent young

---

[2]   The information gathered by means of this survey module is used here with the express authorization of the Secretary General of OEI.

people from taking advantage of the cultural opportunities that these media offer. Section C reviews the role of digital media in promoting access to culture and the development of new means of accessing cultural goods and services. Finally, section D describes a number of different types of cultural programmes and some of the main kinds of initiatives in this area being promoted by the State and civil society.

A.   Access to cultural goods

What kinds of cultural consumption patterns do young people exhibit and how do they compare with those of adults? How unequal is the access to cultural goods of young people in different countries, regions and social strata? In order to answer these questions, a clear understanding of three concepts is needed.

First, cultural consumption occurs during people's "free time", defined as the time left over after paid and unpaid work has been completed (ECLAC, 2013), which, in the case of young people, includes their studies. People's free time is limited and is devoted, among other things, to freely chosen activities that contribute to people's well-being, such as rest, leisure, recreational and creative activities, and sharing time with family members and friends. Cultural consumption is central in the use of free time.

Second, cultural consumption patterns are not a reflection of arbitrary differences in individual preferences but are instead tied in with aspects of class structure that influence the intergenerational reproduction of cultural interests that alter and mould aesthetic preferences (Palma and Aguado, 2010; DiMaggio and Useem, 1978b). Family settings and early socialization through art can increase the frequency with which people attend cultural events. The level of formal education is another factor that influences participation in artistic and cultural activities (DiMaggio and Useem, 1978a, p. 64). According to Bourdieu, socioeconomic stratification and cultural consumption patterns are directly related. Participation by some groups in certain kinds of activities, such the fine arts, is a sign of social distinction and both signals and reinforces their membership to a certain (higher) socioeconomic stratum (Bourdieu, 1984).

Third, as noted earlier, cultural consumption presupposes access to cultural goods. However, access does not guarantee appropriation, which requires certain skills and abilities that are acquired in the course of people's socialization within the family and their formal education. In other words, cultural consumption is bound up with cultural capital. The notion of cultural capital has to do with areas of cultural competence or bodies of cultural knowledge that give rise to specific types of cultural consumption that are associated with a relatively sophisticated classification of culture and symbolic goods (Lee, cited in Gayo, 2011, p. 12). Cultural capital expresses cultural knowledge, tastes and abilities that are closely associated with the arts (Gayo, 2011, p.10). It is also an asset that can be used in playing an active civic role and in communicating within the information society (Hopenhayn, 2008, p. 61) and is therefore a resource of key importance in the attainment of social inclusion.

Figure IV.1 shows the access to different cultural activities enjoyed by three different age groups within the Latin American population: young people (16-29 years), adults (30-50 years) and older adults (51 years and over).[3] Available information indicates that access to cultural goods declines with age: young persons have the highest levels of cultural consumption, followed by adults and then older adults.

Figure IV.1
Latin America (18 countries): persons who have watched or participated in a cultural activity, by age group [a]

(Percentages)

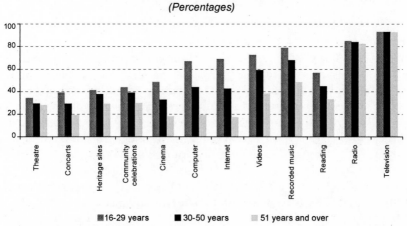

■16-29 years   ■30-50 years   ▓51 years and over

Source: Economic Commission for Latin America and the Caribbean (ECLAC), on the basis of special tabulations of the 2013 Latinobarómetro survey results.

[a] The questions regarding frequency of attendance or participation were not the same for all the different types of cultural goods. For example, for attending the cinema, watching videos and listening to recorded music, the categories of frequency were: daily, at least once per week, at least once per month, at least once every three months and less than once every three months. For computer use, on the other hand, the categories were: several times per day, at least once per day, at least once per week, at least once per month and at least once every three months. The categories for Internet use were: every day, occasionally, almost never and never.

Young people have more access than adults and older adults to all the cultural activities included in the survey (with the exception of television, to which all age groups have equal access). On average, this is the age group

---

[3] The classification of persons 51 years of age or older as "older adults" is used purely for purposes of simplification.

that reads books more frequently (57% as compared with older adults' 33%), attends concerts (40% of young people go to concerts fairly frequently, as compared to 22% of older adults), goes to the cinema (49% of young people go to the cinema fairly frequently, versus 18% of older adults), watches videos (73% do so fairly frequently, as compared to 39% of older adults) and listens to recorded music more often (80% of young people versus 48% of older adults).

These greater access to cultural activities of today's young generation suggest that new social sectors —young people in the middle class and, to some extent, those in low-income sectors— are accessing cultural goods that used to be the reserved for the elite, such as the theatre, museums and concerts. They are also accessing cultural goods produced by the cultural industry, such as books, films, recorded music and videos.

Available information also indicates that young people are also the age group that uses digital technologies most frequently: 67% use computers "fairly frequently", compared to 19% of older adults, and 69% use the Internet "fairly frequently", versus 17% of older adults.[4]

These differences reflect the existence of an intergenerational gap in cultural consumption patterns, with today's young generation in Latin America having greater access to cultural goods and services than older generations. This means that a larger percentage of young people are making use of their right to have access to and participate in cultural activities, which is of fundamental importance to attain more just and equitable societies. The exercise of cultural rights is associated with the higher levels of education attained by the young population in recent decades, which has empowered people in situations of exclusion or vulnerability. In turn, these higher levels of education are also a key factor in modifying the intergenerational reproduction of cultural interests in order to smooth out the distribution of cultural capital (for further information on the advances made in the region in the field of education, see chapter I).

Yet, although progress has clearly been made in terms of young people's access to culture, much more ground needs to be covered. Whereas high indices of participation are found for cultural activities that take place within the sphere of private life (television, radio, video, computers and the Internet), those that take place in the public sphere (theatre, cinema, heritage sites or concerts) have fairly low participation rates (see figure IV.1). While it has to be understood that there are major differences across countries, overall just 34% of young people in Latin America have watched a stage play, 39% have attended a concert, 44% have participated in community celebrations and 49% have gone to the cinema fairly frequently.

---

4   The category "fairly frequently" includes "several times per day", "at least once per day", "at least once per week", "at least once per month" and "at least once very three months" and therefore includes more people than only those who consider themselves to be frequent users.

These relatively low rates of participation in cultural activities that take place in the public sphere point to the existence of access constraints. There are economic, education-related and geographical barriers to access to public cultural activities (theatre, cinema, heritage sites or concerts), which tend to be held primarily in large cities. Undoubtedly, some of these barriers (such as economic ones) also exist in the case of activities that form part of individuals' private lives (computers and the Internet). Consequently, if culture is to play a key role in making the societies of the region more inclusive, policies designed to remove the obstacles that limit the general population's access to such activities will need to be put in place.

Figure IV.2 illustrates the extent of young people's access to various cultural goods in three groups of countries (or subregions): the Southern Cone (Argentina, Chile and Uruguay); the Andean region (Colombia, Ecuador, Peru and the Plurinational State of Bolivia) and Central America (Costa Rica, El Salvador, Guatemala, Honduras, Nicaragua and Panama), in addition to Brazil and Mexico. This information indicates that, although progress has been made, sharp inequalities persist in terms of young people's access to cultural capital in the countries of the region.

Figure IV.2
Young persons (16-29 years) who have watched or participated in a cultural activity, by groups of countries
(Percentages)

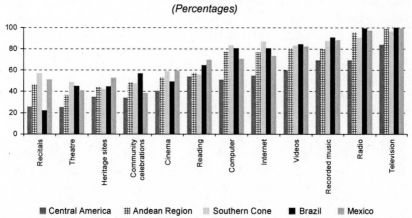

Central America   Andean Region   Southern Cone   Brazil   Mexico

Source: Economic Commission for Latin America and the Caribbean (ECLAC), on the basis of special tabulations of the 2013 Latinobarómetro survey results.

Young people in Central America have less access to all the cultural activities covered (with the exception of concerts) than young people in the other subregions. In addition, in some of these countries (El Salvador, Guatemala, Honduras and Nicaragua), access to cultural activities is far below the averages for that subregion. For example, 22% of young Hondurans participate in community celebrations, 26% go to the cinema, 15% go to the theatre, 13% attend concerts, 41% watch videos, 33% use computers and 36% use the Internet. Young people's ability to exercise their cultural rights in these countries is therefore very limited, possibly owing to lower levels of education, high poverty rates, problems in terms of social integration and a scant supply of cultural goods.[5]

The differences in access across subregions are stark. The fact that Central American youths have lower levels of access across all the categories of cultural activities than young people in the other subregions and countries points up the existence of a critical situation in terms of the exercise of cultural rights. It is also true, however, that an examination of the various types of cultural activities reveals intragenerational differences or gaps in the subregions where higher levels of access are observed. For example, young people in the Southern Cone have greater access to the Internet, computers, concerts and the theatre, while young people in Brazil have higher consumption levels in the case of music, radio and videos and Mexican youths have the highest levels of consumption in the categories of reading and the cinema.

Inequalities in young people's access to culture are undoubtedly linked to their socioeconomic and educational levels. According to the report entitled *Cultura y Desarrollo Económico en Iberoamérica* (culture and economic development in Ibero-America) access to cultural goods that have traditionally been reserved for elite groups, such as museums, the theatre and musical performances or concerts, has been broadened in some countries of the region. Nonetheless, socioeconomic status and level of education still have a bearing on the extent of access to these cultural goods and are associated with inequalities in this respect (ECLAC/OEI, 2014, pp. 230-244). Increasing the level of young people's participation in events involving various types of artistic expression therefore remains a challenge from the standpoint of access.

The situation in relation to the goods produced by the culture industry is similar. According to the above-mentioned report, reading is closely associated with a person's level of education (the more educated a person is, the more likely he or she is to read books) and socioeconomic level (the higher the socioeconomic level, the greater the frequency of reading); these factors therefore continue to limit the access of persons in vulnerable social and economic positions (ECLAC/OEI, 2014, p. 248). The same process is at work in the consumption of other cultural goods, such as the cinema. In this

---

[5]   The levels of access to cultural goods enjoyed by young people in Costa Rica and Panama are far higher than the average for this subregión. For example, 54% of young Panamanians participate in community celebrations, 72% go to the cinema, 40% go to the theatre, 41% attend concerts, 81% watch videos, 70% use computers and 74% use the Internet.

case, too, the higher the socioeconomic and educational levels, the greater the attendance and frequency of attendance (ECLAC/OEI, 2014 p. 259).

Some of the main findings to be drawn from this analysis are listed here.

- More young people than before are exercising their right to access and participate in cultural activities. This is of fundamental importance in forging more inclusive, egalitarian societies. This democratization of access to cultural goods stands in contrast to the intergenerational gap in cultural consumption that is associated with the higher levels of education attained by today's younger generations.

- Intragenerational gaps and inequalities in young people's access to cultural goods in the countries of the region are primarily associated with socioeconomic and educational factors, but there are other elements at work as well.

- The development process in Latin America is a highly unequal one in terms of opportunities for gaining access to cultural activities. There are countries in which young people's rate of participation in various of the cultural activities considered in this analysis is quite high, and there are others (such as some Central American countries) in which access is very limited.

- Young people's greater access to cultural affairs undoubtedly contributes to the social inclusion of new generations. Obstacles remain, however, that limit many young people's access to cultural activities. These obstacles take the form of socioeconomic and educational factors as well as a lack of free time. Formidable challenges therefore remain to be met in order to ensure that culture can play a key role in the achievement of social inclusion, and policies designed to remove these obstacle are therefore needed.

B.   Digital media: access and use

When talking about generational watersheds, the 1960s are seen as marking just such a paradigm shift. There is nothing wrong with that in many ways, but it does reflect the perspective of those of us who are adults now and were young people during those years. Today we are witnessing a turning point of a similar or even greater magnitude, but instead of being an ideological or political shift, it is linked to techno-cultural factors (Balardini, 2014, p. 2).

Section A included a discussion of access to various sorts of cultural goods, including digital media (computers and the Internet). A deeper analysis of access to and use of digital technologies will be undertaken here for a number of reasons. First of all, digital media have come to be such an important part of young people's lives that those media have actually altered the way they live their lives and influenced their social relationships. Second, the use of digital technologies is a must if people are to capitalize upon the opportunities that those technologies open up in the cultural sphere and in other areas of life. Third, the use of digital technologies provides new gateways to cultural activities that give rise to a reorganization of cultural consumption patterns and a restructuring of cultural affairs. Lastly, the use of new technologies is also a cultural practice.

Do young people in the region have equal access to digital media or are there gaps in access and use that prevent many young people from taking advantage of the opportunities offered by these media? Have those gaps, if they exist, widened as digital technologies have come into more widespread use? A few conceptual points need to be clarified in order to attempt to answer these questions.[6]

The first point has to do with the digital divide that separates people who have access to digital technologies from those who do not (OECD, 2001). New lines of thought have recently been presented that focus on ways of broadening and deepening this concept. The Organisation for Economic Cooperation and Development (OECD), for example, has sounded an alarm about the emergence of a "second digital divide" between those who have the necessary skills and capabilities to use digital technologies effectively and those who do not (OECD, 2010). The persons who have developed this idea of a second digital divide contend that the possession of these skills and capabilities is linked to the amount of economic, social and cultural capital that a person has. Professor Selwyn uses the term "access rainbow" to refer to the existence of many different "shades" of access to digital technologies, since the gap that exists is not limited to physical access but also encompasses the way in which people use information and communications technologies (ICTs). He goes on to say that access to technology is meaningless unless people have the skills, knowledge and support that they need in order to use it effectively (Selwyn, 2004, p. 348). In other words, the digital divide exists in the dimension of physical access but also in the dimension of the ability to use digital technologies in meaningful ways.

A second point refers to the concept of a digital culture, which is, in essence, composed of material electronic environments and symbolic digital environments (that is to say, environments that are expressed in binary code) (Lévy, 2007). In the digital culture, the pivotal material environments are composed of computers, informatics hardware, and computer and telecommunications networks, while the basic symbolic digital environments

---

6   For an analysis of the issues dealt with in this section from the standpoint of education, see Sunkel, Trucco and Espejo (2014).

are formed by the immense array of digitized content and information that reside and circulate within the above-mentioned material environments. Symbolic interpretive environments are then shaped by the meanings, interpretations, representations and knowledge that stem from those symbolic digital environments or that have to do with the related legitimizations, objectives or values (Lévy, 2007).

Figure IV.3 depicts the frequency of computer use in three age groups of the Latin American population: young people, adults and older adults. Clearly, young people use computers the most. Adding together the categories "several times per day" and "at least once per day" yields a figure of 44% for young people who are frequent users. This is more than four times as much as the figure for older adults (10%) and is far higher than the figure for adults (26%). A large percentage of older adults (81%) never use computers at all.

Figure IV.3
Latin America (18 countries): frequency of computer use, by age group
(Percentages)

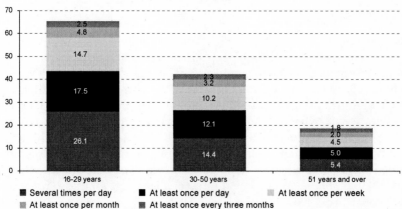

Source: Economic Commission for Latin America and the Caribbean (ECLAC), on the basis of special tabulations of the 2013 Latinobarómetro survey results.

Figure IV.4 shows the frequency of Internet use for these same age groups. Somewhat more than a third of all young people (35%) use the Internet "every day", compared with 19% of adults and just 7% of older adults. The percentage of young people who are frequent users of the Internet is smaller than the corresponding figure for computer use (44%), possibly as a result of the cost of acquiring an Internet connection.[7] The 35% of the younger population that uses the Internet each day is fully integrated into the digital culture, while the 26% who use it "occasionally" are also fairly well integrated and can be assumed to be fully familiar with the codes of the digital culture.

---

[7] For further information on this subject, see ECLAC (2010).

Figure IV.4
Latin America (18 countries): frequency of Internet use, by age group
(Percentages)

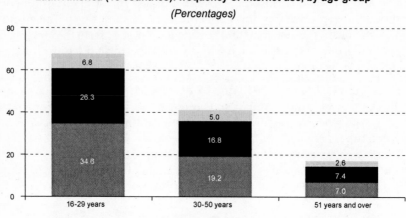

Source: Economic Commission for Latin America and the Caribbean (ECLAC), on the basis of special tabulations of the 2013 Latinobarómetro survey results.

The information presented here points to the existence of a wide intergenerational gap in access to digital media. Unlike adults and older adults, a sizeable percentage of young people in the region have frequent access to digital technologies.[8] The intergenerational digital divide can be thought of in terms of a distinction between "digital natives" and "digital immigrants". Piscitelli argues that today's students are native speakers of the language of interactive television, computers, video games and the Internet, whereas older people, no matter how technologically savvy they may be (or think they are), will always be digital immigrants and, at the most, more or less skilled second-language speakers of the language of technology. He contends that the fact that digital-speak will always be a second language for these immigrants can be seen in everything that they do; it can be likened to an accent that can always be heard as they pursue their activities and that is particularly evident in their academic and professional lives. Adults go on to the Internet when they are unable to find a book that addresses the issue that interests them; before using a new device, they read the manual; before executing a computer program, they need to know what key to press. Native digital speakers do just the opposite: first they act and then they ask (Piscitelli, 2009, p. 46).

The concept of "digital natives" suggests that today's young generation has undergone a radical change relative to its predecessor (whose members are "digital immigrants"). The young people of today are the first generation that has grown up with recent technological advances. They have been immersed in these technologies, having been surrounded since early childhood by

---

[8] Nonetheless, as a regional average, one third of Latin American youths (32%) never use the Internet (see figure IV.4).

computers, videos and videogames, digital music, mobile phones and other digital tools and forms of entertainment. They think and process information in a significantly different way than the digital immigrants who have gone before them and are much more skilled in handling and using technology. Digital natives have been born and have grown up speaking the "digital language" of computer games, videos and the Internet (Balardini, 2004).

Figure IV.5 shows the frequency of Internet use by young people in Latin America, disaggregated by socioeconomic level. It can be seen that, even though the young people of today can, on the whole, be described as "digital natives", a socioeconomically based intragenerational digital divide clearly exists. Nearly half (48%) of high-income youths in the region use the Internet every day, and another 28% do so occasionally. This means that, on average, three quarters of these young people are very familiar with the codes of the digital culture and are clearly digital natives. The frequency of use declines quite sharply as one moves down the socioeconomic ladder, however. Slightly more than one quarter of middle-class young people (27%) use the Internet every day and 28% use it occasionally, which means that somewhat more than half of this population group is immersed in the digital culture. Meanwhile, only 13% of the young people in the poorest population groups use the Internet every day and 18% do so occasionally. In other words, less than one third of young people in a vulnerable situation are immersed in symbolic digital environments.

Figure IV.5
Young people (16-29 years): frequency of Internet use by socioeconomic level [a][b]
(Percentages)

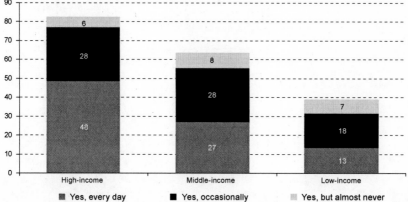

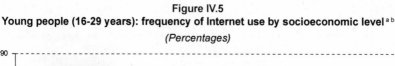

Source: Economic Commission for Latin America and the Caribbean (ECLAC), on the basis of special tabulations of the 2013 Latinobarómetro survey results.
[a] Does not include the "never" category.
[b] In the Latinobarómetro surveys, the socioeconomic level of respondents is based on their own perceptions. The corresponding question asks respondents to evaluate several different aspects of their living conditions.

Looking beyond regional averages affords a view of significant differences across countries with respect to the frequency of Internet use. For example, nearly two thirds (61%) of low-income Chilean youths and over half (55%) of low-income Argentine youths are Internet users (defined as those who use the Internet "every day" or "occasionally"). Thus, a large percentage of young people in vulnerable sectors in these two countries, in which the process of digital inclusion is well advanced, have access to digital media. This stands in sharp contrast to the situation in some Central American countries, where, for example, only 8% of young Salvadorans, 9% of young Hondurans and 9% of young Nicaraguans in low-income sectors are Internet users. Clearly, then, large sectors of the young population in these countries do not have access to digital technologies.

The intragenerational digital divide is also associated with different levels of access to technologies. The home is where people can access these technologies the most frequently and can use them most intensively, since that is where they can have a permanent connection. Figure IV.6 shows how much Internet connections in the home differ by socioeconomic level, with high-income youths being nearly four times more likely to have an Internet connection in their homes than low-income youths owing to connection costs. Cybercafés are an option for those who do not have Internet connections in the home, but this arrangement affords more limited access in terms of both the frequency and intensiveness of Internet use. The possibility of using the Internet in the workplace is subject to even greater constraints.

Figure IV.6
**Latin America (18 countries): Internet connection sites for young people
(16-29 years), by socioeconomic level** [a]

(Percentages)

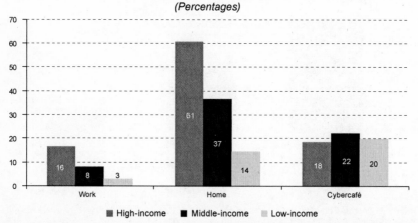

Source: Economic Commission for Latin America and the Caribbean (ECLAC), on the basis of special tabulations of the 2013 Latinobarómetro survey results.
[a] In the Latinobarómetro surveys, the socioeconomic level of respondents is based on their own perceptions. The corresponding question asks respondents to evaluate several different aspects of their living conditions.

Some of the points that can be drawn from the above analysis are as follows.

- The existence of an intergenerational digital divide is due to the fact that, unlike adults and older adults, a considerable percentage of young people in the region have access to digital technologies and use them often. A much larger percentage of the young generation than adult generations is part of the digital culture because they are digital natives that have grown up with the new advanced technologies.

- There is also an intragenerational digital divide, since not all young people have equal access to digital media. These inequalities in access are associated with a variety of factors, including socioeconomic ones. As a result, lower-income youths use the Internet much less often than higher-income youths do and are therefore less a part of the digital culture. This situation, in turn, is associated with the fact that the home is where people can access this technology most often and can use it most intensively and that connections in the home are concentrated in higher-income sectors due to the cost involved.

- The gap separating young people who have access to the opportunities afforded by digital technologies and those who do not —the access gap— continues to be a critical issue in Latin America despite the prodigious efforts that have been made to rectify this situation. In some countries of the region, many youths do not have access to digital media and are therefore left on the sidelines of the "techno-culture". This prevents them from capitalizing upon the opportunities opened up by these media and may therefore help to widen this gap even further.

- The headway made by some countries of the region in broadening access and developing digital network infrastructure poses new challenges. For these countries, as for the more developed countries, the problem has ceased to be one of access —or one involving the availability of Internet-connected digital devices— and has instead become one involving the use and appropriation of new technologies. This has come to be called the "second digital divide" (or "use gap"), which has to do with the differences between one group and another in terms of their skills or abilities to use technologies effectively. The challenge now is to stop this second divide from deepening further so that more young people can take advantage of the opportunities offered by these new technologies.

C. Access to culture through digital technologies

Access to digital media and their use are preconditions for taking advantage of the opportunities opened up by new technologies in the cultural domain and elsewhere. From this standpoint, the role of digital media in promoting access to culture and their contribution to the exercise of cultural rights warrant some attention. Do digital technologies help to democratize access to culture? Do they create opportunities for promoting access to culture or have they instead opened up new gaps between one group of young people and another?

In order to answer these questions, account has to be taken of the fact that digitization —the cornerstone of the digital culture— has had a strong impact on the production and circulation of goods in various types of cultural domains, ranging from the heritage sector (which includes museums and theatre arts) to cultural industries (publishing, music, film), including the media (radio and television). The music industry pioneered this process and exemplifies the scale of the impact that digitization has had. It has been said that the true revolution engendered by the technological advances of the late 1990s in the music industry is associated with the enormous potential unleashed by the emergence and spread of digital support technology around the world and, most of all, with the possibilities opened up by the capability to distribute content over digital networks (Palmeiro, 2004). Some of the chief factors that made this revolution possible were the development of PC hard discs that use sophisticated audio file compression techniques (such as MP3) to store extremely high-quality recordings of thousands of songs and the spread of high-speed Internet connections that provide enough bandwidth to distribute music quickly and efficiently to people's homes.

The digital paradigm radically alters the very essence of musical recordings. Digitization transforms what were once tangible goods (CDs, tapes or vinyl records) into mere sequences of zeros and ones that are packed into a digital file. The digital distribution of music has upended established supply structures, since users can now choose, store and listen to their preferred songs at the drop of a hat without leaving their homes. Digitization also makes it possible to produce a perfect copy of a song at no cost whatsoever (Palmeiro, 2004).

The number of research projects focusing on the impact of digitization on the production and distribution of various forms of culture is growing. One example is a study conducted by Dosdoce.com that analyses how museums, cultural centres and art galleries can make better use of state-of-the-art technologies to improve their services and operations by using virtual materials and content to enrich their visitors' experience (Dosdoce.com, 2013). Another example is the compilation entitled *Anuario AC/E de cultura digital*.

Focus 2014: uso de las nuevas tecnologías en las artes escénicas (AC/E, 2014), which looks at the impact that new technologies are having on the theatre arts and, in particular, how the digital culture is changing the way in which theatrical presentations are designed, produced and performed.[9]

Digital media have also opened up new cultural gateways that provide access to a wide array of digitized cultural goods and services. Figure IV.7 depicts Internet use for cultural activities for three age groups in the Latin American population: young people, adults and older adults. Activities are classified according to whether they are associated with the culture industry (music, film, books), heritage (museums), theatre arts or other activities (seeking information, buying or reserving tickets).[10]

Figure IV.7
Latin America (18 countries): persons who have used the Internet to participate in a cultural activity, by age group
(Percentages)

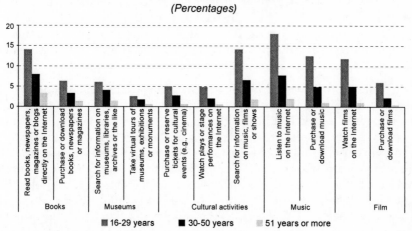

Source: Economic Commission for Latin America and the Caribbean (ECLAC), on the basis of special tabulations of the 2013 Latinobarómetro survey results.

The available information indicates that these cultural activities are engaged in the most on the Internet by young people, followed by adults and older adults. The Latinobarómetro survey results suggest that, on average, young Latin Americans are the age group that listens to music (18%), reads

---

9   For other examples of research projects dealing with the impact of digital technologics on culture industries, see Dosdoce.com (2011), IFPI (2014) and De Luca (2009).

10 The Internet-based cultural activities covered in the Latinobarómetro survey are more varied than those covered in the section on "traditional" means of accessing cultural goods. In addition to such activities as reading books, seeing films or videos, listening to music, and attending concerts, the theatre or other events, they include buying or downloading (with the latter obviously being possible only if the person has an Internet connetion) books, music or films, searching for information on music, films or shows, and buying or reserving tickets to cultural events.

books (14%) and watches films (12%) on the Internet the most. They are also the age group that is most likely to buy or download music (13%), books (6%) and films (6%) on the Internet. Young people also use the Internet a great deal to look for information on music, films and shows (14%) and, although this is a trend that is in its very early stages, they are also the ones who watch stage plays or performances (5%) and who take virtual tours of museums or exhibitions (3%) the most.

Figure IV.7 also shows that some cultural activities on the Internet are engaged in much more than others. Those carried out the most by young people are: listening to music; looking for information on music, films and shows; purchasing or downloading music; reading books; and watching films. Participation in the other categories of activities —purchasing or downloading books, purchasing or downloading films and seeking information about museums or libraries— is still in its earliest stages.

Fewer people use the Internet to gain access to culture than those who use "traditional" (that is, non-digital) methods to do so. However, more and more people are using the Internet for these purposes, and this trend is being heightened by the spread of Internet access and use and the creation of new services that promote access to culture (see box IV.1).

These processes are also changing the ways in which people make use of cultural goods. The rapid growth and expansion of services that allow people to watch films on the Internet, for example, have provided new ways to bring films to their audience. The idea that watching a film is a sort of shared ritual that begins when the curtain rises and that involves discussing it after the viewers leave the movie theatre was already becoming outdated before the rise of the Internet as videos, DVDs and cable television came into widespread use, but the Internet has greatly added to this shift. The region has reached a post-cinematographic stage in which the way that people relate to images is changing very swiftly, and films no longer signify what they did for earlier generations.

The Internet has also brought changes in the way people, and especially young people, read. People are shifting from "plane reading" to "spherical reading", to use the terms employed by Beatriz Sarlo. The latter form of reading involves the ability to handle hypertext, which allows the reader to begin at different points in the text and to then follow any of various paths to different parts of the text or to move from words to images and sounds. Sarlo has pointed out that, while books made us accustomed to the concept of a "page", in hypertext there are no longer individual pages, since hypertexts are simply a group of many different screens that are in no particular sequence and that can be accessed and used in different ways by following nexuses of association, hierarchy, sequence, subject matter or the like or simply by jumping from one to another at will (Sarlo, 1998, p. 70). This constitutes a profound change in the act of reading, especially on the part of young people, who are more intimately familiar with new communication technologies and have a greater affinity with them. According to Martín-Barbero, this affinity involves an enormous capacity to absorb information via television or computer games (which erodes the role of schools as the only legitimate vehicle for the transmission of knowledge) and a facility for handling and delving into complex informatics networks (Martín-Barbero, 1998, p. 35). Whereas adults exhibit resistance to the hypertext culture, young people not only demonstrate greater instrumental expertise in navigating through it but also display a greater expressive affinity to it in the stories and images that they produce, with the rhythms, fragmentations and speeds of communication within this new culture forming a language of their own (Martín-Barbero, 1998, p. 35).

Box IV.1
Cultural Internet services

In response to the fact that so many people listen to music on the Internet —and as a way of trying to deal with illegal downloads— subscription services that allow people to stream music from the Internet for a flat monthly fee are on the rise.[a] One of these service is the *Spotify* streaming service, which was launched on 7 October 2008 in Europe and in other countries in 2009. This Swedish company is based in Stockholm and has signed agreements with Universal Music, Sony BMG, EMI Music, Hollywood Records and Warner Music, among others. As of March 2013, it had more than 24 million registered users, of whom 6 million were paying clients.[b]

Grooveshark and Deezer are also music streaming subscription services, and these kinds of ventures are boosting the number of users who are paying for the music that they listen to. Many users are shifting from pirate services to a licensed music environment that pays artists and rights holders (IFPI, 2014, p. 7).

Cinemas have taken a similar tack. As the Internet takes on greater and greater importance as a medium for watching films —and, here again, in an attempt to deal with illegal downloads— subscription services have been set up that provide on-demand access to multimedia streaming functions (primarily for films and television series) on the Internet. One of these services, *Netflix*, which has been available in Latin America since 2011, offers subscribers an enormous catalogue of films and television series that can be viewed on a variety of Internet-connected devices, such as computers, tablets or television sets. This subscription business model is having the effect of increasing the number of people who pay for the films and television shows that they watch, thereby boosting the number of people who are ceasing to watch pirated shows and are instead moving into a legal viewing environment.

Source: International Federation of the Phonographic Industry (IFPI), *Digital Music Report 2014*, 2014, and Wikipedia.
[a] The term "streaming" can be defined as the digital distribution of multimedia content over a computer network in a manner that allows the user to view the product (generally a video or audio file) while it is being delivered. This distinguishes it from downloading, since, with the latter option, files must be fully downloaded before the user can access their content. See [online] https://en.wikipedia.org/wiki/Streaming_media.
[b] See [online] http://en.wikipedia.org/wiki/Spotify.

There is also an intergenerational gap in this new, digital, Internet-enabled way of accessing cultural goods. Young people have greater access to the cultural domain via the Internet than older generations do and they therefore exercise their right to access and participate in culture by digital means.[11] Young people's access to traditional forms of cultural consumption is associated with the higher educational levels achieved by this population group in recent decades, while their new Internet-based means of access are associated with new types of techno-cultural assets that take the form of people's attitudes towards technology, their ability to adopt it and certain areas of competence, knowledge and skills (O'Keeffe, cited in Gayo, 2011, p. 11).

There are two sets of digital skills that are of particular importance in amassing techno-cultural capital (Claro, 2008). First there are the functional skills that are generally understood as those that constitute "digital literacy", that is, the set of skills needed in order to use certain computer applications, such as word processing software, spreadsheets, e-mail and Internet browsers. The second set is composed of "digital learning skills", which go beyond the functional manipulation of certain applications to encompass the creative use of those applications in ways that enable the user to acquire new knowledge. These skills include the ability to navigate, search, evaluate on a critical basis and extract meaning from the information garnered through digital media.

The techno-cultural assets comprising these two types of digital skills are of fundamental importance in gaining access to cultural activities and participating in them through the Internet. The youth of today, whose lives have been permeated by these new technologies, are in a clearly advantageous position in this respect. This suggests that the tendency to use the Internet as a new gateway to culture —a trend that is just beginning in the case of some activities and that is quite advanced in others— is opening up opportunities for young people who previously did not participate because of economic factors, physical distance or other reasons and that this new gateway is therefore helping to mainstream access to cultural activities.

Figure IV.8 shows the cultural activities that young people engage in via the Internet in three groups of countries (or subregions): the Southern Cone (Argentina, Chile and Uruguay); the Andean region (Colombia, Ecuador, Peru and the Plurinational State of Bolivia) and Central America (Costa Rica, El Salvador, Guatemala, Honduras, Nicaragua and Panama). Information for Brazil and Mexico is given separately. The data point to the existence of sharp intragenerational inequalities in the use of the Internet as a means of accessing cultural activities in the various countries of the region.

---

[11]   The percentage of older adults who engage in cultural activities via the Internet is marginal for all of the activities considered.

Figure IV.8
Latin America (18 countries): young people (16-29 years) who have used the Internet
to participate in a cultural activity, by groups of countries
(Percentages)

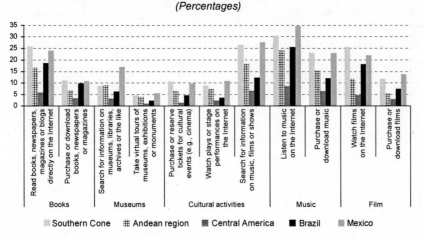

Source: Economic Commission for Latin America and the Caribbean (ECLAC), on the basis of special tabulations of the 2013 Latinobarómetro survey results.

Young people in the Central American countries use the Internet to access all of the cultural activities listed above much less than their peers in the rest of the region do. The use of the Internet to listen to, purchase or download music, books and films is in its very early stages, particularly in countries such as El Salvador, Guatemala, Honduras and Nicaragua. This information fits in with the data reported previously regarding the consumption of culture and the development of the digital culture in the countries of the region.

The use of the Internet as a gateway to culture is greater in the other subregions, although it varies from one to another. Internet use for this purpose by young Mexicans and young people in the Southern Cone is greater than elsewhere. For example, 35% of young people in Mexico and 30% of those in the Southern Cone listen to music on the Internet, and 24% and 26%, respectively, read books on the Internet. In Mexico, 22% of young people watch films on the Internet, while the figure rises to 25% in the Southern Cone. These significant levels of Internet use for cultural activities reflect a clear-cut and ongoing trend.

Unfortunately, the information that would be needed in order to undertake a more detailed analysis of the factors involved in the intragenerational gaps or differences in Internet use as a medium for accessing cultural activities is not available. It is known, however, that the possibility of taking advantage of the opportunities offered by the Internet in the cultural domain is necessarily tied to the level of access to digital media and their use. As discussed, there are inequalities in terms of access to digital media, and a gap therefore exists between those who can take advantage of these opportunities and those who cannot. This gap is widened by the fact that many young people lack the digital skills that they would need in order to capitalize upon those opportunities. Broadening Internet access to cultural activities is therefore a challenge that can only be met by closing the digital divide and endowing the entire population with the necessary techno-cultural assets.

Some of the points that can be drawn from the above analysis are as follows.

- There is a growing tendency to use the Internet as a new, digitally mediated way of accessing cultural activities. The Internet allows a very significant portion of the population to engage in a wide array of these activities. Changes in the ways that people are consuming culture are also taking place. This is an ongoing process that is engendering new types of services that heighten people's access to culture.

- The trend towards increased Internet use as a means of gaining access to cultural activities is being led by the younger generation. This gives rise to an intergenerational digital divide, since adults are using the Internet much less than their younger counterparts for these purposes, whereas a significant percentage of young people are exercising their right to access and participate in cultural activities through digital media.

- The use of the Internet as a means of gaining access to cultural activities is associated with a stock of techno-cultural capital that is composed of a variety of digital skills. This is a resource that differs from the ones traditionally used to access culture inasmuch as it is associated with the higher educational levels attained by the younger generation and the ability of young people, as digital natives, to use digital media. These kinds of cultural assets, or "cultural capital", are making it possible for young people who used to lack those assets (because they lived in remote areas, for example) to take part in the cultural sphere, but they are still unequally distributed among the region's households.

- There are sharp intragenerational inequalities in terms of the use of the Internet as a means of accessing cultural activities in the countries of the region. Whereas a broad spectrum of young people in some countries are beginning to participate in certain types of cultural activities via the Internet, in other countries, such as those of Central America, this kind of access is still very limited. These inequalities are a reflection of other types of differences, such as those existing in the extent to which the coverage of these new technologies is expanding.

- The use of the Internet to access cultural activities is not supplanting the more traditional forms of cultural consumption. Digital media are simply opening up another gateway to culture, and it is quite possible that they will put such goods within the reach of people who had previously been excluded from this domain. The main point, in any case, is that a larger percentage of young people use both traditional means and new digital media to exercise their right of access to cultural activities.

D.   Cultural programmes: the promotion of well-being

The above analysis shows that young people have greater access to cultural activities than adults do thanks to higher levels of education and to their possession of techno-cultural assets or capital in the form of certain types of digital skills. This situation is manifested in a democratization of access to cultural rights and the exercise of those rights. Because there are still a number of obstacles that block many young people's access to culture, however, challenges remain to be surmounted before cultural activities can play a key role in the promotion of social inclusion.

Have cultural policies or programmes been developed to promote access to cultural activities and support the exercise of cultural rights? Has culture been used as a resource for enhancing the social inclusion of young people? Have inclusive digital programmes been put in place that will contribute to a more equitable distribution of techno-cultural capital?

Nationwide cultural programmes for young people and, more specifically, programmes designed to enhance their access to cultural activities, are generally lacking in the countries of the region (Interarts, 2012). There are, however, a wide range of programmes, projects and initiatives focused on increasing young people's access to culture and on promoting social inclusion. Public initiatives of this type are primarily being launched by youth institutes, ministries of culture or cultural councils, ministries of education and municipalities.

There are various types of cultural programmes. A recent study has categorized such programmes on the basis of the subject area that they address, as follows: artistic training; audiovisual training and development; public cultural events for young people; social inclusion; improvements in education and health services; and human rights, including cultural rights (Interarts, 2012). This section examines three of these types of programmes: those aimed at promoting access to cultural activities; those designed to use art and culture as a mechanism for social inclusion; and those focusing on the development of digital skills that can be used for purposes of cultural expression and production.[12]

It is important to point out that this analysis does not cover other types of cultural programmes (such as, for example, training programmes and programmes for the development of public venues for youth-oriented cultural activities or other cultural arrangements) that may be quite relevant but that fall outside the scope of this analysis. Nor does it cover policies aimed at closing the digital divide in spheres other than culture (such as ICT policies in education or other policies that form part of countries' digital inclusion agendas).

The programmes discussed here do not cover all the various kinds of cultural projects that can be undertaken or even all of the existing initiatives aimed at providing access to cultural activities. The programmes examined here do not even represent the majority of these initiatives. Instead, the limited number of initiatives that are described below are presented with the sole purpose of illustrating the kinds of actions that are being taken under a specific type of cultural programme.[13]

1.   Promotion of access to culture

Initiatives intended to promote access to cultural activities generally seek to foster social inclusion by democratizing access and, in particular, helping socioeconomically or educationally disadvantaged youths to gain access to cultural activities. Three emblematic cases will be explored here in order to provide a picture of this type of policy line.

One project that illustrates this type of policy line quite well is the Abono Cultural (cultural subscription) project in Uruguay. Under the Socio Espectacular (show subscriber) project run by the El Galpón and Circular de

---

[12]   No programmes dealing with Internet use as a means of accessing cultural goods was identified.

[13]   Most of the projects described here are being run by the public sector or by public-private partnerships, although some are being implemented by the not-for-profit or community sector. In order to identify these intiiatives, searches were carried out on the oficial websites of youth institutes and the ministries of culture of the countries of the region. Other reference materials included the realtively few available documents that provide information on cultural projects considered to represent good practices, such as: "Acceso de los jóvenes a la cultura en Iberoamérica: Tendencias, obstáculos y experiencias" (Interarts, 2012); *Cultura, común denominador para el desarrollo. 18 prácticas exitosas* (OAS, 2011); *Arte para la inclusión and la transformación social. Documento de experiencias e iniciativas en este ámbito* (Bizkaia Observatory, IV Factoría Creativa, 2011) and the Internatioal Fund for Cultural Diversity (IFCD) of the United Naitons Educaitonal, Scientifi and Cultural Organization (UNESCO). IFCD supports projects aimed at creating a dynamic cultural sector by working to facilitate the introduction or developmnent of policies and strategies to conseve and promote a diverse range of forms of cultural expression. See [online] http://www.unesco.org/new/es/culture/themes/cultural-diversity/diversity-of-cultural-expressions/international-fund/.

Montevideo theatre companies, and in partnership with the Social Security Bank (BPS), the National Institute for Youth (INJU) has created a card (the Abono Cultural Card) that is associated with the Tarjeta Joven (youth card). The Tarjeta Joven provides access to cultural activities for a period of one year to young people attending formal or informal public educational institutions who would otherwise be entirely or partially excluded from the consumption of cultural goods and services. This project, which was launched in 2009 and serves 5,000 young people, is intended to democratize access to cultural goods and services such as theatre productions, films, sports events, concerts, carnival and other forms of cultural expression. The underlying assumption is that the democratization of access to a diverse range of cultural goods is a decisive factor in social integration processes. The recipients are selected students in secondary school, juvenile centres or special-purpose classrooms who are trying to complete their education (Interarts, 2012).[14]

Cultura Viva para la Nueva Lima (live culture for the new Lima) is another project that is being implemented along the same lines. This project is run by the Office of the Assistant Manager for Culture of the Municipality of Lima and is aimed at bringing artists together in order to strengthen cultural productions in the city and thereby help to build greater awareness of its inhabitants' civic role. As part of this project, different artistic and cultural events and shows are offered for the entire community in freely accessible public venues every week. Funding is provided to the actors and actresses, visual artists, musicians, dancers, creators of audiovisual content and narrators or storytellers (whether they are professionals, amateurs or students) whose exhibition or event proposals are selected. The subject categories from which they can choose are: democracy, gender equity, celebrating diversity, integrity, cultural identities, environmental conservation, human rights and championing change (Interarts, 2012).

The National Reading Plan of Panama seeks to coordinate, publicize, strengthen, develop and promote activities that will encourage children, young people and adults in all regions of the country to read, while respecting diversity, in order to inculcate critical thinking skills among the country's men and women. Its lines of action include: reading as a public policy issue; training for cultural advocates; promoting the creation of reading materials; actions for the improvement of children's, public, school, university and specialized libraries; strengthening reading and writing in the educational system; and the media and reading. This nationwide project began in 2008 and is administered by various public and private institutions. The wide range of activities that it conducts in order to encourage reading (such as conventions and fairs) include such innovative schemes as reading circles,

---

14   See [online] http://www.socioespectacular.com.uy/abono.html.

literary cafés, the "siembra de lectores" ("cultivating readers") programme and book caravans (Interarts, 2012).[15]

There are also projects that seek to bring art to the public by organizing activities such as theatre festivals, which have played an influential role in expanding the audience for this form of cultural expression. One outstanding example, although it is not specifically targeted at young people, is the Santiago a Mil Theatre Festival, which has been held every January in Santiago, Chile, since 1994. This event has grown steadily over time and has now succeeded in transforming the streets of Santiago into an open-air stage. Since its creation more than 20 years ago, millions of people have had the opportunity to see plays and other theatrical presentations during an entire month out of the year and has thus brought this form of art within the reach of the general public.[16]

2.   Art and culture as a mechanism of social inclusion

These initiatives focus on promoting the social inclusion of young people in vulnerable situations through their participation in artistic and cultural activities. The underlying assumption is that different forms of expression are a dimension and a fundamental right of all persons and that artistic and cultural expression is one of the best ways for people, and particularly those in vulnerable situations, to develop this dimension and exercise this right on both an individual and a collective basis (Bizkaia Observatory, 2012, p. 6). Some of these initiatives are discussed in the following paragraphs.

Dunna: Creative Alternatives for Peace is a project run by the Granitos de Paz (little seeds of peace) Foundation in conjunction with the Ministry of Culture of Colombia and the Educational Institution of the Republic of Lebanon and is a good example of this line of policy. Its objective is to introduce a mental health service model based on psychotherapy through dance and movement as a means of helping adolescents belonging to vulnerable sectors of Colombian society to manage episodes of depression and anxiety. Sessions involve different exercises in which movement is used as a creative process to foster the participants' emotional, cognitive, social and physical integration. The project is based on the belief that the management of mental health issues paves the way for the participants' personal and social reintegration while at the same time helping to build a new peaceful, tolerant and harmonious society in Colombia (Interarts, 2012).

---

[15] See [online] http://www.binal.ac.pa.
[16] Along these same lines, the UNESCO International Fund for Cultural Diversity has recently been funding the South African Theatre4Youth programme, which seeks to bring the theatre arts to young people.

Another project working in this area is the Social Circus of the South (CSS) in Buenos Aires, a not-for-profit organization that works with young people in the most vulnerable sectors of society with the aim of bringing about personal and social transformations through art. Its target population is children and young people who live in poor households subject to nutritional shortfalls and serious environmental and sanitary risks. The project uses circus arts and culture as the basis for its strategy for engendering new forms of production, a sense of belonging, education and community organization and new drivers for the development of creative capacities and autonomy in the groups of children and young people with which it works. CSS sets up activities in various grassroots community organizations in Villa 21-24 and Ciudad Oculta involving different artistic disciplines that provide the community with opportunities for belonging, learning and participating (Bizkaia Observatory, IV Factoría Creativa, 2011).

Another initiative that exemplifies this line of action is the YIP-Colombianos Renaciendo en el Hip-Hop (Colombians being reborn through hip-hop) project, which works within the framework of the Bogotá District's development plan, "A Positive Bogotá: Living Better", to counter behaviours associated with crime and violence. The project was devised by an international cooperation agency, Young in Prison International (YiP IN), in the Netherlands that has been introducing similar strategies in other countries that revolve around hip-hop. The objective is to contribute to the social reintegration of young offenders and to transition them into non-criminal forms of behaviour. The project's target population is made up of young women and men in prisons and detention centres in Bogotá and other municipalities in the Department of Cundinamarca, those who have recently been released from such institutions, young people who are in drug rehabilitation programmes and children in institutions housing abandoned children or children who have been victims of abuse. The project uses the high-impact Ayara training methodology, which covers four different areas of artistic expression through hip-hop (graffiti, breakdance, rap and DJ), as well as providing psychosocial guidance aimed at strengthening personal skills in the areas of self-esteem, social capacity and conflict resolution. The programme also offers training in areas related to capoeira, the production of clothing for hip-hoppers and media (audiovisual techniques and journalism). The choice of this methodology for working with these young people is a response to the fact that Bogotá, like other cities in Colombia, has lacked attractive programmes for the prevention of criminal behaviour and the reintegration of young people.

The YIP project is included in the Best Crime Prevention Strategies in Latin America and the Caribbean catalogue of the Centre for Studies on Public Safety of the Chilean Institute of Public Affairs of the University of Chile, which partners with the Inter-American Development Bank (IDB) and the Open Society Institute.[17] Another project in that catalogue that focuses on the use of cultural activities to spur the inclusion of young people in society is the Escuelas para la Convivencia (schools for living together) project in El Salvador. This project uses a methodology for attracting young participants that is based on sports, art and culture, conflict resolution, gender issues and vocational training.

Another noteworthy initiative is the Conchalí Big Band in Santiago, Chile. This educational project was launched in 1994 when the Municipality of Conchalí, which is one of the districts of the Metropolitan Region whose inhabitants are at the greatest risk, set up a series of sports and art workshops. Under this project, young people between 12 and 18 years of age join a large jazz orchestra. The project has been in place for over 20 years and has introduced more than 400 adolescents and young people to musical performance careers. Participation in musical events and learning to play musical instruments, together with other cultural learning experiences, help these young people to learn how to engage in the self-discipline that is an important factor in successful performance in school and in the workplace (ECLAC/OIJ, 2014).

The Symphony of Peru is another social inclusion and preventive programme that seeks to involve children and young people in orchestras so that, through music, children can discover their talents and can be motivated to advance in their personal development and to renounce violence. This project was launched in 2011 by the Peruvian government in an effort to combat violence among the children and young people of Peru and to equip them with tools for personal expression and a safe, secure environment in which they can develop and grow. The work of the Symphony of Peru involves translating art and education into a language that is meaningful to the young generation and that is accessible to them in an entertaining manner and that can be expressed through their own musical creations. This paves the way for the creation of settings in which they can distance themselves from the increasing violence and danger to which many of the country's young people are exposed.

3.   Building digital skills for the production of cultural goods and cultural expression

Building the digital skills involved in producing cultural goods and creating forms of cultural expression requires an investment in techno-cultural capital. Some of the projects in this area are focusing on promoting the social inclusion of young people through employment. Three of the projects that provide examples of this line of action are described below.

---

[17]   See [online] http://seguridadenbarrios.cl/buenaspracticasenprevencion.org/bbp.html.

One example of the efforts being pursued in this area is provided by a project focusing on the provision of training in the audiovisual arts to indigenous youths in Guatemala. This project is being implemented by the International Relations and Peace Research Institute (IRIPAZ), a Guatemalan non-profit organization, with support from the UNESCO International Fund for Cultural Diversity. Participants from the Maya, Garífuna and Xinca indigenous peoples have acquired audiovisual production, script-writing, film-direction, lighting and photography, camera-work, editing and post-production skills in a new audiovisual training centre set up by the University of San Carlos. Classes have also been given on the cultural rights of indigenous peoples, gender equality and capacity-building for the community. Students who did internships in TV Maya had the opportunity to gain hands-on experience. The Centre is continuing to organize short workshops, which are offered free of charge, on intercultural audiovisual communication. After finishing the course, students have embarked on a variety of professional paths, with some of them working as graphic directors for television channels, others as cultural advocates in their communities or cultural promoters for the Ministry of Culture and Sports. Some of the graduates of the course have also formed indigenous artistic groups that have gone on to produce short films and music videos dealing with their cultures and are sharing their creations on the Internet and social media; some local television stations have also broadcast their work. Other graduates have started up their own media businesses. "Destinos cruzados" ("overlapping fates"), the first short film to have been produced entirely by a team of indigenous Guatemalan youths, has been one of the prime successes of this training initiative. In September 2012 it was screened at the Icaro Film Festival in Guatemala City. A longer version that incorporates five musical pieces is in the pipeline. One of the members of the team recently said: "In addition to teaching us how to use the relevant technologies, the course gave us the audiovisual tools we need to express our own cultural identity…to show people how our Xinca, Garífuna and Maya communities actually live. We are just starting out and, thanks to this project, we have been given the benefit of a valuable training opportunity."[18]

Another project along these same lines, *Wapikoni Mobile*, was launched in 2004. This initiative originally targeted the First Nations of Quebec, Canada, and involved the Council of the Atikamekw Nation and the Youth Council of the First Nations of Quebec and Labrador. *Wapikoni Mobile* is a study being carried out by a team that visits different communities and trains young people in the use of various audiovisual media. The project takes an educational approach in its efforts to meet regional demands and

---

[18]   See [online] http://www.unesco.org/new/es/culture/themes/cultural-diversity/diversityVéa-of-cultural-expressions/international-fund/.

address the serious problems faced by First Nations communities, which include domestic violence, suicide and addiction. As of 2012, *Wapikoni Mobile* had carried out many different training events in indigenous communities (including video and music composition and production workshops) and has produced nearly 360 music recordings and 450 short films or video clips, some of which have been translated into a number of different languages. The project has also organized conferences, held hundreds of outreach activities at festivals and received over 40 national and international awards. It has also set up a number of studios where it provides training on an ongoing basis. The first one of its kind, the Wetomaci Studio, opened in 2006. The workshops use a practical "learning by doing" method of instruction, with the long-term goal being to enable participants to reaffirm their identities through language, skill-building and the use of communication tools to put an end to their isolation and to create a network of producers in the First Nations and in other locations that will help to combat prejudice among immigrants. Ten years after its founding, *Wapikoni Mobile* is a leading creator of documentaries and multidisciplinary materials that is active throughout North America (OAS, 2011).

Habla ("speak"), which is being implemented in Bangladesh and Peru, is another project that is working in this area. This initiative, which was developed in collaboration with the Anesvad Foundation, gives individuals and communities a voice and provides them with a means of telling other people about their living situation through the use of video. In the organization's own words: "We launched the Habla Project as a pioneering initiative in the field of social communication. Community-produced videos, recorded on mobile telephones by the vulnerable population with whom we work, document their own reality. This is communication at the service of the community. This ground-breaking social communication initiative enables the vulnerable populations who are working with the project to tell their own truths, first-hand, in recordings made using mobile telephones. The Habla Project is a participatory, documentary exercise that introduces a social dynamic aimed at raising awareness about the problems experienced by countries in the South and about their struggle to gain access to health services (for example, to combat tuberculosis). The intention is also to generate a critical line of thought that will help to reverse the situations of inequality and social injustice around the world that prevent people from exercising their basic rights" (Bizkaia Observatory, IV Factoría Creativa, 2011).

4.   Recommendations

The foregoing analysis permits a number of conclusions to be drawn regarding the way forward in terms of policy proposals for promoting young people's access to culture and opportunities for them to participate in cultural activities, which are of fundamental importance for their well-being. Some of the recommendations based on these findings are presented below.

(a) Define the institutional structure to be responsible for implementing cultural policies and programmes targeting the young population

The countries of the region do not have youth-oriented cultural policies on a national scale or policies designed to help young people to gain access to or participate in cultural activities. Nor do they have an institutional structure for the implementation of such policies. In the public sector, the existing initiatives are primarily run by youth institutes, ministries of culture, cultural councils, ministries of education and municipalities. Thought should therefore be given to ways of linking up the different institutions that contribute to young people's cultural well-being so that the various initiatives now in place —many of which operate on a small scale— can be incorporated into broader policies. Thought should also be given to the development of public-private partnerships and alliances that include the not-for-profit or community sector.

(b) Ensure that young Latin Americans have access to and can participate in cultural activities

More young people than older persons are exercising their right of access and their right to participate in cultural activities. This situation is undoubtedly associated with the higher levels of education attained by the younger generation. Further progress needs to be made, however, since there are still obstacles that limit many young people's access to cultural activities and their participation in cultural affairs. In order to ensure that young Latin Americans have access to cultural goods and can participate in cultural activities, policies are needed that will remove these obstacles, many of which take the form of socioeconomic and educational factors, and that will bring about a redistribution of cultural capital.

(c) Use culture as a key resource for achieving the social inclusion of vulnerable young people

Culture can be used as a tool for combating poverty, building capacity and expanding the range of opportunities open to vulnerable groups. Within the domain of public policy, these goods can be used as a valuable resource for the inclusion of young people who are at risk because of their proximity to violence, delinquency, drug trafficking, drug use or other harmful situations. The cultural sphere is a key "place" in which to carry out these types of efforts because it is attractive to young people and provides an ideal setting for fostering participation, promoting conflict resolution and engendering resilience.

(d) Contribute to a redistribution of techno-cultural capital

As has been discussed, not all young people have access to digital technologies. In many countries of the region, however, the main problem is what has been called the "second digital divide", that is, a lack of the capabilities or skills needed to use these technologies effectively. In order to take advantage of the cultural opportunities offered by new technologies, people need to have techno-cultural assets that take the form of certain digital skills. The cultural sphere offers a key platform for redistributing this techno-cultural capital by training young people in the use of these digital skills for the production of cultural goods and for cultural expression. This would also help to narrow the second digital divide.

(e) Improve systems for gathering information on youth and culture

Information is needed in order to devise sound policies, yet, as noted earlier, statistics on cultural matters are in short supply. National youth surveys could be used to gather information on the habits and behaviours of young people in this regard and could serve as a useful source of other data if a module with relevant questions about cultural matters were included in such surveys. The same set of questions should be included in the various countries' youth surveys in order to ensure the comparability of the results.

(f) Develop policy approaches tailored to the specific needs of some of the Central American countries

Throughout this chapter it has been seen that there is a great deal of inequality in terms of the opportunities for gaining access to culture and to digital technologies in Central America. Young people in some Central American countries have very little access to cultural goods and cultural activities and are therefore unable to exercise many of their cultural rights. The above recommendations are certainly valid for these countries as well as for those of the rest of Latin America, but, given their special features, specific policy approaches for these countries should be developed.

Bibliography

AC/E (Spain's Public Agency for Cultural Action) (2014), *Anuario AC/E de cultura digital. Focus 2014: uso de las nuevas tecnologías en las artes escénicas* [online] http://www.accioncultural.es/es/publicacion_digital_anuario_ac_e_cultura_digital_focus_2014.

Balardini, Sergio (2014), "Viejas y nuevas formas de ser joven", *Diálogos del SITEAL*, May.

_____(2004), "De deejays y ciberchabones. Subjetividades juveniles y tecnocultura", *Revista de Estudios sobre Juventud*, año 8, No. 20.

Bourdieu, Pierre (1984), *Distinction: A Social Critique of the Judgement of Taste*, Harvard University Press.

ECLAC (Economic Commission for Latin America and the Caribbean) (2014a), *Social Panorama of Latin America 2014* (LC/G.2635-P), Santiago.

___(2014b), *Preliminary reflections on Latin America and the Caribbean in the post-2015 development agenda based on the trilogy of equality* (LC/L.3843), Santiago.

___(2013), *Social Panorama of Latin America, 2013* (LC/G.2580), Santiago.

___(2010), "Avances en el acceso y uso de las tecnologías de la información y la comunicación en América Latina y el Caribe 2008-2010", *Project Documents*, No. 316 (LC/W.316), Santiago.

ECLAC/OEI (Economic Commission for Latin America and the Caribbean/Organization of Ibero-American States for Education, Science and Culture) (2014), *Cultura y desarrollo económico en Iberoamérica*, Madrid.

___(2012), "Avanzar en la construcción de un espacio cultural compartido. Desarrollo de la Carta Cultural Iberoamericana" [online] http://www. culturasiberoamericanas.org/documentos_trabajo.php.

ECLAC/OIJ (Economic Commission for Latin America and the Caribbean/Ibero-American Youth Organization) (2014), *Invertir para transformar. La juventud como protagonista del desarrollo*, Santiago, October.

___(2004), *La juventud en Iberoamérica, tendencias y urgencias* (LC/L.2180), Santiago.

Claro, Magdalena (2008), "ICT related skills and competencies. Approaches to identification, definition and assessment in the Chilean context", unpublished.

De Luca, Luiz Gonzaga Assis (2009), *A hora do cinema digital. Democratização e globalização do audiovisual*, São Paulo, Imprensa Oficial.

DiMaggio, Paul and Michael Useem (1978a), "Cultural democracy in a period of cultural expansion: the social composition of arts audiences in the United States", *Social Problems*, vol. 26, No. 2, Oxford, Oxford University Press.

___(1978b), "Social class and arts consumption", *Theory and Society*, vol. 5, No. 2, Springer.

Dosdoce.com (2013), "Los museos en la era digital. Uso de las nuevas tecnologías antes, durante y después de visitar un museo, centro cultural o galería de arte" [online] http://www.dosdoce.com/articulo/estudios/3820/museos-en-la-era-digital/.

___(2011), "Indústria editorial 2.0: tendències, oportunitats i reptes davant la digitalització del llibre", *Les diagnosis de L'observatori de prospectiva industrial*, N° 08.

Gayo, Modesto (dir.) (2011), "Consumo cultural y desigualdad de clase, género y edad: un estudio comparado en Argentina, Chile y Uruguay", *Avances de Investigación*, No. 62, Madrid, Fundación Carolina.

Hopenhayn, Martín (2008), "Inclusión y exclusión social en la juventud latinoamericana", *Pensamiento Iberoamericano*, No. 3, Madrid.

IFPI (International Federation of the Phonographic Industry) (2014), *Digital Music Report 2014* [online], http://www.ifpi.org/downloads/Digital-Music-Report-2014.pdf.

Interarts (2012), "Acceso de los jóvenes a la cultura en Iberoamérica. Tendencias, obstáculos y experiencias" [online] http://www.interarts.net/descargas/interarts1241.pdf.

Lévy, Pierre (2007), *Cibercultura: la cultura de la sociedad digital*, Barcelona, Anthropos Editorial.

Martín-Barbero, Jesús (1998), "Jóvenes: des-orden cultural y palimpsestos de identidad", *Viviendo a toda. Jóvenes, territorios culturales y nuevas sensibilidades*, Humberto Cubides, María Cristina Laverde and Carlos Eduardo Valderrama (eds.), Bogota, Siglo del Hombre Editores.

Música Popular, "Conchalí Big Band" [online], www.musicapopular.cl/3.0/index2. php?op=Artista&id=487.

Observatorio Bizkaia (2012), "Arte para la inclusión y la transformación social" [online] www.3sbizkaia.net.

Observatorio Bizkaia, IV Factoría Creativa (2011), *Arte para la inclusión y la transformación social. Documento de experiencias e iniciativas en este ámbito* [online] http:// www.3sbizkaia.org/Archivos/Documentos/Enlaces/1174_Documento%20 de%20experiencias.pdf.

OECD (Organisation for Economic Cooperation and Development) (2010), *Are the New Millennium Learners Making Their Grade? Technology Use and Educational Performance in PISA*, Paris.

___(2001), *Understanding the Digital Divide*, Paris.

OAS (Organization of American States) (2011), *Cultura, común denominador para el desarrollo. 18 Prácticas exitosas* [online] http://scm.oas.org/pdfs/2012/CIDI03698S01.pdf.

Palma, Luis Antonio and Luis Fernando Aguado (2010), "Economía de la cultura. Una nueva área de especialización de la economía", *Revista de Economía Institucional*, vol. 12, No. 22, Bogota, Universidad Externado de Colombia.

Palmeiro, César (2004), "La industria discográfica y la revolución digital", Buenos Aires, Universidad de Buenos Aires.

Piscitelli, Alejandro (2009), *Nativos digitales*, Santillana.

Sarlo, Beatriz (1998), "Del plano a la esfera: libros e hipertextos", *Cultura, medios y sociedad*, Jesús Martín-Barbero and Fabio López de la Roche (eds.), Bogota, Universidad Nacional de Colombia.

Selwyn, Neil (2004), "Reconsidering political and popular understandings of the digital divide", *New Media & Society*, vol. 6, No. 3, SAGE.

Sinfonía por el Perú [online] www.sinfoniaporelperu.org.

Sunkel, Guillermo, Daniela Trucco and Andrés Espejo (2014), *La integración de las tecnologías digitales en las escuelas de América Latina. Una mirada multidimensional*, Libros de la CEPAL, No. 124 (LC/G.2607-P), Santiago, Economic Commission for Latin America and the Caribbean (ECLAC).

UNESCO (United Nations Educational, Scientific and Cultural Organization) (2012), "Culture: a Driver and an Enabler of Sustainable Development", United Nations System Task Team on the Post-2015 United Nations Development Agenda.

___(2010), *The Power of Culture for Development*, Paris.

Chapter V

Political participation, commitment to democracy and priority issues for young people in Latin America, 2000-2013

Carlos F. Maldonado Valera[1]

Introduction

Inequality and social inclusion are two major challenges for all of Latin America and for its young people in particular. As discussed throughout the analysis presented in this volume, political participation is one of the main vehicles for the social inclusion of young people, together with education, employment, health, culture and a life free of violence. This is both because participation in political affairs is in itself a fundamental human right and because the exercise of that right is an essential pathway towards the genuine enjoyment of other human rights. The use of a rights-based approach as a cornerstone for public policies designed to guarantee such rights is therefore also linked to the creation of real opportunities for participation for all.

[1] The author, a Social Affairs Officer in the Social Development Division of ECLAC, is grateful for the support and valuable inputs provided for this chapter by Matías Sálces, a Research Assistant in the Social Development Division, and for the extremely helpful comments and observations made by Andrés Espejo, Fabiana Pierre, Humberto Soto, Guillermo Sunkel, Daniela Trucco and Heidi Ullmann. The contents of the final version of this chapter are, however, the sole responsibility of the author.

Numerous studies conducted by the Economic Commission for Latin America and the Caribbean (ECLAC) and by other agencies and specialists have pointed to the fact that young people in Latin America, like their counterparts in other regions of the world, feel alienated from politics, mistrust politicians and participate less than other segments of the population as voters and as candidates in elections and as members of political parties and the social organizations that have traditionally channeled the demands and given voice to the interests of different groups within society (IDEA International, 2013; ECLAC/OIJ, 2008; ECLAC/UNFPA, 2011). It often happens that, based on the somewhat arbitrary dividing line of the age of majority as a criterion in determining the full exercise of political citizenship, the established political order tends to regard young people —and especially those who are still minors— as political subjects but not active ones (Reguillo, 2003). And even when they reach voting age, it is often the case that policymakers view their priorities as important only if the electorate as a whole agrees with them, or, in other words, when "parents vote for the interests of their children" (UNFPA, 2014, p. 7). As observed by the Inter-Parliamentary Union (IPU), an international institution comprising legislators from around the world, young people, as compared to other age groups, face a variety of very real obstacles or barriers when seeking to play an active part in political and electoral affairs by conventional means (see box V.1).

On the other side of the coin, many young people tend to be indifferent to traditional forms of political action or even to reject them outright while at the same time often taking the lead in mobilizing through informal or unconventional types of political participation. Many young people are utilizing new types of channels for communication and coordination, such as social media, in new and creative ways to spur major changes in politics and policy. In fact, by networking and taking part in collective discussions (which sometimes go "viral"), today many young people are inventing and unveiling their own identity as political subjects, as citizens. Examples of this may include the student movement of 2011 in Chile, the emergence of the #YoSoy132 ("I am number 132") movement during the 2012 presidential elections in Mexico and, looking a bit further back, the movement that led to the convocation of the Constituent Assembly of Colombia in 1990-1991. It was not in vain that, on 15 September 2014, the International Day of Democracy, the Secretary-General of the United Nations made special reference to the imperative need to forge a closer bond between youth and political participation as a means of renewing and consolidating democracy around the world.[2]

---

[2]   By its resolution A/62/7 of 2007, the General Assembly of the United Nations declared 15 September of each year to be the International Day of Democracy in order to encourage governments to strengthen national programmes designed to promote and consolidate democratic systems in their countries. See [online] http://www.un.org/es/events/democracyday/.

Box V.1
Constraints on young people's participation in political affairs in today's democracies

Young people are not taken seriously by the political system and are regarded as immature and inexperienced.

Young people also face legal obstacles to their participation in politics, which include the minimum legal age for voting and the minimum legal age for standing as a candidate. In many countries, people between the ages of 16 and 21 and, in some cases, those up to the age of 25 (which represents a significant percentage of the young population) cannot take part in their country's political life.

Young women and men who are involved in politics do not always have access to the social networks of older politicians, which often present formidable entry barriers to newcomers.

Young people who are involved in politics are confronted with greater financial challenges than their older peers who have longer track records.

The image that young people have of politics as a conflictive, corrupt sphere of activity makes it clearly unattractive, as is their image of major political leaders.

Source: Inter-Parliamentary Union (IPU), *Taking Democracy to Task*, Geneva, 2014.

Discussions about the participation of young people in political affairs is taking place within a regional setting that exhibits certain specificities. While the different countries in the region have taken a wide diversity of political paths, most of the countries share a legacy of long periods of autocratic governments or outright dictatorships followed by a gradual return to electoral democracy starting in the 1980s. In a majority of these countries, the most recent phase of democracy has been the longest-lasting, most stable period of democratic rule. Nonetheless, challenges clearly remain for the translation of the formal equality of all people that is set out in the law into concrete, effective mechanisms of social inclusion and equality, especially in the case of the younger generations. The sharp inequalities characteristic of the region therefore raise serious questions as to the value of the role played by life in democracy as an effective vehicle for social inclusion and as to the work that remains to be done in this connection. A suspicion that the role of democracy in attaining equality is more a legal fiction than an actual social condition of members of the population raises questions in the minds of citizens as to the value of democracy and undermines people's commitment to democratic principles and values.

The past two decades have witnessed the configuration of a widely varying political map in the region, with some countries recently changing their constitutional systems under the leadership of charismatic figures (the Bolivarian Republic of Venezuela, Ecuador and the Plurinational State of Bolivia), the emergence of new centre-left governing coalitions in others (Argentina, Brazil, El Salvador, Nicaragua, Peru and Uruguay), the continuation of political orders crafted during transitions to democracy with relatively little subsequent change (Chile and Colombia) and the sustained presence of signs heralding a loss of legitimacy and protracted crises (or outright collapses) of long-standing party systems in yet others (Costa Rica, Guatemala, Honduras, Mexico and Paraguay) (Luna, 2014).

Meanwhile, at least in South America and in contrast to the 1980s and 1990s, when countries returned to democracy, the past decade has been a time of rapid economic growth that has given rise to tangible social and economic advances, as well as to new and greater expectations on the part of citizens. These improvements and these new expectations, which transcend formal and electoral bounds, add greater urgency to the call for qualitative improvement of the region's democracies (Morlino, 2014).

Against the backdrop of these two or more decades of life in democracy, what evidence can be gathered about young people's interest in taking part in political affairs in general and their commitment to democracy in Latin America? What kind of changes have taken place in this respect over time? Can any common patterns throughout the region be identified? Are democratic policies and democratic life seen as vehicles for the inclusion of young people and for the introduction of greater equality for them? What are young people's public policy priorities? Have clear-cut differences between the characteristic patterns of young people and their older peers remained over time? Information that may help to answer these questions will be presented in this chapter.

Drawing on data from the Latinobarómetro surveys (2000 and 2013) and secondary bibliographic sources, a regional overview will be provided on the perceptions and participation of young segments of the population in the region's public affairs. This approach has methodological advantages and disadvantages that should be explained at the start. The Latinobarómetro data are collected by means of opinion polls using large national samples that do not, however, provide a statistically representative sample of the young population and that may therefore not offer a fully accurate picture of the opinions of a majority of the region's youth. Yet there are very few sources of information that can be used to compare the situations in the countries of the region on the same terms and on the same subjects, much less at two different points in time. Weighing these different aspects and giving priority to the search for information and its comparison at the regional level, a choice has therefore been made to develop a dynamic picture of the changes occurring between 2000 and 2013 in the patterns of participation of persons between 16 and 29 years of age and those aged 30 and over. While accepting that the data are not drawn from a fully representative sample, the focus will be on providing inputs for the debate and further research on the political participation of younger generations and their main concerns, in the context of the countries' young democracies and the inequalities that are characteristic of the region.

As will be seen in the following sections, in most of the countries young people vote less often than adults do, are more distrustful of institutions such as the legislature or political parties than of others, express dissatisfaction with the way the democratic system functions and, in most cases, are less convinced than before that this is invariably the best form of government. The situation in the region is highly diverse, however, and there are a number of indicators that suggest that the differences between adults and young people are not so sharp as might be thought. For example, young people do not show a great deal less interest in politics than adults do, nor are they unaware of the important role played by the legislature and political parties in a well-functioning democracy. In fact, they show themselves to be more willing to mobilize in order to address a series of issues than adults are, and this greater willingness, along with their involvement in new types of activism, draws attention to the fact that opportunities for young people to participate in political affairs should be expanded in order to achieve a greater degree of social inclusion of this segment of the population.

A.   The electoral participation and mobilization of young people

Young generations show little interest in politics, although it is also true that adults of 30 years of age and older do not show much more than the younger cohorts (see figure V.1). Data from the 2013 Latinobarómetro survey indicate that 72% of young people said that they were not at all interested in politics or were interested very little, while the average for the entire adult population was virtually the same (71%).[3] The percentages of respondents giving these answers ranged from 88% in Chile to 66% in Paraguay, with the Bolivarian Republic of Venezuela being the only country in which no more than half of all young people said they were not interested or interested very little. The comparison of the degrees of interest expressed by young people and those declared by the adult population varies across countries. The least interest in politics relative to the level of interest of adults was exhibited by youths in Chile and Uruguay. There were also a number of countries in

---

[3]   Simple average for 18 countries on the basis of the results of the 2013 Latinobarómetro survey. The question in the survey was phrased as follows: How interested are you in politics? Originally, the multiple-choice responses were: "do not know", "no answer", "very interested", "somewhat interested", "not very interested" and "not interested". In compiling the data, however, the options have been collapsed into "very or somewhat interested" and "not very or not interested".

which young people showed themselves to be more interested in politics than those aged 30 or over (Colombia, Costa Rica, the Plurinational State of Bolivia, Nicaragua (where levels of interest in politics were the lowest for all age groups) and Peru). Overall, however, the differences between the levels of interest displayed by adults and young people were —with the exception of the Bolivarian Republic of Venezuela— generally small, with the predominant feature for all age groups being a lack of interest in the subject.

Figure V.1
Latin America (18 countries): little or no interest in politics on the part of persons between the ages of 16 and 29 years and those aged 30 or over, 2013 [a]
(Percentages)

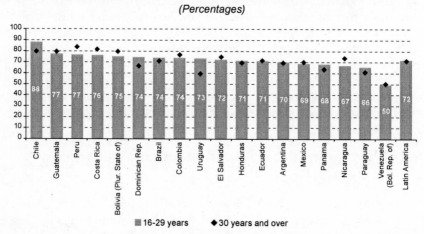

■ 16-29 years   ◆ 30 years and over

Source: Economic Commission for Latin America and the Caribbean (ECLAC), on the basis of special tabulations of the results of the 2013 Latinobarómetro survey.
Note: The question in the survey was phrased as follows: How interested are you in politics? Originally, the multiple-choice responses were: "do not know", "no answer", "very interested", "somewhat interested", "not very interested" and "not interested". In compiling the data, however, the options have been collapsed into "very or somewhat interested "and "not very or not interested".
[a] The results by country are given in descending order according to the percentage of young people in 2013 who stated that they were not at all interested in politics or not interested in it very much.

Another, much more informative indicator of political participation has to do with voting in the most recent presidential elections. Most young people reported that they had voted, but the percentage was much lower than it was for adults. Part of the reason for this has to do with age restrictions, but self-exclusion on the part of persons who meet the age and other administrative requirements is also a factor. In Chile and a number of Central American countries, the percentage of young people who vote is close to or even less than 50% (see figure V.2).

Some countries have witnessed a steep reduction over the past decade in the percentage of young people who go to the polls. This trend has become evident in Chile and Uruguay in the Southern Cone, where it dovetails with the decline in the portion of this population group that is interested in politics, and in Costa Rica, El Salvador, Guatemala and Panama in Central America. Just the opposite kind of trend has been seen over the past decade in some other countries, however, such as the Bolivarian Republic of Venezuela, Ecuador, Peru and the Plurinational State of Bolivia, where the percentage of young people who are participating in elections has risen sharply.

Figure V.2
Latin America (17 countries): young people and adults who say that they voted in the latest presidential elections, 2000-2013 [a]

(Percentages)

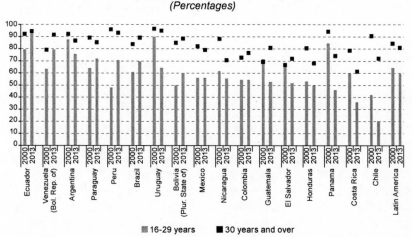

■ 16-29 years   ■ 30 years and over

Source: Economic Commission for Latin America and the Caribbean (ECLAC), on the basis of special tabulations of the results of the 2000 and 2013 Latinobarómetro surveys.
Note: The percentages that make up the total of non-voters also include those who were unable to get to the polls, those who did not meet the requirements and those who decided not to vote, among others.
[a] The results by country are given in descending order according to the percentage of young people in 2013 who stated that they had voted in the most recent presidential elections.

The small number of young respondents to the 2013 survey who said that they were working for a party or candidate (ranging from slight over 14% in Brazil to just 3% in Chile) (see figure V.3) is another indication of the low level of interest among the young population in conventional politics. In practically every case, more persons 30 years of age or older said that they had worked for a party or candidate, with the sharpest differentials being seen in Costa Rica, the Dominican Republic, Honduras and Panama. The difference between young people and adults in this respect is smaller in most of the other countries, however, and, as a result, at the regional level the average is 8% for young people and 10% for adults.

Figure V.3
Latin America (18 countries): percentage of persons who have worked for a political party or candidate, by age group, 2013 [a]

(Percentages)

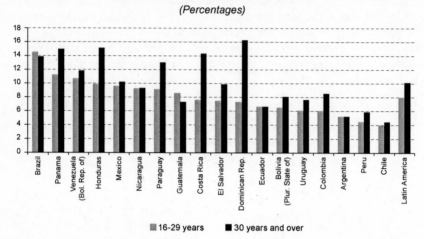

Source: Economic Commission for Latin America and the Caribbean (ECLAC), on the basis of special tabulations of the results of the 2013 Latinobarómetro survey.
[a] The countries are listed in descending order of the percentages of young respondents in the 2013 survey who reported that they often worked for a political party or candidate.

Numerous studies have also found that young people are less involved than before in other, non-political types of organizations as well. The United Nations Educational, Scientific and Cultural Organization (UNESCO) has stated that "the vast majority of young people in Latin America and the Caribbean stand outside existing youth associations and movements (between 5% and 20% participate, depending on the country, with sporting and religious organizations accounting for the overwhelming majority), in what could be seen as a transition to new forms of youth participation and new understandings of civic engagement or action" (ECLAC, 2014, page 154).

Young people's involvement or non-involvement in social movements and their decision as to whether or not to vote are indicators of their engagement, indifference or rejection of public life and democracy. In the case of the younger members of this age group, however, a failure to vote may not necessarily signal indifference or a refusal to do so but may instead be a manifestation of the political exclusion of persons who have not reached the required age for full political engagement. In principle, at least, social mobilization is not subject to comparable formal restrictions, however. One way of gauging the extent of social mobilization is to look at the percentage of young people who reported having taken part in a demonstration at least once during the past year (see figure V.4). At the regional level, that percentage held at around 26% for 2000-2013, which was slightly higher than the figure recorded for persons aged 30 or more.

Figure V.4
Latin America (17 countries): young persons and adults who report having participated in demonstrations at least once during the past year, 2000-2013 [a]

(Percentages)

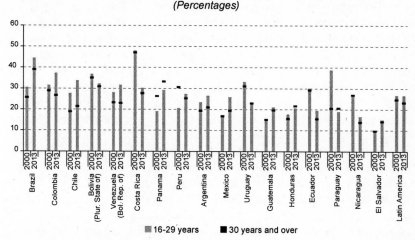

16-29 years   30 years and over

Source: Economic Commission for Latin America and the Caribbean (ECLAC), on the basis of special tabulations of the results of the 2000 and 2013 Latinobarómetro surveys.
[a] The countries are listed in descending order of the percentages of young respondents in the 2013 survey who reported that they often worked for a political party or candidate.

The figures vary a great deal across countries, however. In 2013, the percentage of respondents who said that they had taken part in a demonstration at least once during the past year ranged from 44% in Brazil to 15% in El Salvador. In 11 countries, the percentage increased over the period in question, while in 6 others, it declined considerably. In the Bolivarian Republic of Venezuela, Brazil, Chile, Colombia, Costa Rica and the Plurinational State of Bolivia, the rate of participation in demonstrations was 30% or more, but in most of the Central American countries, the rate was around 20% or less. The rate of participation in demonstrations in Costa Rica remained relatively higher than it was in neighbouring countries, but nonetheless dropped by nearly 18 percentage points between 2000 and 2013.

How large is the group of young people who do not vote and do not participate in social movements? A number of different studies have sought to link voting activity and participation in social mobilizations (FLACSO/ IDEA International, 2013) as a means of identifying the groups of young people who: (i) vote and participate in social mobilization; (ii) vote but do not participate in social mobilization; (iii) do not vote but do participate in social mobilization; and (iv) do not vote and do not participate in social mobilization (with this latter group being characterized to some extent as those who remain on the sidelines of political life). Those who both vote and participate in social mobilization make their voice heard in the public arena through conventional forms of political participation as voters but also through direct forms of participation as mobilized citizens (Hirschman, 1995). The profile of those who vote but do not take part in demonstrations can be characterized as having a "voice with loyalty" as active members of the electorate who thereby perform one of the basic duties of citizens in a democracy but whose degree of participation does not extend to participation in collective mobilizations. Meanwhile, those who take part in demonstrations but do not vote correspond to a strategy that can be characterized as being based on having a "voice without loyalty", since they take an active, direct part in public life but do not necessarily engage in conventional forms of electoral participation. Finally, those who neither vote not take part in social mobilizations can be characterized as a marginalized group that stands apart from elections and social movements, whether out of indifference, out of dissatisfaction with the existing channels for participation or because they are excluded from those channels. The above does not mean, however, that any of these groups may not include individuals who are creating and making an active use of other channels of expression and means of searching for meaningful participation.

A comparison of the patterns of participation of young people and persons aged 30 or over during the period 2000-2013 sheds light on the extent of differences in attitudes towards political participation and the size of the subcategory of young people who neither vote nor participate in demonstrations (who can be characterized as being "marginalized"). As shown in figure V.5, most young people fall into one of two categories: the largest one is composed of people who vote but do not participate in social movements (42% in 2013); the other is made up of people who are on the sidelines of political activity inasmuch as they neither vote nor take part in demonstrations (31.3% in 2013). The next-largest category is made up of people who vote and who have taken part in a demonstration at least once (17.4% in 2013), followed by the category of people who do not vote but have taken part in demonstrations (9.3%). The main changes seen during this period are a slight rise in the percentage of people who neither vote nor take part in demonstrations (from 27.3% to 31.3%) and a decrease in the number of those who vote but do not take part in demonstrations (from 45.9% to 42.0%). The main differentiating features of persons in the 30-and-over age group is that many fewer people neither vote nor participate in social movements and that very few of the people in this group do not vote but have participated in demonstrations.

Figure V.5
Latin America (simple average of 17 countries): young persons and adults
who report having voted in the most recent elections and having taken part
in a demonstration at least once in the past year, 2000-2013
(Percentages)

A. Persons between the ages of 16 and 29

2000

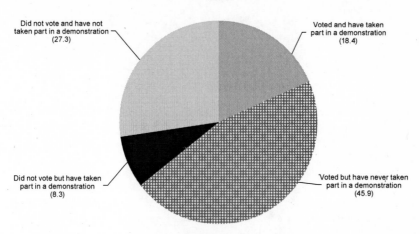

2013

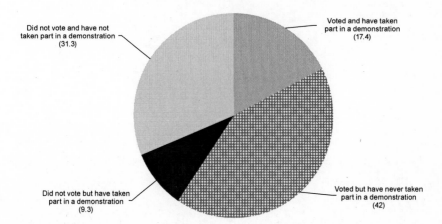

Figure V.5 (concluded)

B. Persons aged 30 or over

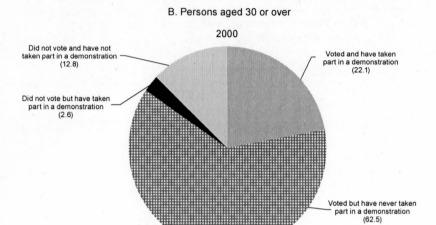

2000

Did not vote and have not taken part in a demonstration (12.8)

Did not vote but have taken part in a demonstration (2.6)

Voted and have taken part in a demonstration (22.1)

Voted but have never taken part in a demonstration (62.5)

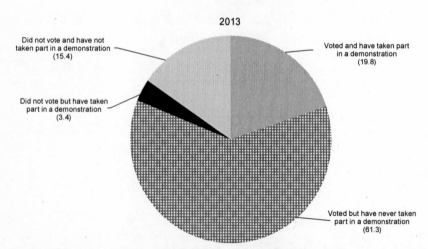

2013

Did not vote and have not taken part in a demonstration (15.4)

Did not vote but have taken part in a demonstration (3.4)

Voted and have taken part in a demonstration (19.8)

Voted but have never taken part in a demonstration (61.3)

Source: Economic Commission for Latin America and the Caribbean (ECLAC), on the basis of special tabulations of the results of the 2000 and 2013 Latinobarómetro surveys.
Note: The figures for those who did not vote include people who were unable to go to the polls, those who were not eligible to vote and those who did not wish to vote.

The sizes of the groups of people who have remained on the sidelines of political activity (the marginalized group) and who have not voted but who have participated in demonstrations vary considerably from one country to the next (see figure V.6). At one end of the spectrum, there are Chile, where 54% of young people neither voted nor had taken part in a social movement in 2013, and most of the Central American countries, where the percentage ranges from 38% to 48%.[4] At the other extreme, with much smaller percentages for these groups, there are Argentina, the Bolivarian Republic of Venezuela, Brazil and Ecuador. In almost all cases and for both survey years, the percentages of young people who did not vote and did not take part in demonstrations were higher than the corresponding figures for adults. These results attest to the former group's lower level —whether owing to their exclusion by society or their exclusion by their own choice— of political participation. The trend over time exhibited by the category of persons who neither voted nor participated in demonstrations in one group of countries stands in contrast to the trend in another group. In many countries of Central America and the Southern Cone (Argentina, Chile, Costa Rica, El Salvador, Guatemala, Nicaragua, Panama and Uruguay), the percentage has climbed, whereas it has fallen in five other South American countries: the Bolivarian Republic of Venezuela, Brazil, Ecuador, Peru and the Plurinational State of Bolivia. The case of Chile is noteworthy in that a very large percentage (26%) of young people said that they had not voted but that they had taken part in demonstrations; this set of circumstances is discussed in box V.3.

Figure V.6
Latin America (17 countries): young persons and adults who did not vote in the most recent elections, disaggregated by participation and non-participation in a demonstration in the past year, 2000-2013 [a]
(Percentages)

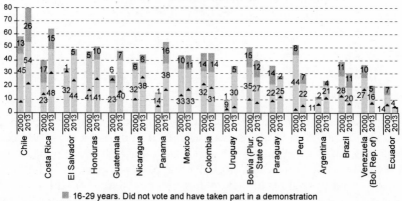

▨ 16-29 years. Did not vote and have taken part in a demonstration
▨ 16-29 years. Did not vote and have never taken part in a demonstration
▲ 30 years and over. Did not vote and have never taken part in a demonstration

Source: Economic Commission for Latin America and the Caribbean (ECLAC), on the basis of special tabulations of the results of the 2000 and 2013 Latinobarómetro surveys.
[a] The countries are listed in descending order of the percentages of young respondents in the 2013 survey who reported that they did not vote and had not taken part in a demonstration.

---

[4] In the case of Chile, however, the fact has to be borne in mind that in the intervening period between the two surveys, changes were made in electoral laws. The voluntary voter registration and mandatory voting system was replaced by an automatic voter registration system for all citizens over 18 years of age while voting was made voluntary. This may be the reason why a much larger number of people (both young people and the rest of the voting-age population) did not vote.

These data suggest that there is scope to promote an expansion of political participation among young people. An effort could therefore be made to seek out different channels for participation in social movements and in elections, especially in countries where young people have been distancing themselves from conventional forms of political activity in the past decade. This point will be discussed further in the section on recommendations for ways of removing existing barriers to participation, beginning with the alignment of the age requirements for voting and for standing for election. This also raises the question of how these patterns of political participation tie in with individuals' attitudes, their confidence in institutions or their lack thereof, and their commitment to democracy —all of which may vary quite markedly from one country to another. The trend in this regard has been quite negative in the countries of the Southern Cone (Argentina, Chile and Uruguay) and in Central America but quite positive in the Bolivarian Republic of Venezuela, Brazil and Ecuador.

In short, there are clear signs among the young population of disaffection with conventional forms of political participation; this is not to say, however, that the extent of this sentiment is necessarily greater among this group than it is in the adult population, since, overall, there is very little interest in politics and few members of either age group become actively involved in working for political parties. The differences between age groups are greater in the case of electoral participation, since young people vote less often and are less involved in these conventional forms of political participation and mobilization.

B.   Individual attitudes, trust in institutions and commitment to democracy

Young people's apparent disaffection with conventional forms of political participation is reflected in their questioning and mistrust of institutions, despite the fact that a number of studies have found that young people have a more positive, optimistic outlook that older persons do and that they tend to believe that their skills and capacities will enable them to attain better living conditions in the future both for themselves and their countries (OIJ and others, 2013; ECLAC/UNFPA, 2012). Be that as it may, and as will be discussed below, in recent years young people have become less trustful of the institutions that surround them, particularly the political ones, and have become less committed to democracy.

The existence of a continuing trend of disaffection and lack of trust in democratic institutions is corroborated by the survey results regarding the countries' economic conditions and outlook for the coming year. The opinions expressed about these factors, which are of course subjective, relate not only to trends in the material living conditions reflected, for example, in economic growth or absolute poverty rates but also to feelings of empowerment or agency and comparisons of respondents' living conditions with those of other people and of the overall population of the country in question (Corporación Latinobarómetro, 2013).

Young people's assessments of their country's economic situation was more positive in both 2000 and 2013 than those of people aged 30 or over (see figure V.7). Perceptions of each country's economic situation improved between 2000 and 2013 at the regional level, since the percentage of people who viewed the situation as poor declined considerably and the percentage that viewed it as fair or good rose. In both cases, however, differences are to be observed between the young and adult populations, with fewer young people tending to regard the situation as being poor and more of them tending to evaluate the situation as good or fair in both survey years.

Figure V.7
Latin America (simple average of 17 countries): assessment of the economic situation of the country, 2000-2013
(Percentages)

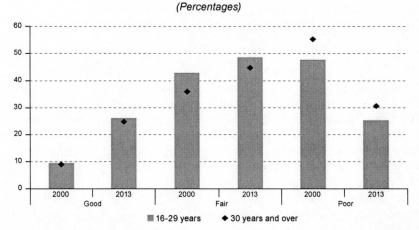

16-29 years   ◆ 30 years and over

Source: Prepared by the author on the basis of special tabulations of the 2000 and 2013 Latinobarómetro surveys.

Young people had a more positive attitude regarding the economic outlook for themselves and their families over the coming 12 months in 2013 (see figure V.8). In most of the countries, more than 50% of the respondents thought that the situation would improve. The Bolivarian Republic of Venezuela, El Salvador and Honduras were exceptions in this respect. These positive expectations were more prevalent among young people than among the adult population except in the Bolivarian Republic of Venezuela and Paraguay.

Figure V.8
Latin America (18 countries): belief that the personal and household economic situation will be better or slightly better in the coming 12 months, by country and age group, 2013 [a]

(Percentages)

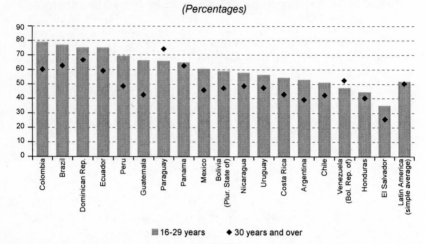

■ 16-29 years   ◆ 30 years and over

Source: Prepared by the author on the basis of special tabulations of the 2013 Latinobarómetro survey.
[a] The countries are listed in descending order of the percentages of young respondents who believed that the economic situation would be better or slightly better.

As noted earlier, young people's generally optimistic view about their personal situation continues to be associated with a considerable degree of mistrust and disaffection with regard to various social and, in particular, political institutions. They are much less trustful of national legislatures and political parties than they are of other institutions that have traditionally been viewed as legitimate, such as the Church (although they are more mistrustful of the Church than in the past) and the media (television, in particular) or institutions such as the armed forces or the police (see figure V.9). With the exception of the Church, the comparison of the responses given during the first decade of the twenty-first century points to a slight easing of this negative assessment. The decline in trust of the Church is sharper among adults than among young people, while this group's increased confidence in television and the armed forces is somewhat greater. In any case, over the period of time covered by these results, it continued to be the case that national legislatures and political parties inspired less confidence than other institutions among both adults and young people.

Figure V.9
Latin America (simple average of 17 countries): persons between the ages of 16 and 29 years and those aged 30 or over who state that they have a great deal of confidence or no confidence in selected institutions, 2000-2013
(Percentages)

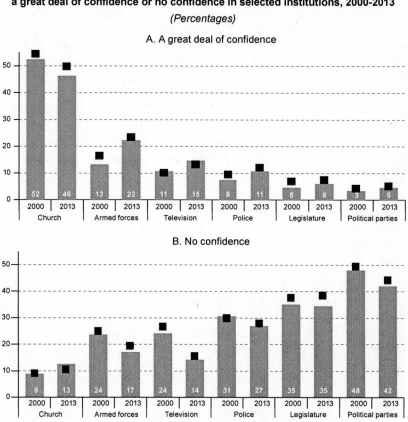

A. A great deal of confidence

B. No confidence

■ 16-29 years   ■ 30 years and over

Source: Prepared by the author on the basis of special tabulations of the 2000 and 2013 Latinobarómetro surveys.

The number of young survey respondents who felt that a democracy can function without a legislature or political parties indicates how little this segment of the population values two of the basic institutions of representative democracy which are supposed to represent the pluralistic views and interests of the citizenry while at the same time providing checks and balances for the executive branch of government. This mistrust of legislatures and political parties does not entirely eclipse an appreciation of their importance, however. At the regional level, 56% and 53% of young people responding to the surveys for these two years felt that a democracy cannot function in the absence of these institutions, although the figures varied sharply across countries. Some of these variations are noteworthy. The percentage of respondents who viewed the national legislature as a necessary institution rose steeply from a very low percentage to a very high one in Ecuador and the Bolivarian Republic of Venezuela (28% to 78% and 30% to 58%, respectively). A similar trend was seen in respect of the perception of the role of political parties, with the corresponding percentages climbing from 26% to 84% in the Bolivarian Republic of Venezuela and from 27% to 57% in Ecuador. By contrast, in a number of Central American countries (Costa Rica, El Salvador and Panama) and countries in the Southern Cone (Chile and Uruguay), a sizeable decrease was seen in both indicators.

In sum, the responses of the young people surveyed by Latinobarómetro in 2000 and 2013 attest to the presence of very little confidence in political institutions as such in comparison to institutions such as the Church or the armed forces or media such as television.

Another standard question in opinion polls deals with the respondents' opinion as to whether democracy is the best form of government under any circumstances, whether authoritarian governments might be preferable in certain cases or whether the respondents have no preference between one and the other. Those who choose the first option are exhibiting a commitment to democracy as the preferable system of government at all times, regardless of any particular circumstance or short-term crisis, while the second option reflects more ambivalent attitudes regarding the possibility that it may be acceptable to turn away from democracy, at least under extreme conditions, which signifies that this system is not viewed as necessarily the best or only legitimate form of government. The third alternative (indifference) points to another type of ambivalence that is associated with a lack of interest in or commitment to political activity as such or even an aversion to politics and a questioning of the legitimacy of any political order. The preferences expressed by young people in the region will be explored in the following pages.

Generally speaking, a similar percentage of young people and adults regard democracy as the best form of government (see figure V.10), with the exceptions of Chile and Uruguay, where more adults than young people display a commitment to this form of government. The percentage of young people in the region who believe that democracy is the preferable form of government shifted from 57.7% to 53.7% over this period. In 2013, less than half of the young people in eight countries saw it as the best system (Brazil, El Salvador, Guatemala, Honduras, Mexico, Nicaragua, Panama and Paraguay). The level of support fell between 2000 and 2013 in most of the countries, however. In one group of countries, the decline amounted to between 6 and 32 percentage points (Costa Rica, El Salvador, Honduras, Mexico, Nicaragua, Panama, Peru, the Plurinational State of Bolivia and Uruguay), while substantial increases were observed only in the Bolivarian Republic of Venezuela, Brazil and Ecuador (see figures V.10 and V.11).

Figure V.10
Latin America (17 countries): support for democracy as the best form of government by persons between 16 and 29 years of age and by persons aged 30 or over, 2013 [a]

(Percentages)

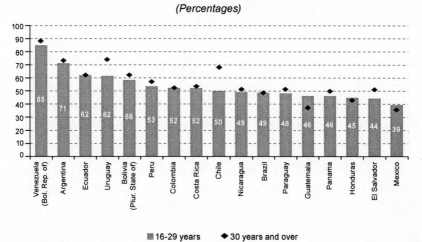

■ 16-29 years   ◆ 30 years and over

Source: Economic Commission for Latin America and the Caribbean (ECLAC), on the basis of special tabulations of the results of the 2013 Latinobarómetro survey.

Note: The question was worded as follows: "With which of the following do you agree the most?" The options were: "Democracy is preferable to any other form of government"; "Under some circumstances, an authoritarian government may be preferable to a democratic one"; and "For people like us, it doesn't matter whether the government is democratic or not". In the 2013 survey, the options "do not know" and "no answer" were added to cover 100% of all cases.

[a]   The countries are listed in descending order of the percentages of young respondents in the 2013 survey who said that democracy was preferable to any other system of government.

Figure V.11
Latin America (17 countries): support for democracy as the best form of government by persons between 16 and 29 years, 2000 y 2013 [a]

(Percentages)

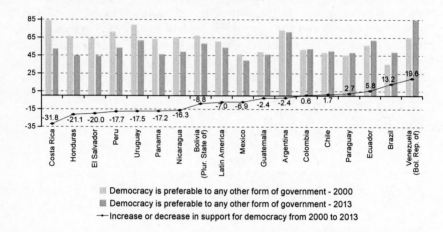

▨ Democracy is preferable to any other form of government - 2000
▓ Democracy is preferable to any other form of government - 2013
━Increase or decrease in support for democracy from 2000 to 2013

Source: Economic Commission for Latin America and the Caribbean (ECLAC), on the basis of special tabulations of the results of the 2013 Latinobarómetro survey.
Note: The question was worded as follows: "With which of the following do you agree the most?" The options were: "Democracy is preferable to any other form of government"; "Under some circumstances, an authoritarian government may be preferable to a democratic one"; and "For people like us, it doesn't matter whether the government is democratic or not". In the 2013 survey, the options "do not know" and "no answer" were added to cover 100% of all cases.
[a] The countries are listed in descending order of the percentages of decreases in support of democracy.

Figure V.12 provides an overview of these various trends. The countries shown above the diagonal line are those in which the young population's preference for democracy as the best form of government strengthened over the period 2000-2013. The most positive trends include those exhibited by the young population in the Bolivarian Republic of Venezuela, Brazil and Ecuador, where support for democracy increased considerably. The countries situated below that line are those in which the advocacy of democracy as the best form of government declined during this period; they include Costa Rica, El Salvador, Honduras, Mexico, Nicaragua and Panama in Central America and, in South America, Peru, the Plurinational State of Bolivia and Uruguay.

However, variations in the extent of support can be seen when the overall levels of that support at the start and ending dates of the period of analysis are compared. For the countries located to the left of the vertical axis and below the horizontal axis of figure V.12, the level of support for democracy as the best system of government was below 50%. In Brazil, support for democracy rose from 35% to 48%, but it remained in the category of countries where the level of support is fairly low. Of the countries in which the level of support in 2013 was below 50%, those that are the greatest cause of concern are the countries in which this low level of support was present at both the starting and end years of the period in question. In Mexico, for example, advocacy of democracy as the best form of government stood at 45% in 2000 but slid further, to 39%, in 2013. By the same token, the countries to the right of the vertical axis and above the horizontal axis are countries that, while following differing paths, have maintained a level of support for democracy of over 50%. While sharp declines were seen in both Costa Rica and Uruguay, both of these countries nonetheless remained in the latter group. The situation in Costa Rica is explored in greater detail in box V.2.

Figure V.12
Latin America (17 countries): changes in the extent of support for democracy as the best form of government among persons between the ages of 16 and 29, 2000-2013

(Percentages)

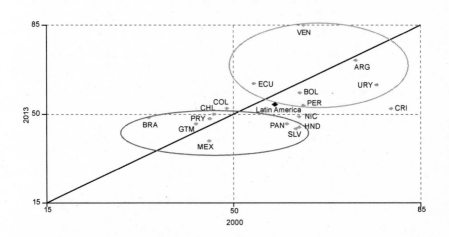

Source: Economic Commission for Latin America and the Caribbean (ECLAC), on the basis of special tabulations of the results of the 2000 and 2013 Latinobarómetro surveys.
Note: The question was worded as follows: "With which of the following do you agree the most?" The options were: "Democracy is preferable to any other form of government"; "Under some circumstances, an authoritarian government may be preferable to a democratic one"; and "For people like us, it doesn't matter whether the government is democratic or not". Data for the Dominican Republic were not included because figures were available only for 2013. In the 2013 survey, the options "do not know" and "no answer" were added to cover 100% of all cases.

Box V.2
Costa Rica: disinterest on the part of young people in electoral participation and democracy, 2013

The results of the 2013 National Youth Survey and the findings of a number of studies on abstentionism and participation confirm that levels of confidence and participation in conventional forms of political activity have declined among Costa Rican youth since the late 1990s. According to García Fernández and others (2005), electoral abstentionism and the associated causes during the past 50 years can be divided into three periods. First of all, in the 1950s, a new political and electoral system was in the process of being consolidated. Then, in the 1960s, the percentage of the electorate who did not vote stabilized at around one fifth of those who were eligible to vote, and that situation remained more or less the same until the 1998 elections, when 30% of the people on the electoral rolls did not vote. In the 2002 elections, a larger proportion of young people had never voted than was the case among the adult population, while the percentage of people who always voted declined. Thus, many of the young people who said that they had never voted did not vote in 2002, or even in 1998 and 2002, which means that they did not vote either the first or the first two times that they were eligible to do so.

Both the 2013 National Youth Survey and the 2013 Latinobarómetro Survey showed up a decrease in the belief that democracy is the best form of government among persons between the ages of 15 and 35 (the age group defined as corresponding to the young population in Costa Rica) and an increase in indifference in respect of this issue. A waning level of confidence in the country's leaders was also detected.

Costa Rica: rating of the democratic system by persons between the ages of 15 and 35 in the 2007 and 2013 National Youth Surveys
(Percentages)

Question	Agree		Neither agree nor disagree		Disagree	
	2007	2013	2007	2013	2007	2013
"Democracy is the best of all political systems"	52.4	37.4	9.5	17.1	12.2	14.8
"I have confidence in the leaders of Costa Rica"	14.1	10.7	14.2	15.6	34.1	30.5

Source: Prepared by the author on the basis of the results of the first (2007) and second (2013) National Youth Surveys.

A number of studies suggest that the increase in abstentionism is chiefly due to political variables that have prompted people to feel uneasy about politics and to distance themselves from traditional political parties. People began to become more and more disenchanted with traditional political parties in the 1990s, and it has also been observed that parties have lost more followers when they are in power. The move away from the two main political parties is most notable in more educated, higher-income groups. One of the explanatory factors in this respect is the differing life experiences of one generation relative to those of the preceding generation. There are differences, for example, in the strength of party loyalty that correspond to the temporal proximity of the events that gave rise to the party system. In Costa Rica, the major political forces of the second half of the twentieth century had their origin in the armed

Box V.2 (concluded)

conflict of 1948. The young people of today did not live through that time, and their parents have not passed on their memories of it. The research done by Fournier, Cortés and Zeledón (1999) on the 1998 elections turned up evidence of a weakening of family political traditions. In a similar vein, Gutiérrez Espeleta and other authors have characterized the breakdown of electoral traditions as the main factor accounting for the results of the 2002 elections and have hypothesized that the most likely origin of that breakdown was in the younger generations, whose members are not emotionally engaged with the political forces of 1948. Another factor is that, unlike their parents, young people have no experience or memory of the period during which the welfare State was at its height (the 1970s) and may therefore not see the State in such a favourable light as the members of the generations that grew up during the second half of the twentieth century. In addition, the younger generations' entry into the labour market has been more difficult than it was for earlier generations.

Historically, the political culture in Costa Rica has been a strong proponent of democracy (Alfaro-Redondo, Vargas-Cullel and Seligson, 2015), but its advocacy of this system of government has weakened considerably over the past three decades.

Source: Prepared by the author, on the basis of Jorge E. Segura Arias "Gobiernos locales y participación de las personas jóvenes en puestos de elección popular en Costa Rica, 2010", *Revista Derecho Electoral*, No. 15, January-June 2013; National Council of the Public Policy of Young Persons, *Segunda Encuesta Nacional de Juventudes: Informe de principales resultados*, San Jose [online] http://www.cpj.go.cr/component/docman/doc_download/41-segunda-encuesta-nacional-de-juventudes-informe-de-principales-resultados-costa-rica-2013; United Nations Population Fund (UNFPA), *1era Encuesta Nacional de Juventud: Costa Rica 2008. Informe integrado*, San Jose, 2009 [online] http://www.cpj.go.cr/docs/encuesta/Informe-final-encuesta.pdf; Jorge Raúl García Fernández and others, *Abstencionistas en Costa Rica: ¿Quiénes son y por qué no votan?*, Editorial de la Universidad de Costa Rica, 2005 [online] http://biblioteca.clacso.edu.ar/Costa_Rica/iis-ucr/20120725041855/abstencion.pdf; Gerardo Berthin, *Explorando la dinámica de la participación política juvenil en la gobernabilidad local en América Latina*, Regional Centre for Latin America and the Caribbean, Panama City, 2013; Ronald Alfaro-Redondo, Jorge Vargas-Cullell and Mitchell A. Seligson, "Cultura política en Costa Rica: el declive de largo plazo de las actitudes que favorecen una democracia estable continúa", *Perspectivas desde el Barómetro de las Américas: 2015*, No. 111 [online] http://www.vanderbilt.edu/lapop/insights/IO911es_V2.pdf; Ana Lucía Gutiérrez Espeleta and others, "Resquebrajándose una tradición electoral", *Revista de Ciencias Sociales*, No. 98, San Jose [online] http://163.178.170.74/wp-content/revistas/98/04-.pdf; and Marco Fournier, Alberto Cortés and Fernando Zeledón, "Elección nacional de 1998: Encuesta de opinión. Informe final", 1999.

One indicator that points to the existence of a low level of support for democracy is the change in the percentage of young people who stated that they are satisfied with the way that the democratic system has functioned (see figure V.13). At the regional level, this figure was just 36% in 2000 and stood at 39% in 2013. The 10 countries in which the level of satisfaction with democracy increased are plotted above the diagonal line (Argentina, Brazil, Chile, Ecuador, El Salvador, Nicaragua, Paraguay, Peru, the Plurinational State of Bolivia and Uruguay). Another five countries —most of them in Central America— are below that line because the level of satisfaction of respondents in those countries decreased (the Bolivarian Republic of Venezuela, Costa Rica, Guatemala, Honduras and Mexico). In 2013, a majority of the young respondents in each country —with the exceptions of Argentina, Ecuador, Nicaragua and Uruguay— said that they were not satisfied. The level of satisfaction with democratic systems also declined in five countries, most of which were in Central America.

Figure V.13
Latin America (17 countries): change in the number of persons between the ages of 16 and 29 who state that they are satisfied with the workings of the democratic system, 2000-2013

(Percentages)

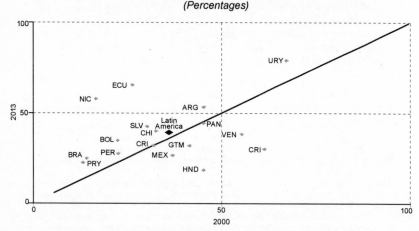

Source: Economic Commission for Latin America and the Caribbean (ECLAC), on the basis of special tabulations of the results of the 2000 and 2013 Latinobarómetro surveys.
Note: The question was worded as follows: "With which of the following do you agree the most?" The options were: "Democracy is preferable to any other form of government"; "Under some circumstances, an authoritarian government may be preferable to a democratic one"; and "For people like us, it doesn't matter whether the government is democratic or not". Data for the Dominican Republic were not included because figures were available only for 2013. In the 2013 survey, the options "do not know" and "no answer" were added to cover 100% of all cases.

With the alternatives to democracy as the best system of government being characterized as indifference (no preference) or as a preference for a non-democratic system, in most cases a majority of people said that they had no preference (see figure V.14). In 2013, as many as 35% of young people in Mexico said that they did not care what system of government was in place. One positive trend that can be discerned is that, in the countries where support for an authoritarian form of government was relatively high in 2000, sharp decreases in that level of support were seen in 2013. Examples include the Bolivarian Republic of Venezuela (from 23% to 9%), Brazil (from 27% to 18%), Chile (from 18% to 12%), Colombia (from 23% to 16%) and Paraguay (from 38% to 31%). The percentages of young people who favoured authoritarian forms of government under certain circumstances rose considerably only in Peru (from 11% to 19%) and in three Central American countries: Costa Rica (from 7% to 18%), El Salvador (from 12% to 20%) and Nicaragua (from 7% to 21%).

Figure V.14
Latin America (17 countries): support for democracy as the best form of government among persons between the ages of 16 and 29, 2000-2013
(Percentages)

A. 2000

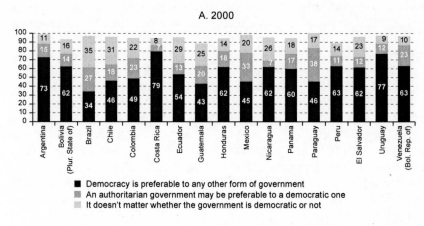

■ Democracy is preferable to any other form of government
▓ An authoritarian government may be preferable to a democratic one
░ It doesn't matter whether the government is democratic or not

B. 2013

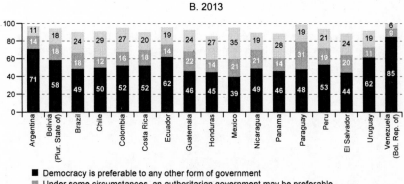

■ Democracy is preferable to any other form of government
▓ Under some circumstances, an authoritarian government may be preferable
░ For people like us, it doesn't matter whether the government is democratic or authoritarian

Source: Economic Commission for Latin America and the Caribbean (ECLAC), on the basis of special tabulations of the results of the 2000 and 2013 Latinobarómetro surveys.
Note: The question was worded as follows: "With which of the following do you agree the most?" The options were: "Democracy is preferable to any other form of government"; "Under some circumstances, an authoritarian government may be preferable to a democratic one"; and "For people like us, it doesn't matter whether the government is democratic or not". Data for the Dominican Republic were not included because figures were available only for 2013. In the 2013 survey, the options "do not know" and "no answer" were added to cover 100% of all cases.

A final indicator of people's perceptions of the representative capacity of democratic systems is their views as to who is actually running the country (see figure V.15). In 2013, in most of the countries, 70% or more of young people responding to the survey said that powerful groups run the country for their own benefit. There were only three countries in which most young people thought that their countries were governed for the good of the people (Ecuador, Nicaragua and Uruguay), while the corresponding figures for the Plurinational State of Bolivia, El Salvador and the Bolivarian Republic of Venezuela were somewhat below that 70% mark, at 55%, 59% and 60%, respectively. In all of these countries, new coalitions on the left of the political spectrum have taken office and remained in power, in most cases under the helm of charismatic leaders, since 2000. On this point, the rather pessimistic views of young people are in line with those of people aged 30 and over. These perceptions are also in keeping with the findings of several studies that have found that, if the periods during which political parties fell into disrepute hastened the collapse of the party system that then paved the way for the emergence of strong leadership figures not associated with any established party, the next phase —if associated with vigorous social mobilizations and protest movements— could well be one in which stable party ties are re-established (UNDP/AECID, 2014). Be this as it may, the prevailing view in most of the countries is that the government has not been run with the intention of upholding the interests of the majority of the population.

Figure V.15
Latin America (18 countries): persons between the ages of 16 and 29 and persons aged 30 or over who believe that powerful groups, rather than the people, are running the government of their country, 2013 [a]

(Percentages)

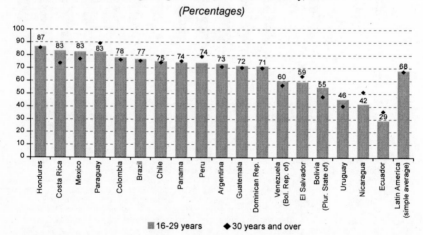

Source: Economic Commission for Latin America and the Caribbean (ECLAC), on the basis of special tabulations of the results of the 2013 Latinobarómetro survey.

Note: The survey question was worded as follows: "Generally speaking, would you say that (the country) is governed by a few powerful groups for their own benefit or is governed for the benefit of all?".

[a] The countries are listed in descending order of the percentages of young persons who said that the government was run by powerful groups for their own benefit in 2013.

In sum, the results of the 2000 and 2013 Latinobarómetro surveys trace a downward trend in young people's support for democracy as the best form of government, with much of this support giving way to indifference (with some exceptions, such as the Bolivarian Republic of Venezuela, Brazil and Ecuador). The results for the Central American countries and Mexico are particularly worrisome, since the level of support for democracy was already low in 2000 in those countries and has continued to decline since then. It should not be forgotten, however, that these trends reflect political cycles and dynamics in each country that influence the attitudes of different groups and that changes in governing coalitions may lend greater legitimacy or detract from the legitimacy of democratic systems, as well as fuelling or dampening indifference regarding forms of government or the acceptance of authoritarian regimes.

The question then arises: What is democracy identified with? Representative democracy entails an everlasting tension between individual freedom and the quest for equality (Bobbio, 1996). Upholding individual freedom involves the use of a series of safeguards for protecting people's rights against arbitrary decisions or actions by the State, private and public organizations and other people, whereas attaining equality for all persons entails the establishment of conditions for people's existence and interaction that will generate similar results or levels of enjoyment of human rights. The way in which different people think about democracy will tend to place priority on one or the other of these two values. In the early 2000s, a number of opinion polls in Latin America indicated that, in this recently democratized region, people tended to place greater priority on equality than on safeguards for human rights as such, with the emphasis being more on improvements in social, economic and other conditions than in the case of their peers in North America (Moreno, 2001). They also indicated that young people tended to associate democracy more often with liberty, the protection of minorities and freedom of expression rather than with material or electoral factors (Moreno, 2001).

One way of approaching this subject is to look at the types of conditions that young people associate with democracy. The 2013 Latinobarómetro survey included a number of questions in which respondents were asked to associate democracy with different elements. For each of these questions, the possible answers included options that alluded to individual freedom, the exercise of political power, material well-being and public policy. At the regional level, the most frequently selected option (although it did not represent an absolute majority of the answers in all cases) related to individual liberty and freedom of expression (see figure V.16).

Figure V.16
**Latin America (18 countries): average of the four main elements associated
with democracy by young persons, 2013**
(Percentages)

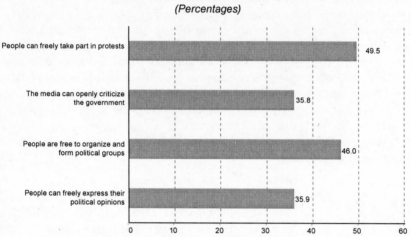

Source: Economic Commission for Latin America and the Caribbean (ECLAC), on the basis of special tabulations of the results of the 2013 Latinobarómetro survey.

Note: The survey question was worded as follows: "If you could choose only one of the following four sentences, which one would you choose as being the one that best describes a democracy?". Each question had four possible answers (in addition to "no answer", "do not understand the question" and "cannot decide"), but those possible answers were repeated for four different questions.

Table V.1 shows the data for the various responses given at the country level to the question "If you could choose only one of the following four sentences, which one would you choose as being the one that best describes a democracy?". It should be borne in mind, however, that a number of variations and different interpretations of the concept of democracy were involved. Overall, the most frequent answer had to do with freedom: "The media can openly criticize the government". The second-most popular option had to do with material conditions: "The government makes sure that job opportunities are available to everyone"; this answer was the preferred one in Mexico and Paraguay. In the Dominican Republic, Ecuador and El Salvador, the second-most favoured option was "The government upholds law and order". In Uruguay, the second-most frequently chosen option was: "Many different parties compete fairly and openly with each other in the elections".

In the light of this diverse situation where, nonetheless, the general trend is towards a low level of participation, a disaffection with political institutions and tenuous support for democracy in many countries, the question that arises is to what extent are the traditional channels for youth participation reshaping paths for the direct mobilization of young people and for their participation by unconventional means?

Table V.1
Latin America (18 countries): averages for the four main aspects
of democracy attributed to it by young people, 2013
(Percentages)

Country	The media can openly criticize the government	The government makes sure that job opportunities are available to everyone	The government upholds law and order	Many different parties compete fairly and openly with each other in the elections
Argentina	42.4	19.4	9.7	19.1
Bolivia (Plurinational State of)	35.7	20.9	15.5	10.2
Brazil	48.4	14.6	12.4	12.1
Colombia	34.5	22.5	20.2	17.1
Costa Rica	38.6	18.3	15.4	17.1
Chile	26.5	23.0	15.8	11.1
Dominican Republic	29.1	16.5	26.8	21.2
Ecuador	30.1	21.8	29.6	8.6
El Salvador	36.4	14.1	27.8	9.2
Guatemala	31.7	27.1	22.2	12.7
Honduras	50.2	18.8	8.0	10.7
Mexico	29.6	30.1	16.6	15.5
Nicaragua	35.7	24.3	17.2	14.5
Panama	40.9	15.1	11.9	20.8
Paraguay	22.8	28.5	15.7	15.4
Peru	43.1	20.4	14.5	10.3
Uruguay	31.8	19.2	11.6	22.8
Venezuela (Bolivarian Republic of)	37.3	17.5	17.3	15.6
Latin America	35.8	20.7	17.1	14.7

Source: Economic Commission for Latin America and the Caribbean (ECLAC), on the basis of special tabulations of the results of the 2013 Latinobarómetro survey.
Note: The survey question was worded as follows: "If you could choose only one of the following four sentences, which one would you choose as being the one that best describes a democracy?". Each question had four possible answers (in addition to "no answer", "do not understand the question" and "cannot decide"), but those possible answers were repeated for four different questions. The figures do not add up to 100% because the fairly small percentage of answers corresponding to the options of "do not understand the question" and "cannot decide" have not been included for the sake of clarity.

C. Unconventional forms of participation and new platforms for expression, mobilization and advocacy

Even though many young people have distanced themselves from the political and electoral systems, young people are opting for new, unconventional ways of participating in political affairs and are exhibiting a growing potential to dispute and influence the public political agenda. Forceful youth-led social movements have appeared on the scene in recent years that attest to young people's desire to have their voices heard and to play an active part in the development of their societies. New ways of mobilizing and organizing members of the younger population are emerging in which technological tools play a key role (e.g. social media). This is reflected in the use of Internet platforms in Latin America: of the 12 countries in the world in which social media are used the most, 5 of those countries are in the Latin American and Caribbean region, and most of the users of those platforms are adolescents and young adults (ECLAC, 2014).

The communications model used by social media is very different from the model used by traditional mass media, which broadcast a single message to an indefinite group of individuals. In the case of social media, the users are the ones who create and send out messages to an (also) indeterminate number of people, and the interactivity of that mode of communication is enhanced by their ability to create networks and establish contacts. This new model brings about a substantial change in the way that people interact among themselves and with institutions, either as individuals or as members of communities or movements (Pavez, 2014). These social networks are playing an increasingly important role in the way that adolescents and young adults exert influence and make their opinions, concerns and ideas known, and they are opening up new pathways for the organization of social movements and communities (UNDP, 2013).

In recent years a three-pronged revolution has been taking place: the extension of Internet access to large sectors of the world's population has gone hand in hand with the emergence of virtual social networks as leading new forums for social interaction and with the burgeoning use of portable digital devices (mobile phones and tablets). The younger generations in Latin America are at the forefront of this process in their role as both "democratic natives" and "digital natives". In a 2014 study, Bianchi speaks of a new generation of activists who are making new and different uses of the forums and tools available to them. These activists include many young people who are naturalized practitioners of democratic methods but who nonetheless challenge the status quo (Bianchi, 2014).

This information confirms the observation that young people are more likely to abstain from participating in elections or in other conventional forms of political participation than adults. Among those who do decide to participate, however, there is a clear tendency to use direct, non-electoral channels for participation. This is reflected in the results of the First National Youth Survey of Guatemala, which was conducted in 2011. The responses of under-age young people indicated that they preferred to participate in organizations that were supporting specific causes (see figure V.17).

Figure V.17
Guatemala: participation in unconventional organizations,
by age group and reason, 2011
(Percentages)

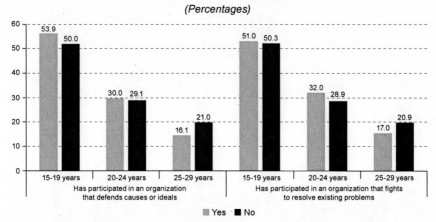

Source: Economic Commission for Latin America and the Caribbean (ECLAC), on the basis of special tabulations of the results of the First National Youth Survey of Guatemala (ENJU), 2011.

The situation in Chile is a case apart since, as noted in earlier sections, its population exhibits very high levels of disaffection with electoral participation and youth mobilizations but, at the same time, there was a striking increase in the percentage of young people in 2000-2013 who stated that they had taken part in demonstrations but had not voted. Portions of these results are in keeping with the data collected by the 2012 National Youth Survey of Chile (see box V.3).

Box V.3
Chile: unconventional forms of mobilization among young people, 2012

Associative behaviour, understood as participation in intermediate social organizations of various types, has been weak ever since Chile's return to democracy (Ríos Tobar and Ajenjo Martínez, 2014). Just the opposite is true, however, of less conventional forms of political participation, such as participation in marches. Various studies have found that young people, unlike adults, prefer to engage in social movements in the form of "taking politics to the streets", protests and direct political action (Flisfisch and Miranda, 2014). In 2011 and 2012, a broad student movement took shape in which large numbers of young people —particularly university students in the country's large urban centres— took part.

Some of the results of the Seventh National Youth Survey are quite interesting (see the following figures). First of all, the great majority of young Chileans do not participate in this form of mobilization. Three unconventional types of participation were listed in the survey (marches, strikes and takeovers), and the respondents who stated that they had engaged in these types of activities represented 23%, 18% and 10% of the sample, respectively. Most of the young people who do choose to participate in these kinds of protests are males

---

Box V.3 (concluded)

between the ages of 15 and 24 in higher-income groups (who therefore are
likely to have greater access to a university education) residing in urban areas
(the main areas of action of the student movement has been in major cities
where universities are located). These findings indicate that, at least during the
period covered by the survey, a sizeable number of young people who had not
reached voting age chose unconventional avenues of political participation.

**Chile: youth participation in different forms of unconventional political
action during the preceding 12 months, by age group, social stratum,
sex and geographical area, 2012**
(Percentages)

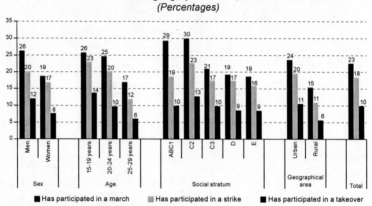

Source: National Youth Survey, 2012.

**Chile: youth participation in different forms of unconventional political action
during the preceding 12 months, by age subgroup**
(Percentages)

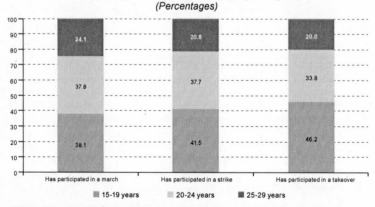

Source: National Youth Survey, 2012.

Source: Prepared by the author, on the basis of National Institute for Youth, *7ma
Encuesta Nacional de Juventud 2012*, Santiago, 2013; Marcela Ríos Tobar and Felipe
Ajenjo Martínez, "Evolución de la participación social y política en Chile", *Electoras y
electores, movimientos, partidos*, Ángel Flisfisch (comp.), Santiago, FLACSO Chile,
2014; and Ángel Flisfisch and Lucía Miranda, "Análisis comparativo de niveles de
confianza en instituciones y agentes políticos: Chile y América Latina", *Electoras y
electores, movimientos, partidos*, Ángel Flisfisch (comp.), Santiago, FLACSO Chile, 2014.

The low indicators for conventional forms of political participation in Chile are thus counterbalanced by the scope of the 2011 student movement, which succeeded in putting issues on the political agenda that traditional politicians had sidestepped or addressed only partially. One of their main demands was that an end should be put to for-profit activities within the educational system and especially in the universities; this principle was already set forth in the relevant legislation, but was not being upheld in practice. In the face of the denials and proposals made by the government, the student demonstrations garnered broad-based, lasting support from, among others, thousands of families and members of other social sectors, and exceptionally large demonstrations were held that were widely covered by the media. Most opinion polls indicated that there was widespread support throughout the country for the causes espoused by the student movement and that this support was maintained over time. The country's leaders made changes in the cabinet and introduced some significant measures, but the need for a complete overhaul of the educational system and the need for a tax reform package that would bring in the necessary funds were firmly positioned on the public agenda. The issues raised by the movement were of such importance that many of them were a central focus of attention during the next presidential campaign and figured prominently in the platform of the coalition that won the elections. Another important outcome was that many of the leaders of the student movement —persons below 25 years of age— succeeded in launching congressional candidacies as members of different political parties or as independents, and a number of them won seats in the Chamber of Deputies in 2013. Thus, another significant aspect of the 2011 student movement was that it contributed to the emergence of new, young, popularly elected leaders who have risen to influential positions within the government.

Another noteworthy case is the #YoSoy132 movement organized by young Mexican university students during the 2012 presidential campaign (see box V.4).

Brazil is another country in which social discontent has been expressed and shaped into an organized movement with the help of the Internet. In June 2013, the media began to report on demonstrations that were being held by thousands of persons, most of whom were young university students, to protest such things as the high cost of public transportation or the costs involved in mounting the FIFA World Cup. These demonstrations mushroomed into one of the largest protest movements to arise in many years. This movement also used social media (mainly Facebook) to underscore the need to meet the new demands for social inclusion of many students and other young people, who focused attention on the fact that public transportation plays an essential role in enabling people to take advantage of educational and employment opportunities, especially in the country's vast urban centres.

As is also true of the Mexican student movement, the participants made sure that this mobilization was organized horizontally and without party affiliations or formal leaders (Pavez, 2014).

Box V.4
Mexico: the #YoSoy132 movement during the 2012 presidential campaign

In the course of the 2012 presidential and congressional campaigns in Mexico, a vibrant movement led by young students at public and private universities coalesced around demands for the democratization of the media and for the holding of a third debate among presidential candidates and the repudiation of what was seen as attempts by certain media to impose a presidential candidate on the public.

On Monday, 14 May, an incident occurred during a campaign event at the Ibero-American University in which students protested the presence of a police contingent and of an outside group of one of the candidate's supporters. Media coverage of the event emphasized that the protests had not been carried out by students of that university but rather by outside elements. In reaction to what they saw as a distortion of the facts, a group of students from that private university made and publicized a video in which 131 of them displayed their student cards, which showed their names and registration numbers, to demonstrate that they had in fact been present. The video circulated widely on YouTube and, just a few minutes later, became a trending topic on Twitter (see [online] http://www.youtube.com/watch?v=P7XbocXsFkl).

This movement spread almost immediately to other universities, with other students identifying themselves as Student No. 132 on Twitter (hence the name of the movement ("Yo Soy" means "I am")). The movement gave rise to public demonstrations that called upon students to remain informed, upon the media to refrain from manipulating the news and to provide information on an independent, neutral basis, and upon the public to hold forums open to all young people who wished to take part in them. A debate was also organized to which all the presidential candidates were invited and which was moderated in an innovative way that included relaying questions posed on Twitter and via Skype. Thanks to the inclusive potential of these technologies, the movement's message was not confined to groups that have traditionally been interested in politics but was instead broadcast to a much larger, varied and hitherto unknown audience. This movement thus successfully used virtual social media to channel the indignation of many members of the electorate at what was seen as biased media coverage.

The initial impact of this movement can partially be accounted for by the fact that it filled a void of information and participation for many young people and other members of the electorate. Two of the factors underlying the eruption of the #YoSoy132 movement were the scarcity of formal avenues for participation via political parties and the political class's reluctance to expand the scope of the available channels for participation (González, 2012, p. 99). Once the elections were over, however, the movement grew weaker —a fact that attests to the difficulty of consolidating this type of movement and achieving its continuity over the long term through the construction of new organizational structures.

Source: Prepared by the author, on the basis of Luis Josué González, "#YoSoy132. Participación política 2.0 en México", *Diálogo Político*, No. 2, 2012.

The non-traditional movements, demonstrations and social organizations in which young people are playing a key leadership role are making use of new forms of communication, new ways of calling for collective action and new avenues for participation. They use social media to organize themselves and to draw the attention of the mass media and their governments (Pavez, 2014). These same features militate against their continuity over time, but they nonetheless constitute a new vehicle for high-impact forms of social mobilization to address specific issues that is now being used on a continuing basis. The importance of these new forms of communication lies in their ability to supplement the existing unsuitable or insufficient avenues for the representation of young people and their diverse views that are afforded by the conventional channels associated with representative democracies. These modalities are engendered by social conflicts that oblige formal political systems to address demands and mount responses to issues and demands that are overlooked or actively stonewalled by established institutions (Calderón Gutiérrez, 2011 and 2012). It is therefore important to explore this subject in order to determine which issues are capable of mobilizing young people and which ones are perceived as being the most urgent.

D.   Issues that mobilize youth and young people's priorities for the public agenda

An exploration of the issues that prompt young people to organize and take part in mobilizations provides a different perspective on the subjects dealt with in this chapter. The results of the 2013 Latinobarómetro survey pinpoint a number of issues that young people appear to be much more willing to champion than older members of the population (see figure V.18). In fact, the percentage of young respondents who said that they were "not willing at all" to take collective action to address the issues identified in the survey was much smaller than the corresponding percentage of the older population. The issues that aroused the most interest among the young population were education and health, followed by higher wages and better jobs, the protection of democratic rights, land ownership and the harvesting of natural resources. Greater priority appears to be placed on issues relating to opportunities for individuals (health, education, wages and employment) than on less tangible causes such as the protection of democratic rights. Issues that have traditionally figured prominently in social struggles, such as those relating to society-wide discussions about land ownership or the harvesting of natural resources and the appropriation of the revenues that they generate and their environmental impact appear to elicit less enthusiasm.

Figure V.18
Latin America (simple average of 18 countries): persons between
the ages of 16 and 29 and persons aged 30 or over who stated
that they were "very willing" or "not willing at all" to join
movements in order to champion selected issues, 2013 [a]

(Percentages)

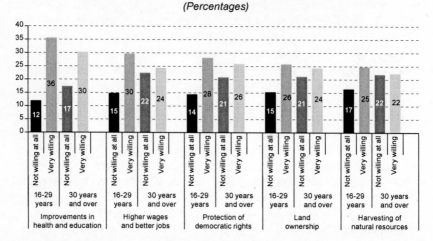

Source: Economic Commission for Latin America and the Caribbean (ECLAC), on the basis of special
tabulations of the results of the 2013 Latinobarómetro survey.
[a] In order to provide as clear a picture as possible of the strength of respondents' feelings about each
issue, results are reported only for those who said that they were "very willing" or "not willing at all"
to join a movement; the 2013 Latinobarómetro questionnaire included eight other possible responses
between these two options.

While the answers varied from country to country, overall the same
order of priority was apparent, as was the gap between the younger population
and those aged 30 or over. Except in a few countries, more respondents
aged 30 or over said that they were "not willing at all" to mobilize on
behalf of given issues than their younger counterparts (see figure V.19). In
other words, a lack of confidence, greater indifference and smaller voter
turnouts for elections do not per se signify less of a willingness on the
part of young people to join social movements. In the case of health and
education, more people aged 30 or over said that they were not at all willing
to join a social movement except in Honduras and Panama. And there were
no exceptions at all to this rule in the case of higher wages and better jobs
or of the protection of democratic rights. With regard to land ownership
and the harvesting of natural resources, the only case in which slightly
more people between the ages of 16 and 29 than those aged 30 and over
chose the response "not willing at all" was in Panama. The overall results
therefore indicate that those under 30 years of age are less averse to joining
a social movement, in line with this group's greater level of enthusiasm,
as mentioned earlier.

Figure V.19
Latin America (simple average of 18 countries): persons between the ages
of 16 and 29 and persons aged 30 or over who stated that they were
"not willing at all" to join movements in order to champion selected issues, 2013 [a]
(Percentages)

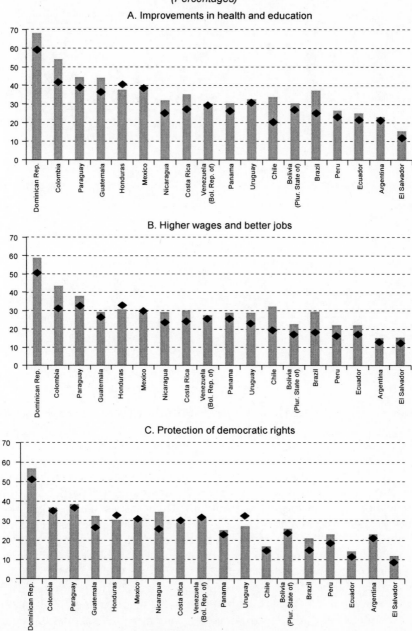

A. Improvements in health and education

B. Higher wages and better jobs

C. Protection of democratic rights

▨ 16-29 years   ◆ 30 years and over

Figure V.19 (concluded)

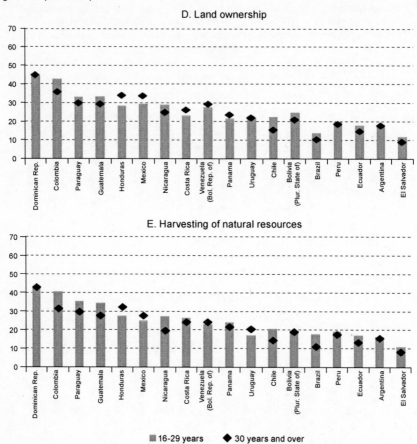

D. Land ownership

E. Harvesting of natural resources

■ 16-29 years   ◆ 30 years and over

Source: Economic Commission for Latin America and the Caribbean (ECLAC), on the basis of special tabulations of the results of the 2013 Latinobarómetro survey.
ª In order to provide as clear a picture as possible of the strength of respondents' feelings about each issue, results are reported only for those who said that they were "not willing at all" to join a movement.

In addition to examining the positions adopted by young people in terms of conventional and unconventional forms of political participation and in relation to democracy as such, along with the issues that are more likely to spur them to action, it is also informative to look at which issues are the highest on the public agenda and how those priorities may have shifted in recent years. At the regional level, the main problems identified by young people changed between 2000 and 2013 (see figure V.20). In 2000, the issues on which priority was placed were unemployment (21.2%), education (20.7%) and corruption (9.7%), followed by poverty (8.1%) and crime (7.7%). In 2013, on the other hand, the top three issues were crime (23%), unemployment (15.9%), and education and corruption (each with 6.3%). Thus, unemployment was the only issue that remained among the top priorities, while the issue of crime gained ground in terms of its standing among the issues listed in the survey.

Figure V.20
Latin America (17 countries): averages of responses of persons between the ages of 16 and 29 regarding the most important issue in their country, 2000 y 2013

(Percentages)

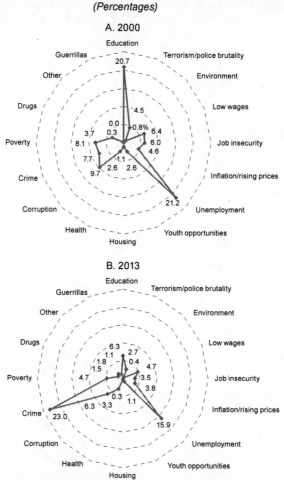

A. 2000

B. 2013

Source: Economic Commission for Latin America and the Caribbean (ECLAC), on the basis of special tabulations of the results of the 2000 and 2013 Latinobarómetro surveys.

Note: The question on the survey form is worded as follows: "Of the list of problems that I am going to show you, which do you think is the most serious in your country?" In order for the results for the two survey years to be comparable, only the responses that were present on the forms for both years are reported. The options "do not know", " no answer", " none", "transportation", "human rights violations", "drug trafficking", "supply shortages", "global warming", "basic services", "the economy/financial problems", "the political situation", "income distribution", "racial discrimination", "border disputes", "problems with neighbouring countries" and "energy problems" account for 100% of the survey responses in 2013.

While there are differences across countries, there are also some general patterns that warrant attention (see table V.2). In 2000, education was identified as one of the two most important issues in 13 of the 17 countries for which information is available. Unemployment was also placed near the top of the list by respondents in a majority (11) of the countries.

Table V.2
Latin America (17 countries): the two problems identified as being the most important by persons between the ages of 16 and 29, 2000 and 2013

Country	2000	2013
Argentina	Unemployment	Crime and public safety
	Education	Inflation and rising prices
Bolivia (Plurinational State of)	Education	Crime and public safety
	Unemployment	The economy and financial problems
Brazil	Unemployment	Health problems
	Drugs	Problems with education [a]
Chile	Unemployment	Problems with education
	Job instability	Crime and public safety
Colombia	Terrorism and political violence [a]	Unemployment
	Unemployment	Violence and gangs
Costa Rica	Education	Corruption
	Corruption	Unemployment
Ecuador	Education	Crime and public safety
	Corruption	Unemployment
El Salvador	Poverty	Crime and public safety [a]
	Education	Low wages
Guatemala	Education	Crime and public safety [a]
	Low wages	Unemployment
Honduras	Education	Unemployment
	Crime [a]	Crime and public safety [a]
Mexico	Inflation and rising prices	Crime and public safety
	Education	Unemployment
Nicaragua	Education	Unemployment
	Unemployment	Low wages
Panama	Unemployment	Transportation
	Education	Low wages
Paraguay	Unemployment	Unemployment
	Education [a]	Crime and public safety
Peru	Unemployment	Crime and public safety
	Education	Poverty
Uruguay	Unemployment	Crime and public safety
	Low wages	Unemployment
Venezuela (Bolivarian Republic of)	Education	Crime and public safety
	Unemployment	Supply shortages, food shortages and hoarding

Source: Prepared by the author on the basis of special tabulations of the 2000 and 2013 Latinobarómetro surveys.
[a] These responses were worded somewhat differently in the two survey forms, but it can be assumed that they mean the same thing.

In the 2013 survey, crime (including gang activity) and public safety were ranked as one of the two top-priority issues in 13 out of 17 countries. Unemployment was rated this highly in 9 countries, with other issues that were mentioned less often being economic and financial problems, corruption and education. There is thus a degree of concordance among the results at the individual country level with the region-wide averages, with unemployment being rated as a top-priority problem by young respondents to both the 2000 and 2013 surveys, while crime was mentioned as one of the respondents' primary concerns in the 2013 survey.

E. Policies and programmes for promoting youth participation and mobilization

Young people's participation in politics, their engagement in public debates and discussions and their possible involvement in direct collective action are processes that are not likely to be heavily influenced by specific policies or measures. It is difficult to imagine a way of heightening their involvement "by fiat" or through the introduction of targeted policy measures alone. Participation stems from an interest in public affairs, and the decision to vote and to join social movements is the product of a personal awareness of their importance and of a willingness to assume the costs that may be associated with civic activism.

Youth participation and mobilization are spurred by specific demands and causes at a given point in time that may mark a generation but that may not necessarily ensure that its members remain involved in the future (see boxes V.3 and V.4). To some extent, each new generation seeks out and finds a place for itself within the environment that it happens to find itself in: one in which there is faster or slower economic growth, greater or lesser redistributive tensions and a greater or lesser presence on the public and governmental agenda of the issues of importance to them. The patterns that have emerged of young people's disaffection with political participation and democracy have prompted a number of researchers (including the authors of this study) to posit that, while there are certainly particular sets of circumstances in different countries that merit an in-depth examination, the main problem shared by all the countries in this respect has to do with the need to include young people in the operation and processes of a representative democracy.

Tables V.3 and V.4 provide an overview of some of the programmes that have been implemented in the region in an effort to foster political and social participation by young people. Generally speaking, these initiatives fall into one or the other of two main categories: programmes focusing on the organization of forums for political dialogue and participation on the part of young people (see table V.3) and programmes that are intended to promote young people's political participation by direct means (see table V.4).

Table V.3
Programmes focusing on the creation of youth forums for political dialogue and communication

Country	Policy, programme or project	Responsible institution or agency	Objective
Argentina	*Mutuales del Bicentenario* (bicentenary mutual groups)	National Youth Department	Creation of channels and pathways for enhancing the social and political participation and organization of persons between the ages of 21 and 36 within the context of more than 40 mutual associations throughout the country.
Brazil	*Estação Juventude* (youth stations)	National Youth Secretariat	Introduction of public centres for persons between the ages of 15 and 29 years in vulnerable sectors within the country.
	Participatório (Observatório Participativo da Juventude) (participatory youth observatory)	National Youth Secretariat	Promotion of participation in virtual environments, youth mobilization and the generation of knowledge networks.
Chile	*Escuelas de ciudadanía* (citizenship schools)	National Institute for Youth (INJUV) of the Ministry for Social Development	Fostering of a greater commitment to democratic, civic and citizen action and engagement among young people. Promotion of a culture of civic engagement through the development of hands-on civic activities as a means of bringing new leaders to the fore who are willing to work to improve their surroundings. This initiative targets over 10,500 students in the fourth year of private, subsidized or municipal secondary schools in 60 "citizenship schools".
Colombia	*Mesa Nacional de Consejeros y Consejeras* (national board of counsellors)	Colombia Joven (Young Colombia), a presidential programme making up part of the National Youth System	Provision of a forum for dialogue and consensus-building for governmental agencies of Colombia in representation of youth and the practices of youth organizations with a view to safeguarding, upholding and ensuring the enjoyment or recovery of the rights of young people, building their capacities and expanding the integral, sustainable development opportunities for them. The target population for this initiative is young people who are involved in youth and political organizations in the country.
Ecuador	*Proceso de articulación de los jóvenes para su participación política en el Ecuador* (coordination of young people's political participation in Ecuador)	National Secretariat for Policy Management	Consolidation of forums around the country for political participation by young people.

Source: Prepared by the author on the basis of information concerning the policies and programmes implemented by youth agencies in the region.

Table V.4
Programmes for the promotion of direct political participation on the part of young people

Country	Policy, programme or project	Responsible institution or agency	Objective
Chile	*P.A.I.S. Joven (Programa de Apoyo a Iniciativas Sociales Jóvenes)* (support programme for social youth initiatives)	National Institute for Youth (INJUV) of the Ministry of Social Development and the Ministry of Planning	Promotion of the participation of young people in the country's development effort. The target population is composed of young people who wish to participate or who already are participating in political affairs.
Colombia	*Innovación Social creada por Jóvenes* (youth-driven social innovation)	Colombia Joven (Young Colombia), a presidential programme making up part of the National Youth System	Promotion of a culture of innovation among persons between the ages of 14 and 28 so that they can become agents of change in their communities and can take an active part in the consolidation of peace in Colombia.
Costa Rica	*Democracia Participativa* (participatory democracy)	Spanish Agency for International Development Cooperation (AECID)	Promotion of an equitable society while strengthening the institutions of the State as a means of bringing the State and the citizenry closer together and improving public administration. Building capacity in vulnerable collectives as a means of enhancing their integration and participation in society.
	Participación Ciudadana (civic engagement)	National Commission for the Improved Administration of Justice (CONAMAJ)	Strengthening of the link between the judiciary and the citizens as a means of democratizing and optimizing the administration of justice. Reinforcement of the democratic system in Costa Rica and a deepening of knowledge about the needs and potentials of civil society in relation to the judicial system. Improvement of the judicial system's responsiveness to local needs and a reinforcement of ties between the community and judicial institutions.
Ecuador	*Diálogo con los gobiernos autónomos y descentralizados en el Ecuador* (a dialogue with autonomous and subnational governments in Ecuador)	National Secretariat for Policy Management	Support for governance at subnational levels and within the framework of the democratic reform of the State.
Mexico	*Impulso Mexico* (driving Mexico forward)	Mexican Youth Institute (IMJUVE) of the Secretariat for Social Development (SEDESOL)	Stimulation of creativity, the acquisition of social capital and the formation and participation of youth groups and organizations through the exercise of their rights and support for actions undertaken to promote the integral development of people between the ages of 12 and 29.
Peru	*Cuota de Jóvenes* (youth quota)	Standing Committee of the National Congress	Promotion of the active participation of persons under the age of 29 in local and municipal governments.
	Ley del Consejo Nacional de la Juventud (National Youth Council Act)	Standing Committee of the National Congress	Establishment of an institutional and policy framework to guide State and societal action in the area of youth policy and to promote the participation and democratic representation of persons between the ages of 15 and 29, without discrimination in terms of their rights, duties and responsibilities, with a view to the promotion and integral development of the young population.

Table V.4 (concluded)

Country	Policy, programme or project	Responsible institution or agency	Objective
Uruguay	*Fondo de Iniciativas Juveniles* (youth initiative fund)	National Institute for Youth (INJU) of the Ministry for Social Development	Support for youth involvement and leadership in associative forms of behaviour. Reinforcement of the capacities and associative networks of youth organizations, groups and collectives as a strategy for enhancing the influence that they are able to exert in public and political forums in shaping the country's agenda. Promotion of the widest possible range of expression for young people by supporting inclusive proposals relating to their organization in groups and their initiatives. Configuration of an experience of networking and information sharing among youth collectives as a basis for the establishment of local and departmental youth boards. The target population is composed of people between the ages of 15 and 29 throughout the country who submit social projects.

Source: Prepared by the author on the basis of information concerning the policies and programmes implemented by youth agencies in the region.

Most of the programmes falling into the first of these two categories are implemented by youth institutes or secretariats, whereas most of those in the second category are run by various offices in the legislative or judicial branches of government or in the executive branch itself. All of these initiatives attest to the efforts being made to provide young people with greater opportunities for social and political participation. As will be discussed below, although these programmes are valuable and should be provided with adequate funding and assisted in achieving broader coverage, there are also many other spheres of action that should be explored.

Looking beyond the scope of sectoral youth policies, it is important to note that this analysis of conventional and unconventional patterns of youth participation based on a review of international experiences points to a way of delineating a number of possible lines of action that may help to ensure that the institutional environment and the way that the political system operates provide as many pathways as possible for young people to contribute and participate. The different types of steps that can be taken range from changes in national justice and electoral systems to measures that can open up opportunities for young people to engage in dialogue, participate and exert influence at the community level, in political parties and in civil society organizations. Parallel progress along these strategic lines can give shape to a political and institutional framework that is more open to the assumption of a political role by young people.

The measures set out in various studies for encouraging young people to take an interest in politics and to participate in political affairs include the introduction of school curricula that provide information on the workings of electoral systems and channels for political participation. They also include the organization of youth congresses or special sessions of national legislatures that could be opened up to young people (Beetham, 2006; IPU, 2014). Box V.5 lists a number of the specific measures recently proposed by the Inter-Parliamentary Union for spurring interest and political participation on the part of young people. Rather than contending that all of these measures would be useful in every context, a more useful approach is to bear this wide array of options in mind as starting points for a determination of the viability of their implementation in specific cases.

Box V.5
Robust measures to strengthen young people's involvement in politics

---

Set quotas for young people in the legislature and in political parties.

Set quotas at the local level so that a new political class can emerge and establish itself in leadership positions at the national level.

Consider the possibility of lowering the minimum voting age and the minimum age of eligibility to run for office.

Bring the minimum age of eligibility to run for office into line with the minimum voting age.

Consider the possibility of forming youth political parties if this is feasible under the relevant country's Constitution and laws.

Because people often elect candidates who are like them and because the more young people there are in congress, the more young people will vote, include more young people in political parties' lists of candidates and executive bodies.

Establish youth committees in legislatures and empower them to consider every piece of draft legislation and every policy, regardless of whether or not it has a direct bearing on youth.

Monitor the implementation of youth policies; allocate funds for youth, education and training policies; and take young people into account in preparing national budgets.

Include young people in international debates rather than only in forums that focus on youth.

Introduce training programmes for young politicians in order to address young people's overall lack of political experience.

Establish postgraduate or university programmes for young political hopefuls in order to compensate for their lack of experience.

Include youth involvement in political decision-making, governance and peace among the Sustainable Development Goals as requested by the Youth Forum of the United Nations Economic and Social Council.

Source: Inter-Parliamentary Union (IPU), *Taking Democracy to Task*, Geneva, 2014.

In the light of these recommendations, it is to be noted that the age requirement for candidates for elected office is higher than the voting age requirement (see table V.5) in 19 of the 24 countries in Latin America and the Caribbean covered by this analysis. In 11 countries (Argentina, Brazil, Colombia, the Dominican Republic, Haiti, Paraguay, Peru, the Plurinational State of Bolivia, Saint Lucia, Trinidad and Tobago, and Uruguay), people have to be 25 years or older to take up a seat in the Chamber of Deputies, which leaves a large segment of the young population without the ability to engage in this form of political participation. In addition, in countries that have higher chambers or senates, the age requirements for holding seats in these bodies are even higher. In fact, in 9 de the 13 countries with a higher congressional chamber (Argentina, Brazil, Chile, Colombia, Mexico, Paraguay, the Plurinational State of Bolivia, Saint Lucia and Uruguay), the whole of the young population is ineligible for election to these bodies (since the age requirements are 30 years or higher). There are only four countries in which the minimum voting age is the same as the minimum age for standing as a congressional candidate (Grenada, Guatemala, Guyana and Suriname). Therefore, in order to expand the opportunities for young people to be elected to public office, thought should be given to a discussion of the possibility of at least narrowing the gap between these two age requirements in most of the countries of the region.

Table V.5
Latin America and the Caribbean (24 countries): minimum ages for voting and for standing as a candidate in national legislative elections

Country	Chamber	Seats	Minimum election age	Minimum voting age
Argentina	Upper	74	30 years	18 years
	Lower	257	25 years	
Bolivia (Plurinational State of)	Upper	36	35 years	18 years
	Lower	130	25 years	
Brazil	Upper	81	35 years	16 years
	Lower	513	25 years	
Colombia	Upper	102	30 years	18 years
	Lower	165	25 years	
Costa Rica	Assembly	57	21 years	18 years
Chile	Upper	38	40 years	18 years
	Lower	120	21 years	
Dominican Republic	Lower	190	25 years	18 years
Ecuador	Assembly	137	18 years	16 years
Guatemala	Lower	158	18 years	18 years
Honduras	Lower	128	21 years	18 years
Mexico	Upper	150	30 years	18 years
	Lower	500	21 years	
Nicaragua	Assembly	92	21 years	16 years

Table V.5 (concluded)

Country	Chamber	Seats	Minimum election age	Minimum voting age
Paraguay	Upper	45	35 years	18 years
	Lower	125	25 years	
Peru	Lower	130	25 years	18 years
Uruguay	Upper	30	30 years	18 years
	Lower	99	25 years	
Dominica	Assembly	31	21 years	18 years
Grenada	Upper	13	18 years	18 years
	Lower	16		
Guyana	Assembly	65	18 years	18 years
Haiti	Upper	30	25 years	18 years
	Lower	95		
Jamaica	Upper	21	21 years	18 years
	Lower	63		
Saint Lucia	Upper	11	30 years	18 years
	Lower	18		
Saint Kitts and Nevis	Assembly	16	21 years	18 years
Suriname	Assembly	51	18 years	18 years
Trinidad and Tobago	Upper	31	25 years	18 years
	Lower	42		

Source: Prepared by the author, on the basis of official electoral registers of the countries and María García, "Jóvenes políticos en los parlamentos latinoamericanos", *Elites Parlamentarias Latinoamericanas. Boletín Datos de Opinión*, No. 6, University of Salamanca, 2009 [online] http://americo.usal.es/oir/elites/Boletines_Analisis/6_Garc%C3%ADa.pdf; Mariana Llanos and Detlef Nolte, "Los Congresos en América Latina: legislaturas reactivas, potencialmente activas", *Política*, No. 47, Santiago, University of Chile [online] http://www.revistapolitica.uchile.cl/index.php/RP/issue/view/1651.

Another area in which each country might devise measures and reforms to foster youth participation, not only in terms of policy but also with a view to the entire electoral cycle, has been outlined in a recent comprehensive study of the subject (UNDP, 2013). This area of action involves systematic efforts to help young candidates to overcome the shortfalls they face in terms of resources and experience in order to build the necessary skills. It is therefore important to keep channels for participation and influential action open at the community level on an ongoing basis, since this is the level that tends to offer the greatest opportunities for people to take the first steps in building their political and social leadership skills.

Youth programmes that are guided or managed by young people themselves constitute a third strategic area for youth skill-building (e.g. project management structures that provide for collaboration with youth-led initiatives and the systematic inclusion of persons under 29 years of age in national and local consultations and dialogues). In order to ensure that project activities are relevant to the interests and priorities of the people involved in each case, these initiatives need to be geared to the national and local conditions and the diverse situations of the young people involved. Box V.6

lists some of the measures that can be used to foster the participation of young people in the different phases of the electoral process, all of which involve interactions among electoral laws and regulations, the bylaws of the various political parties and the rules and practices of civil society organizations.

Box V.6
Strategic actions for promoting young people's political participation and mobilization in the various stages of the electoral process

1. Pre-election measures

In civil society organizations, community affairs and forums for public debate

- Encourage continuous youth participation and civic education in schools and universities.

- Design training programmes to serve as incubators for projects that will help to inculcate democratic values, build leadership capacities, foster teamwork and encourage young people to assume their roles as citizens and agents of change in their societies.

- Support youth-led community development and volunteering organizations.

- Provide flexible support that helps to lower access barriers for innovative, small-scale youth projects.

- Bridge the digital divide with the use of mobile phones and radio broadcasts focusing on the discussion of specific issues of interest to young people.

- Use online platforms for knowledge-sharing and networking among politically engaged youth.

At the level of political parties

- Promote affirmative action measures, such as quotas for youth and women in political parties.

- Support the development of strong youth components or teams in political parties.

- Provide capacity-building for young members of political parties in a multi-partisan setting.

- Address training and mentoring needs of young women belonging to given political parties on a separate basis.

2. Measures for promoting the participation and mobilization of young people during the electoral cycle

- Ensure youth involvement in all phases of voter education campaigns.

- Use attractive multimedia strategies to draw young people's attention.

- Include youths on electoral management body advisory boards, as poll station workers and election observers.

- Develop interactive online tools in order to reach out to young computer-literate voters.

Box V.6 (concluded)

---

3. **Measures for promoting the political mobilization and participation of young people during the post-electoral stage**

- Make the voices of youth heard in congress and government.
- Facilitate the operation of youth-led national youth councils and congresses.
- Invite youth groups to visit and learn about the day-to-day work of national legislatures.
- Start up student internship programmes in national legislatures.
- Train and support young members of the legislature.
- Launch and support youth councils at the local level.

Source: United Nations Development Programme (UNDP), *Enhancing Youth Political Participation throughout the Electoral Cycle. A Good Practice Guide*, New York, 2013 [online] http://www.undp.org/content/dam/undp/library/Democratic%20Governance/Electoral %20Systems%20and%20Processes/ENG_UN-Youth_Guide-LR.pdf.

Many of these measures have been advocated by young people themselves in various forums. For example, in the Youth Declaration of the Fourth Young Americas Forum in April 2015, the participants set forth the following priorities: "We propose electoral quotas for young people to ensure our participation and influence, institutionalize mechanisms for ongoing discussion, social TIC's, consultations and participation in the public policy cycle. Additionally, evaluate those that already exist to reform them, providing public education on leadership, public participation, management and political/ social control." (Youth Declaration, Fourth Young Americas Forum, 2015, p. 7).

F. Conclusions

At this point, when most of the Latin American countries are experiencing the longest-lasting period of democracy in their history, in most cases people appear to feel that the channels for political participation lack legitimacy. This situation is compounded by the difficulties and shortcomings of democratic governments in the region, which continue to be subject to the strong tensions created by the coexistence of formally constituted electoral democracies with societies marked by sharp inequalities. In the vast majority of the countries, for example, survey data demonstrate that over two thirds of young people and adults believe that their countries are governed by powerful groups for their own benefit. Seen in this light, it is clear that these democracies are far from being regarded as mechanisms of inclusion or as means of achieving greater equality or improving people's lives.

The attitudes and perceptions of young people explored in this chapter have changed in recent years, in all probability in step with events and with the political and economic trends in each country. In one country after another, the data have corroborated the findings of many previous studies regarding a decline in the extent to which people trust social and especially political institutions, a decrease in participation in conventional political channels and in voter turnouts, a lack of interest in politics, less support on the part of young people for the proposition that democracy is the best form of government and a tendency to associate democracy with individual liberty and freedom of expression. Some of these views are not only held by young people, however; in many countries, young people and adults alike exhibit little interest in politics and are highly distrustful of political institutions.

The survey results indicate that young people are more optimistic and more enthusiastic than adults about the possibility of taking part in movements to support demands relating to health, education, better jobs and more opportunities. This enthusiasm goes hand in hand with a greater willingness on the part of young people to take part in demonstrations and other forms of action, although a majority of the members of this age group are nonetheless indifferent or reluctant to do so. Generally speaking, more young people than adults do not vote, whether because they do not meet age requirements or because they choose not to go to the polls, and more of them have never taken part in a social movement. At the same time, however, young people have been at the forefront of non-conventional forms of political mobilization that have influenced the public agenda and have played a pivotal role in championing demands that have been sidelined or ignored in conventional spheres of political activity. Another general feature at the regional level has to do with the issues that are of greatest concern to young people and how they have changed over time. In 2000, the problems that were seen as requiring the most urgent attention were unemployment, education and corruption. Thirteen years later, the focus was on crime and public safety, with unemployment remaining a major concern, along with, to a lesser degree, education and corruption.

The profiles of young people in the region have not remained static, nor have they changed in the same way in all of the countries. In fact, apart from the general features mentioned above, sharp differences are observed from one country to the next. Levels of trust, participation and commitment to democracy are fairly high in some countries (Argentina, the Bolivarian Republic of Venezuela, Costa Rica and Uruguay) whereas in others, such as Brazil, Chile, Mexico and a number of Central American nations, they were found to be fairly low in both 2000 and 2013. The changes that have taken place in these views have varied widely, however. In some cases there are multiple indicators of a simultaneous decrease in electoral participation and in social mobilization as well as in trust in political institutions, in democracy and in the government's response capacity. Examples include Mexico, Paraguay and most of the Central American countries, with the case of Costa Rica being notable for the initially high level of trust and commitment to democracy that was found to exist in that country in 2000. The case of Uruguay is also noteworthy, since the initially high levels of trust and commitment to democracy reflected in the 2000 survey results have since declined, although less sharply than in Costa Rica.

There are also countries in which the levels of trust and commitment to democracy among young people were very low in 2000 but were found to have risen by the time of the 2013 survey, with cases in point including Brazil and particularly the Bolivarian Republic of Venezuela and Ecuador. This suggests that economic upswings and political alternation or constitutional reforms mitigated the distrust and reluctance to participate in politics displayed by young people around the start of the 2000s in some countries. This appears to have been the case in Argentina, the Bolivarian Republic of Venezuela, Brazil, Colombia, Ecuador and, to a lesser extent, Uruguay. The situation in Chile is more ambiguous, since it remained one of the countries in which young people gave signs of having less trust in political institutions and democracy but in which a sizeable minority of them were more likely to take part in social movements. This indicates that, in contrast to what a number of other studies have posited on the basis of information gathered at one set point in time, young people's attitudes and their patterns of political participation are not destined to follow a single path but may alter course, in either positive or negative ways, over time. While the pronounced and growing disaffection of young people in some cases (Mexico and Central America) is a cause of concern, the situation in others, especially in South America, is quite positive.

It has been proposed here that there is an array of options in terms of norms, policies and programmes for promoting participation, organization and social mobilization among young people. It has also been argued that efforts should be made to open up opportunities and remove barriers to participation by young people —not as a means of mechanistically reversing patterns of exclusion or self-exclusion from conventional channels for participation, but rather as a way of helping to ensure that the mobilization of young people and the contributions they have to make can be incorporated into each political and institutional setting. In almost all of the countries a good starting point would be to open up the discussion concerning eligibility requirements, i.e. concerning what is in some cases a very large gap between the age requirements for voting and for standing as a candidate.

Bibliography

Beetham, David (2006), *Parliament and Democracy in the Twenty-First Century. A Guide to Good Practice*, Geneva, English Inter-Parliamentary Union.

Bianchi, Matías (2014), *Democracia en los márgenes de la democracia. Activismo en América Latina en la era digital*, Asuntos del Sur.

Bobbio, Norberto (1996), *Liberalismo y democracia*, Mexico City, Fondo de Cultura Económica.

Calderón Gutiérrez, Fernando (coord.) (2012), "La protesta social en América Latina", *Cuadernos de Prospectiva Política*, No. 1, Buenos Aires, Siglo Veintiuno Editores, July.

___(2011), *Understanding Social Conflict in Latin America*, United Nations Development Programme (UNDP)/Latin American Conflict Analysis Unit of Fundación UNIR Bolivia, September.

Corporación Latinobarómetro (2013), *Informe 2013*, Santiago, November.

ECLAC (Economic Commission for Latin America and the Caribbean) (2014), *Social Panorama of Latin America 2014* (LC/G.2635-P), Santiago.

ECLAC/OIJ (Economic Commission for Latin America and the Caribbean/Ibero-American Youth Organization) (2008), *Juventud y cohesión social en Iberoamérica. Un modelo para armar* (LC/G.2391), Santiago, October.

ECLAC/UNFPA (Economic Commission for Latin America and the Caribbean/United Nations Population Fund) (2012), *Informe regional de población en América Latina y el Caribe 2011. Invertir en Juventud* [online] http://www.cepal.org/cgi-bin/getProd.asp?xml=/publicaciones/xml/8/47318/P47318.xml&xsl=/tpl/p9f.xsl.

FLACSO/IDEA International (Latin American Faculty of Social Sciences/International Institute for the Development of Electoral Assistance) (2013), *Youth and Political Participation in Latin America. Current State and Challenges*, Santiago, November.

Hirschman, Albert (1995), *Bonheur privé, action publique*, Paris, Fayard.

IDEA Internacional (International Institute for the Development of Electoral Assistance) (2013), *Annual Democracy Forum 2013. Youth Participation in Politics and Elections. Background Paper*.

IPU (Inter-Parliamentary Union) (2014), *Taking Democracy to Task*, Geneva, October.

Luna, Juan Pablo (2014), "Partidos políticos y pactos sociales en América Latina", unpublished.

Moreno, Alejandro (2001), "Democracy and mass belief systems in Latin America", *Citizen Views of Democracy in Latin America*, Roderic Ai Camp (ed.), Pittsburgh, University of Pittsburgh Press.

Morlino, Leonardo (2014), *La calidad de las democracias en América Latina. Informe para IDEA Internacional*, San José, International Institute for the Development of Electoral Assistance (IDEA).

OIJ (Ibero-American Youth Organization) and others (2013), *El futuro ya llegó. 1ª encuesta iberoamericana de juventudes. Informe ejecutivo*, Madrid, July.

Pavez, María Isabel (2014), "Los derechos de la infancia en la era de Internet. América Latina y las nuevas tecnologías", *Políticas Sociales series*, No. 210 (LC/L.3894), Santiago, Economic Commission for Latin America and the Caribbean (ECLAC), September.

Reguillo, Rossana (2003), "Ciudadanías juveniles en América Latina", *Última Década*, vol. 11, No. 19, Santiago, Centro de Estudios Sociales (CIDPA), November.

UNDP (United Nations Development Programme) (2013), *Human Development Report for Latin America 2013-2014. Citizen Security with a Human Face: Evidence and proposals for Latin America*, New York, November.

UNDP/AECID (United Nations Development Programme/Spanish Agency for International Development Cooperation) (2014), *Ciudadanía política. Voz y participación ciudadana en América Latina*, Buenos Aires, Siglo Veintiuno Editores, February.

UNFPA (United Nations Population Fund) (2014), *The State of World Population 2014. The power of 1.8 billion: Adolescents, youth and the transformation of the future*, New York, November.

VII Summit of the Americas (2015), "Youth Declaration IV Young Americas Forum: Youth Partners for Prosperity" [online] http://yabt.net/foro/download/IV-Young-Americas-Forum-Declaration.pdf/.

Chapter VI

Final remarks

In 2013, the Secretary-General of the United Nations appointed the first Secretary-General's Envoy on Youth, with a view to strengthening the commitment of the United Nations system to young people. At the same time, the United Nations Inter-Agency Network on Youth Development was asked to prepare a global strategic plan on youth, bringing together a range of United Nations agencies in order to improve coordination and synergies throughout the Organization in key areas relating to youth development. These measures have helped to increase knowledge and understanding of the challenges and problems facing young people today. There are two challenges for society as a whole: the need to respond, in a way that ensures respect for youth rights, to their demands in the various spheres in which their voices are not being heard, and the importance of treating young people as key players in development by engaging them in this process (ECLAC, 2014).

ECLAC has long been working in this direction. The first and second Ibero-American youth reports, presented in 2004 and 2008 jointly by ECLAC and the Ibero-American Youth Organization (ECLAC/OIJ, 2004 and 2008), contributed to the development of visions, diagnostics and policies on youth in Ibero-America. The reflections set forth in these reports served to identify a series of tensions and paradoxes that young people face in terms of their development and social inclusion, which have become benchmarks in the discussion on youth in the region. Young people in Latin America and the Caribbean are more educated but have fewer work opportunities than previous generations; they have more access to information than ever before, but few opportunities to access power in representative spheres; they are more healthy, but their specific health needs receive less attention in public policies; they have broad access to symbolic consumption, but much greater difficulties regarding access to material consumption. The region needs policies that take an integrated approach to youth in order to reconcile these paradoxes and enable its young people to realize their rights with full inclusion in society and take part in building fairer and more productive societies.

The foregoing chapters have analysed inclusion from the standpoint of different dimensions of young people's lives and have identified the main challenges that must be tackled in order to formulate policies to close the objective gaps regarding youth inclusion in society. Although the analysis has focused chiefly on income inequalities and intergenerational gaps, gender gaps and ethnic and territorial inequalities also offer fertile ground for further analysis and policy action.

This diagnostic contributes to a rich corpus of knowledge on the situation of young people in Latin America and the Caribbean; one that is becoming increasingly consolidated and invites discussion of certain issues which have been neglected hitherto. It also offers a policy analyses by juxtaposing the realities of youth inclusion with the policies that address these realities (or fail to do so). Some common challenges are identified on the basis of the recommendations put forth in each of the areas of action.

First, better information systems are needed to monitor young people's lives and situations and their perceptions in each country and territory, and this information needs to be used to make more informed public investment decisions for this population group. Progress must be made with the adoption of legislation and regulations to safeguard and promote the realization of young people's social rights as regards, for example, access to health and education, decent work opportunities and participation in decision-making on matters of public interest. Lastly, a key challenge is to coordinate the various public policy sectors involved in integrated manner.

This analysis has confirmed the importance and, in some cases, the lack of such an integrated and multidimensional approach to youth in policies for this population group. For example, it was found that there were few linkages between policies on education and employment, the main pillars of social inclusion for young people, and that neither approached family and care issues in a centralized or comprehensive manner. Precisely at this stage of life, when the need to reconcile education and employment is greatest, and the burden of family and care responsibilities can truncate young people's —especially women's— education and work opportunities. The analysis also confirmed the importance of engaging the health, education and security sectors in an integrated manner in addressing violence as a phenomenon challenging youth development and inclusion processes, in order to apply real prevention and support strategies for the youth population.

A suitable institutional setting is required in order to develop policies that are able to address youth in this multidimensional and integrated manner and promote youth inclusion in society. The institutional framework also determines, to a large extent, the type, scope and effectiveness of the policies that can be implemented to promote the inclusion of young people in society. Three dimensions of the institutional structure are crucial in this process: the bodies coordinating youth issues, the normative framework and existence of national youth policies or plans.

It is important to recognize that the way youth is understood is a social construct and, thus the characteristics, definitions and roles attributed to youth vary according to historical and cultural factors in each society. In addition, countries must take into consideration that young people's transitions and life histories are heterogeneous, develop in different ways and at different rates, and do not necessarily follow a linear trajectory (ECLAC/OIJ/IMJUVE, 2014).

The first thing to bear in mind in analysing the institutional context, then, is the approach to youth adopted in policies and programmes to start with. As proposed in the Ibero-American youth reports (ECLAC/OIJ, 2004, 2008; ECLAC/OIJ/IMJUVE, 2014), the complexity embedded in the term "youth" and how it is defined reflect the variability of the policies adopted to address the theme. Apart from the age range used —in most countries between 15 and 24 or between 15 and 29— which determines to a great extent how policies will be implemented, what matters is the substantive definition of this segment and where it is situated, i.e. the place young people occupy within society, which roles are assigned to them and which are barred to them (ECLAC/OIJ/IMJUVE, 2014).

A study carried out by Dina Krauskopf (2003), which is cited in the Ibero-American youth reports (ECLAC/OIJ, 2008; ECLAC/OIJ/IMJUVE, 2014), found that four main paradigms have dominated State suppositions about youth, thereby impacting the formulation of related policies (see table VI.1).

All these paradigms have arisen at different points over the past three decades, but they are not mutually exclusive. Today they coexist in public discourse and policy, and are often combined and fused in different ways. Each of these approaches gives rise to different options in terms of policymaking and the nature of youth programmes (ECLAC, 2009; ECLAC/OIJ/IMJUVE, 2014). The last two approaches, youth citizenship and youth as a strategic development actor, treat young people as social stakeholders, which is the perspective promoted by the United Nations and in this book. The first paradigm should be avoided, because it does not treat young people as having rights and meriting well-being at this stage of life, but only as an adult in the future. The second leads to a narrow and stigmatizing view of the youth population, which can leave public policies limited in terms of their ability to provide new generations with the capacities they need to participate in a development process geared towards achieving equality.

Table VI.1
Paradigms of the youth phase in policy and programme approaches

Paradigm of youth	Policies	Characteristics of programmes	Types	Aims
Transition to adulthood (youth as a preparatory stage)	Geared towards preparation for adulthood Expansion of education coverage Healthy free time and recreation, with low coverage Military service	Universal Non-differentiated Isolated	Educational programmes Leisure-time and sporting, recreational and cultural programmes	Youth integration Strengthening of factors that offer protection in adolescence Violence prevention at a pre-criminal stage
Risk and transgression (youth as a stage that is problematic for society)	Compensatory Sectoral (mainly justice and health) Targeted	Welfarism and control of specific problems Geared towards urban and low socioeconomic status youth Disjointed supply	Rehabilitation programmes Social reintegration programmes Programmes revolving around the jail system	Social oversight of mobilized youth sectors Violence prevention
Youth citizenship (youth as a stage in social development)	Coordinated within public policy Intersectoral Inclusion of young people as explicit bearers of political, social, cultural and economic rights	Comprehensive Participatory Formation of partnership between programmes and executors	National poverty reduction policies Direct or conditional resource transfer programmes Volunteering schemes	Community strategy Violence prevention Participatory strategies Social capital
Youth as a strategic development actor (as a stage in relation to the formation of human capital and contribution to production)	Coordinated within public policy Intersectoral Geared towards inclusion of youth as part of the formation of human and social capital	Equity and institutional mainstreaming Efforts to tackle exclusion Youth contribution to development strategies	Emergency employment programmes Training programmes Production and business development strategies	Violence prevention Labour market integration Economic capital

Source: Economic Commission for Latin America and the Caribbean (ECLAC)/Ibero-American Youth Organization (OIJ), *Juventud y cohesión social en Iberoamérica: un modelo para armar* (LC/G.2391), Santiago, 2008, on the basis of D. Krauskopf, "La construcción de las políticas de juventud en Centroamérica", *Políticas públicas de juventud en América Latina: políticas nacionales*, O. Dávila (comp.), Viña del Mar, CIDPA Ediciones, 2003.

A range of modalities exist with regard to government institutions responsible for coordinating youth-related issues (see annex VI.A1). Within the region, there are ministries (Bolivarian Republic of Venezuela, Dominican Republic, and Nicaragua), vice-ministries (Costa Rica and

Plurinational State of Bolivia), youth secretariats (Brazil, Paraguay and Peru), under-secretariats, institutes (Chile, El Salvador, Honduras, Mexico and Uruguay), departments (Argentina and Ecuador), national youth councils (Guatemala) and other agencies. As noted in ECLAC (2009), in general, these bodies have at least four objectives: systematic knowledge of the youth situation; professionalization of their own technical staff; innovation in programme design and implementation; and communicational capacity-building to promote consensus between the ruling class and public opinion. Annex VI.A1 sets forth the main objectives or missions established by several of the bodies responsible for coordinating youth issues in the region. Most cite as their main mission the coordination of policies, programmes and actions for youth. Some also consider themselves interlocutors with the State in its dialogue with civil society youth organizations.

Most youth institutions in Latin America and the Caribbean have their own website (in 90% of the countries). Generally speaking, they publish news on youth issues and information on policies and programmes under way in the country. Just over half (60%) of these websites give information on relevant legislation and standards, around 40% carry publications linked to research on youth issues carried out by the institution itself or by other agencies, and less than 30% have statistical information on youth in the country.

Regardless of the form they take or the work they carry out to promote the development of their target population in their respective countries, youth institutions tend to be weak, especially compared with the solidity of the related sectoral ministries in the areas of education, labour and health. Their weakness lies in their limited political power, the scant resources they have to carry out their responsibilities and the small impact of their efforts. This being the case, reflection is called for on the essential functions they should fulfil. Accordingly, it is proposed that agencies responsible for youth issues focus on their coordinating role in order to galvanize processes, ensure that youth matters are visible in sectoral policy and develop an integrated approach to youth across the different sectors. This coordinating function is admittedly a difficult one, considering the power asymmetry between youth institutions and ministries. High-level political support is therefore required to emphasize and turn a spotlight on youth issues within ministries, while simultaneously strengthening and empowering youth institutions.

Clearly, it must be made a priority to strengthen coordination between government agencies working on youth development, since disjointed programmes not only make more inefficient use of the (few) resources available, but are also more costly. This is the rationale for implementing integrated policies and programmes coordinated by youth institutions, agreed on by the stakeholders involved and designed in such a way as to cater to youth groups within their respective environments. It is also necessary to strengthen local bodies (especially at the municipal level) to carry out youth inclusion initiatives involving greater community participation, during both design and implementation.

A second key component of the institutional structure is a legal framework on youth (see annex VI.A2). This framework, in the form of laws or decrees, serves to create institutions, proclaim rights, identify objectives, set targets, allocate resources and distinguish the levels of responsibility and coordination of the stakeholders. By creating a legal framework on youth, society expresses the commitment to address their needs and specifies how those needs are to be addressed. It obliges the different levels of power to establish polices and programmes to meet the objectives set and allocate budget resources to those ends. The legal framework thus provides public policies on youth with stability, lasting criteria, institutional structure and resources. However, the existence of a legal framework is no guarantee that it will be implemented: a national youth policy or plan is required for that. Such a policy or plan also plays a critical role because it confers an overall vision on all youth-related programmes and activities in the country, while also establishing a vision of what it means to be a young person in the specific historical context.

At the first Global Forum on Youth Policies, [1] some basic guidelines for youth policies were agreed upon. According to the Baku Commitment to Youth Policies, such policies should be:

- Rights-based —designed and implemented within a human rights-based framework, in line with the country's global and regional commitments.

- Inclusive —ensuring equal opportunities for every young person to achieve their full potential in life, including the elimination of barriers of inclusion, especially of vulnerable groups, and enabling civic participation of all young people.

- Participatory —designed, developed, implemented, monitored and evaluated with the meaningful participation of young people, and with the involvement of all concerned stakeholders, from the local to the national level, in both rural and urban settings, and in all development contexts, including post-conflict and transition situations.

---

[1]   The Baku Commitment was the outcome of the first Global Forum on Youth Policies, organized by the United Nations, and held in that city on 28-30 October 2014. The meeting was attended by over 700 participants from 165 countries and its purpose was to provide a platform for diverse stakeholders to evaluate the development, implementation and review of youth policies, share experiences and identify gaps and challenges in this regard.

- Gender-responsive —enabling specific actions to promote gender equality, ensure young women are equal partners to young men, and address gender-based disparities in all settings, from political to socioeconomic and cultural.

- Comprehensive —adopting a holistic approach to youth development, through increased collaboration across policy sectors, ministries and other relevant entities as well as by providing an integrated strategic framework that guides legislation and measures affecting youth.

- Knowledge-based and evidence-informed —developed and regularly updated, based on the collection, analysis and dissemination of quantitative and qualitative information on the situation, needs, challenges and opportunities of young women and men in a given context.

- Fully resourced —have adequate, transparent and dedicated resources for implementation, monitoring and evaluation, and maximizing available resources through coordination and by enabling multi-stakeholder partnerships and shared ownership.

- Accountable —nationally and locally owned and led, and regularly monitored and evaluated, against specific youth development targets and indicators, with the active participation of youth.

Many countries in the Latin American and Caribbean region have developed strategies that treat the youth perspective in terms of citizenship-building or see youth as a strategic actor in development, and some include elements of the Baku Commitment (see annex VI.A3). However, the policies put forward by the sectors that concern the youth population do not necessarily include this perspective, but tend to approach youth as a period of transition or a stage characterized by transgression and risk. This gives rise to two parallel courses in youth policies in the region: those advocated by agencies responsible for youth issues, which propose an integrated approach, on the one hand, and those operating on the basis of non-convergent visions of the youth population, on the other (Rodríguez, 2011).

Despite the advances in youth policies and plans, the resources allocated to this sector in public budgets are still insufficient and, in some cases, there is a mismatch between the plan's budget and its objectives. For example, as noted by Rodríguez (2011), public policy documents on youth prioritize excluded youth, labour market integration, citizenship-building and violence prevention, whereas public budgets continue to prioritize integrated youth and formal education. At the same time, some resources are allocated to health, but relatively few to labour market integration and violence prevention (Rodríguez, 2010).

Most of these efforts to confer an institutional structure on youth action have arisen since the first decade of the 2000s. This suggests that governments in the region have increasingly tried to give visibility and direction to youth-related action, and have become more aware of the importance of suitable legislation and policies for addressing the needs, aspirations and demands of young people. However, the existence of a legal framework on youth issues and a plan or policy for putting it into action is a necessary but not a sufficient condition for promoting youth inclusion, since, despite the advances and commitments, a series of challenges still hinder the implementation of the respective measures.

First, today national youth policies are managed by the respective coordinating bodies which, as noted earlier, have limited resources and political power. At the same time, sectoral ministries tend to act independently on issues that affect youth. This fragmentation represents a significant barrier to policy implementation, follow-up and, ultimately, efficiency.

Another challenge has to do with financing, a topic which has received attention at the global level. The Addis Ababa Action Agenda of the Third International Conference on Financing for Development[2] is the first international instrument to explicitly recognize that investing in youth is critical to achieving inclusive, equitable and sustainable development for present and future generations. This message is echoed in the work of ECLAC and other organizations that promote youth development in the region. In its most recent reports (ECLAC/UNFPA, 2012; ECLAC/OIJ/IMJUVE, 2014), ECLAC has analysed the social investment needed in youth policies and strategies to provide a real guarantee of fulfilment of their rights. ECLAC/ UNFPA (2012) argues that the political will expressed in international agreements and consensuses does not necessarily become enshrined in specific policies or programmes that would provide the conditions for young people to build their capacities and achieve their life plans in an autonomous manner. Estimates prepared for the latest youth report (ECLAC/ OIJ/IMJUVE, 2014) show total social investment in the region in 2012 as being equivalent to 19.1% of GDP (some US$ 660 billion). Out of total public expenditure on social investment, it is estimated that the region allocates around US$ 102 billion to social programmes which directly or indirectly benefit young people (US$ 183 billion PPP at 2005 prices). As noted in the 2014 edition of *Social Panorama of Latin America* (ECLAC, 2014), given the currently small margins for expanding spending on youth, efforts need to be redoubled to improve planning of expenditure and to develop and

---

[2]   The Third International Conference on Financing for Development, organized by the United Nations, was held on 13-16 July in Addis Ababa, Ethiopia. The outcome document, the Addis Ababa Action Agenda, is available at [online] http://www.un.org/esa/ffd/wp-content/uploads/2015/08/AAAA_Outcome.pdf.

strengthen assessment mechanisms with a view to making more efficient and effective use of resources.

Third, the channels of participation through which young people can play an active role in policy formulation, implementation, monitoring and evaluation are inadequate and fail to capture the voice of youth in an inclusive and effective manner. Youth organizations do offer some channels, but these generally lack resources and coordination between them tends to be weak or non-existent. Often, policy implementation does not encourage youth participation throughout the process, but only in an ad hoc manner and at the final stages. What is more, these opportunities for participation arise only when policies are directly linked to the youth population, and not in other spheres. Strengthening youth participation is essential to make all decisions more relevant, sustainable and legitimate.

Developing and implementing inclusive and participatory public policies on youth is no simple task, but takes concerted effort and commitment. It calls for consultations between youth and youth organizations, effective and sustainable cooperation between ministries, sufficient resource allocation and the integration of national youth policy in national development plans. However, as this book has argued throughout, it is crucial to invest in this stage of the life cycle and include youth fully in society in order to achieve development geared towards building the capacities and opportunities for greater equality in Latin America and the Caribbean.

Bibliography

ECLAC (Economic Commission for Latin America and the Caribbean) (2014), *Social Panorama of Latin America*, 2014 (LC/G.2635-P), Santiago.

____(2009), *Social Panorama of Latin America, 2008* (LC/G.2402-P), Santiago.

ECLAC/OIJ (Economic Commission for Latin America and the Caribbean/Ibero-American Youth Organization) (2008), *Juventud y cohesión social en Iberoamérica: un modelo para armar* (LC/G.2391), Santiago, October.

____(2004), *La juventud en Iberoamérica: tendencias y urgencias* (LC/L.2180), Santiago, October.

ECLAC/UNFPA (Economic Commission for Latin America and the Caribbean/ United Nations Population Fund) (2012), *Invertir en juventud: Informe Regional de Población en América Latina y el Caribe 2011* (LC/G.2391), Santiago.

ECLAC/OIJ/IMJUVE (Economic Commission for Latin America and the Caribbean/ Ibero-American Youth Organization/Mexican Youth Institute) (2014), *Invertir para transformar: la juventud como protagonista del desarrollo*, Madrid, September.

Krauskopf, Dina (2003), "La construcción de políticas de juventud en Centroamérica", *Políticas públicas de juventud en América Latina: políticas nacionales*, O. Dávila (comp.), Viña del Mar, CIDPA Ediciones.

Rodríguez, Ernesto (2011), "Políticas de juventud y desarrollo social en América Latina: bases para la construcción de respuestas integradas", paper presented at the Ministerial Forum for Development in Latin America and the Caribbean, San Salvador, 11 - 12 July [online] http://www.unesco.org/new/fileadmin/MULTIMEDIA/HQ/SHS/pdf/Youth%20Policies%20and%20Social%20Development%20-%20Building%20Integrated%20Responses%20ES.PDF.

_____(2010), "Políticas públicas de juventud en América Latina: avances concretados y desafíos a encarar en el Marco del Año Internacional de la Juventud", *Debates SHS series*, No. 1, United Nations Educational, Scientific and Cultural Organization (UNESCO), May.

SNJ/CLACSO (National Youth Secretariat of Brazil/Latin American Social Sciences Council) (2014), *Juventud, participación y desarrollo social en América Latina y el Caribe.*

Annex VI.A1
Latin America and the Caribbean (23 countries): institutions responsible for coordinating youth affairs

Country	Institution	Year established	Stated objective	Website
Antigua and Barbuda	Ministry of Education, Sports, Youth and Gender Affairs		To offer the highest quality education possible to children and young people, from preschool to postgraduate level, working with various stakeholders in society in order to improve and strengthen our educational, sports and youth empowerment institutions to develop productive citizens, who can learn and work independently and corporately to contribute to their national, regional and global communities.	http://www.education. gov.ag/index.php
Argentina	National Youth Department (DINAJU)		To engage young people as protagonists in the building of the nation. To position youth affairs by establishing guidelines for policies aimed at the youth population, from a federal and inter-governmental perspective.	http://www.juventud. gob.ar/
Bahamas	Ministry of Youth, Sports and Culture	1977	To promote the well-being of young people between the ages of 16-24 years at a national level, economically, physically, culturally, spiritually and socially, in the Commonwealth of the Bahamas.	http://www.bahamas. gov.bs/mysc
Barbados	Ministry of Culture, Sports and Youth Division of Youth Affairs		To facilitate the development of confident, proud, self-reliant and creative individuals through involvement in productive activity that contributes to personal, community and national development.	http://www. youthaffairs.gov.bb/
Belize	Ministry of Education, Youth and Sports		The Ministry of Education is charged with the responsibility of ensuring that all Belizeans are given an opportunity to acquire the knowledge, skills, and attitudes required for their own personal development and for full and active participation in the development of the nation.	http://moe.gov.bz/
Brazil	National Youth Secretariat (SNJ)	2004	Formulate, coordinate, integrate and coordinate public policies for youth, as well as promoting cooperation programmes with public and private national and international agencies working on youth policies.	http://www.juventude. gov.br/
Chile	National Institute for Youth (INJUV)	1991	Cooperate with the executive branch on the design, planning and coordination of policies on youth affairs.	http://www.injuv.gob. cl/portal/

Country	Institution	Year established	Stated objective	Website
Colombia	Young Colombia Presidential Programme	2014	Promote public policies for youth; encourage youth participation in the various institutional forums; consolidate the National System of Information and Knowledge Management (SNIGCAJ); coordinate the range of institutional programmes available for youth; and promote opportunities for socioeconomic development for young people.	http://www.colombiajoven.gov.co/Paginas/default.aspx
Costa Rica	Vice-Ministry for Youth Affairs	2002	Direct and coordinate activities within and outside the Ministry of Culture and Youth Affairs, and oversee compliance with the guidelines of the Youth Council for the population aged 12 to 35.	http://www.mcj.go.cr/ministerio/juventud/
Cuba	Union of Young Communists	1962	Ensure the unity of young Cubans, mobilize them under the principles of the Socialist Revolution and contribute to their education.	http://www.ecured.cu/index.php/Uni%C3%B3n_de_J%C3%B3venes_Comunistas#Una_organizaci.C3.B3n_de_j.C3.B3venes_comunistas
Dominican Republic	Ministry of Youth	2000	Promote the integrated development of young people, by formulating, coordinating, monitoring and evaluating the National Youth Policy. In consonance with governmental and non-governmental organizations, the aim is to guarantee the execution of programmes, plans and projects that will lead to the implementation of sectoral policies and the application of youth criteria.	http://juventud.gob.do/
El Salvador	National Institute for Youth	2012	Be responsible for the guidelines of the National Youth Policy, especially on matters of social prevention of youth violence.	http://www.injuve.gob.sv/
Guatemala	National Youth Council (CONJUVE)		Establish systematic processes to facilitate consensus between organized youth sectors and to support the construction of legal frameworks and public policies that respond to the multiple demands of Guatemalan youth.	http://conjuve.gob.gt/
Honduras	National Institute for Youth (INJ)	2006	Establish the legal, political and institutional framework to promote youth development; define State policies on youth; guide action in this area by the State, society and the family; and encourage active, responsible and constant participation by young people in their own development and that of the country.	http://dijuve.gob.hn/

Country	Institution	Year established	Stated objective	Website
Jamaica	Ministry of Youth and Culture		The Ministry of Youth and Culture is mandated to lead social transformation and enhance social well-being through programmes, services and activities geared towards youth development as well as contribute to economic growth and advancement through the development of the cultural industry by generally pursuing policies and programmes which help to boost Brand Jamaica.	http://www.myc.gov.jm/
Mexico	Mexican Youth Institute (IMJUVE)	1999	Formulate public policies in favour of young people to afford them the necessary tools in education, health, employment and social participation.	http://www.imjuventud.gob.mx/index.php
Nicaragua	Ministry of Youth (MINJUVE)		Formulate and implement policies, programmes and strategies to promote mindful and protagonistic participation by Nicaraguan youth in the country's economic, social and cultural development, on the basis of a model grounded in Christian values, socialist ideals and the practice of solidarity.	http://www.minjuve.gob.ni/
Paraguay	National Youth Secretariat		Promote, generate, coordinate and implement inclusive public policies aimed at meeting the priority needs of the country's youth population, with an emphasis on young people living in poverty or vulnerability, in order to ensure improvement in their standard of living and their active participation in all areas of national development.	http://www.snj.gov.py/
Peru	National Youth Secretariat (SENAJU)		Promote, coordinate, monitor and evaluate policies, plans, programmes, projects and actions in benefit of young people aged between 15 and 29, within a participatory, inclusive and democratic framework.	http://www.juventud.gob.pe/
Suriname	Ministry of Youth and Sport			
Trinidad and Tobago	Ministry of Sport and Youth Affairs		To engender positive attitudes that facilitate the delivery of technology-driven, quality services with special emphasis on sport development for recreation, lifestyle and industry.	http://www.sport.gov.tt/
Uruguay	National Institute for Youth (INJU)		Plan, design, advise on, coordinate, oversee and implement public policies on youth and ensure they are implemented.	http://www.inju.gub.uy/
Venezuela (Bolivarian Republic of)	National Institute of the People's Power for Youth		Formulate and implement policies aimed at achieving protagonistic participation by young people, and involving them in processes of change towards a socialist nation, building people's power among youth. To be the governing institution in coordinating youth policies with other State bodies.	http://www.inj.gob.ve/

Source: Economic Commission for Latin America and the Caribbean (ECLAC), on the basis of information from the websites of the respective entities.

Annex VI.A2
Latin America and the Caribbean (17 countries): national legal frameworks for youth issues

Country	Youth law	Year adopted	Stated objective
Argentina	Consejo Federal de la Juventud (Ley núm. 26227)	2007	Collaborate in the design and inter-jurisdictional coordination of youth policies, mapping strategic management in order to build the concept of citizenship in values such as solidarity, equity, commitment, justice, responsibility, ethics and national identity.
Bolivia (Plurinational State of)	Ley de la Juventud (Ley núm. 342)	2013	Guarantee young people the full exercise of their rights and duties, and provide for the design of the institutional framework, forums for youth representation and deliberation, and the establishment of public policies.
Brazil	Estatuto da Juventude (Ley núm. 12852)	2013	Establish youth rights and guidelines for public policies on youth, and the National Youth System (SINAJUVE).
Chile	Ley núm. 19042	1991	Create the national Youth Institute as a functionally decentralized public service with legal personality and its own assets, linked to the Office of the President of the Republic through the Ministry for Planning and Cooperation.
Colombia	Estatuto de ciudadanía juvenil (Ley núm. 1622)	2013	Establish the institutional framework to guarantee all young people the full exercise of youth citizenship in the civic, personal, social and public domains, and the effective enjoyment of rights recognized in domestic legislation and ratified in international treaties.
Costa Rica	Ley General de la Persona Joven (Ley núm. 8261)	2002	Prepare public policy on youth and promote and coordinate its implementation. Coordinate the range of national development policies so that they include the creation of opportunities, access to services and means to enable young people to increase their potential. Foster political, social, cultural and economic participation by young people, on a basis of solidarity, equity and well-being. Promote and implement research on the situation of young people and their families. Protect the rights, obligations and fundamental guarantees of young people.
Cuba	Código de la Niñez y la Juventud (Ley núm. 16)	1978	Regulate participation by children and young people under the age of 30 in building the new society and establish the obligations of individuals, agencies and institutions involved in their education, in accordance with the goal of building communist principles in the young generation.
Dominican Republic	Ley General de Juventud (Ley núm. 49)	2000	Establish the legal, political and institutional framework to guide State actions and society in general towards the establishment and implementation of a set of policies needed to fulfil the needs and expectations of the country's youth population, and achieve effective participation by young people in decision-making processes.
El Salvador	Ley General de la Juventud (Decreto núm. 910)	2012	Implement public policies, programmes, strategies and plans for the integrated development of the youth population.

Country	Youth law	Year adopted	Stated objective
Honduras	Ley Marco para el Desarrollo Integral de la Juventud (Decreto núm. 260)	2005	Establish the legal, political and institutional framework to promote the full development of young people.
Mexico	Ley del Instituto Mexicano de la Juventud	2012	Create the Mexican Youth Institute as a technically, operationally and administratively autonomous, decentralized public agency, with legal personality and its own assets, domiciled in the Federal District.
Nicaragua	Ley de Promoción del Desarrollo Integral de la Juventud y su Reglamento (Ley núm. 392)	2001	Promote the human development of young men and women, ensure the exercise of their rights and obligations, establish institutional policies and mobilize State and civil society resources for youth.
Panama	Ley de la Secretaría Nacional de Niñez, Adolescencia y Familia (Ley núm. 14)	2009	Create the National Secretariat for Childhood, Youth and the Family. Strengthen the institutional framework for the protection and promotion of the rights of children and adolescents, by consolidating the bases and guiding principles for the operation of the System for Comprehensive Protection of Children and Adolescents of the Republic of Panama.
Paraguay	Decreto núm. 262	2013	Create the National Youth Secretariat (SNJ) as an institution under public law, to govern and be responsible for guiding the actions of the State on the array of public policies needed to fulfil the needs and expectations of youth, and to promote youth participation in decision-making processes.
Peru	Decreto Supremo núm. 001-2008-ED	2008	Create the National Youth Secretariat (SENAJU), which will formulate State policies on youth matters, contribute to the integrated development of young people on issues of employability, improved living standards, social inclusion, participation and access to forums in all spheres of human development, and promote and oversee programmes and projects for youth.
Uruguay	Ley núm. 16170	1990	Create the National Youth Institute (INJU), to be responsible for formulating, implementing and evaluating national policies on youth, in coordination with other State agencies; and promote, plan and coordinate the activities of the Youth Information Centre, which will report to the Institute, advising and training staff in local information units.
	Ibero-American Convention on the Rights of Youth (Ley núm. 18270)	2008	
Venezuela (Bolivarian Republic of)	Ley Nacional de la Juventud (Ley núm. 37404)	2002	Govern and develop the rights and duties of youth, in order to give young people opportunities for full development towards productive adult life, including guarantees regarding their training, first job and participation in the development process, through State policies and with participation by the family and society on a basis of solidarity.

Source: Economic Commission for Latin America and the Caribbean (ECLAC), on the basis of information from the websites of the respective entities.

Annex VI.A3
Latin America and the Caribbean (20 countries): national youth policy documents

Country	Document	Website
Antigua and Barbuda	National Youth Policy: Empowering Tomorrow's Leaders Today	http://www.youthpolicy.org/national/Antigua_Barbuda_2007_National_Youth_Policy.pdf
Bahamas	National Youth Policy	
Barbados	National Youth Policy	http://www.youthpolicy.org/national/Barbados_2011_National_Youth_Policy.pdf
Brazil	Política Nacional de Juventude: Diretrizes e Perspectivas	http://library.fes.de/pdf-files/bueros/brasilien/05611.pdf
Chile	Chile se Compromete con los Jóvenes: Plan de Acción en Juventud	http://extranet.injuv.gob.cl/cedoc/Estudios%20del%20INJUV/ESTUDIOS%20PDF/Evaluacion_de_la_Reforma_Escolar.pdf
Colombia	Política Nacional de Juventud: Bases para el Plan Decenal de Juventud 2005-2015	http://cdim.esap.edu.co/BancoMedios/Documentos%20PDF/programa%20presidencial%20colombia%20joven.pdf
Costa Rica	Política Pública de la Persona Joven	http://www.cpj.go.cr/images/POLITICA_PUBLICA_DE_LA_PERSONA_JOVEN_2014_-_2019.pdf
Dominican Republic	Política Pública Nacional para el Desarrollo de la Juventud Dominicana 2008-2015	
Ecuador	Agenda de Igualdad para la Juventud, 2012-2013	http://www.youthpolicy.org/national/Ecuador_2012_Youth_Equality_Policy.pdf
El Salvador	Política Nacional de Juventud 2011-2024 y Plan de Acción 2011-2014	http://planipolis.iiep.unesco.org/upload/Youth/El%20Salvador/El_Salvador_Politica%20Nacional%20de%20Juventud%20de%20El%20Salvador%202011-2024.pdf
Guatemala	Política de Juventud 2012-2020	http://conjuve.gob.gt/descargas/pnj.pdf
Honduras	Política Nacional de Juventud 2007-2021: Por una Ciudadanía Plena	http://planipolis.iiep.unesco.org/upload/Youth/Honduras/Honduras_2007_National_Youth_Policy.pdf
Mexico	Programa Nacional de Juventud 2014-2018	http://www.dof.gob.mx/nota_detalle.php?codigo=5343095&fecha=30/04/2014
Nicaragua	Plan de Acción de la Política Nacional para el Desarrollo Integral de la Juventud 2005-2015	http://planipolis.iiep.unesco.org/upload/Youth/Nicaragua/Nicaragua_National_Youth_Policy.pdf
Panama	Política Pública de Juventud de Panamá	http://planipolis.iiep.unesco.org/upload/Youth/Panama/Panama_2004_National_Youth_Policy.pdf
Paraguay	Plan Nacional de Juventud	http://www.mec.gov.py/cms_v2/adjuntos/7259
Peru	Plan Estratégico Nacional de la Juventud 2014-2021: Rumbo al Bicentenario	http://juventud.gob.pe/media/publications/Plan-Nacional-Juventud-Documento-Trabajo.pdf
Trinidad and Tobago	National Youth Policy 2012-2017	http://www.youthpolicy.org/national/Trinidad_Tobago_2012_National_Youth_Policy.pdf
Uruguay	Plan de Acción de Juventudes 2015-2025	http://www.inju.gub.uy/innovaportal/v/26838/5/innova.front/plan_de_accion_de_juventudes_2015-2025
Venezuela (Bolivarian Republic of)	Misión Jóvenes de la Patria	http://www.youthpolicy.org/wp-content/uploads/library/2013_Venezuela_Youth_Policy_Spa.pdf

Source: Economic Commission for Latin America and the Caribbean (ECLAC), on the basis of information from the websites of the respective entities.

Publicaciones recientes de la CEPAL
ECLAC recent publications

www.cepal.org/publicaciones

Informes periódicos / *Annual reports*
También disponibles para años anteriores / *Issues for previous years also available*

- Estudio Económico de América Latina y el Caribe 2015, 204 p.
  Economic Survey of Latin America and the Caribbean 2015, 196 p.

- La Inversión Extranjera Directa en América Latina y el Caribe 2015, 150 p.
  Foreign Direct Investment in Latin America and the Caribbean 2015, 140 p.

- Anuario Estadístico de América Latina y el Caribe 2015 / *Statistical Yearbook for Latin America and the Caribbean 2015, 235 p.*

- Balance Preliminar de las Economías de América Latina y el Caribe 2015, 104 p.
  Preliminary Overview of the Economies of Latin America and the Caribbean 2015, 98 p.

- Panorama Social de América Latina 2015. Documento informativo, 68 p.
  Social Panorama of Latin America 2015. Briefing paper, 66 p.

- Panorama de la Inserción Internacional de América Latina y el Caribe 2015, 102 p.
  Latin America and the Caribbean in the World Economy 2015, 98 p.

Libros y documentos institucionales / *Institutional books and documents*

- Panorama fiscal de América Latina y el Caribe 2016: las finanzas públicas ante el desafío de conciliar austeridad con crecimiento e igualdad, 2016, 90 p.

- Reflexiones sobre el desarrollo en América Latina y el Caribe: conferencias magistrales 2015, 2016, 74 p.

- Panorama Económico y Social de la Comunidad de Estados Latinoamericanos y Caribeños, 2015, 58 p.
  Economic and Social Panorama of the Community of Latin American and Caribbean States 2015, 56 p.

- Desarrollo social inclusivo: una nueva generación de políticas para superar la pobreza y reducir la desigualdad en América Latina y el Caribe, 2015, 180 p.
  Inclusive social development: The next generation of policies for overcoming poverty and reducing inequality in Latin America and the Caribbean, 2015, 172 p.

- Guía operacional para la implementación y el seguimiento del Consenso de Montevideo sobre Población y Desarrollo, 2015, 146 p.
  Operational guide for implementation and follow-up of the Montevideo Consensus on Population and Development, 2015, 139 p.

- América Latina y el Caribe: una mirada al futuro desde los Objetivos de Desarrollo del Milenio. Informe regional de monitoreo de los Objetivos de Desarrollo del Milenio (ODM) en América Latina y el Caribe, 2015, 88 p.
  Latin America and the Caribbean: Looking ahead after the Millennium Development Goals. Regional monitoring report on the Millennium Development Goals in Latin America and the Caribbean, 2015, 88 p.

- La nueva revolución digital: de la Internet del consumo a la Internet de la producción, 2015, 98 p.
  The new digital revolution: From the consumer Internet to the industrial Internet, 2015, 98 p.

- Globalización, integración y comercio inclusivo en América Latina. Textos seleccionados de la CEPAL (2010-2014), 2015, 326 p.
- El desafío de la sostenibilidad ambiental en América Latina y el Caribe. Textos seleccionados de la CEPAL (2012-2014), 2015, 148 p.
- Pactos para la igualdad: hacia un futuro sostenible, 2014, 340 p.
  Covenants for Equality: Towards a sustainable future, 2014, 330 p.
- Cambio estructural para la igualdad: una visión integrada del desarrollo, 2012, 330 p.
  Structural Change for Equality: An integrated approach to development, 2012, 308 p.
- La hora de la igualdad: brechas por cerrar, caminos por abrir, 2010, 290 p.
  Time for Equality: Closing gaps, opening trails, 2010, 270 p.
  A Hora da Igualdade: Brechas por fechar, caminhos por abrir, 2010, 268 p.

Libros de la CEPAL / *ECLAC books*

138 Estructura productiva y política macroeconómica: enfoques heterodoxos desde América Latina, Alicia Bárcena Ibarra, Antonio Prado, Martín Abeles (eds.), 2015, 282 p.

137 Juventud: realidades y retos para un desarrollo con igualdad, Daniela Trucco, Heidi Ullmann (eds.), 2015, 282 p.

136 Instrumentos de protección social: caminos latinoamericanos hacia la universalización, Simone Cecchini, Fernando Filgueira, Rodrigo Martínez, Cecilia Rossel (eds.), 2015, 510 p.

135 *Rising concentration in Asia-Latin American value chains: Can small firms turn the tide? Osvaldo Rosales, Keiji Inoue, Nanno Mulder (eds.), 2015, 282 p.*

134 Desigualdad, concentración del ingreso y tributación sobre las altas rentas en América Latina, Juan Pablo Jiménez (ed.), 2015, 172 p.

133 Desigualdad e informalidad: un análisis de cinco experiencias latinoamericanas, Verónica Amarante, Rodrigo Arim (eds.), 2015, 526 p.

132 Neoestructuralismo y corrientes heterodoxas en América Latina y el Caribe a inicios del siglo XXI, Alicia Bárcena, Antonio Prado (eds.), 2014, 452 p.

Copublicaciones / *Co-publications*

- Gobernanza global y desarrollo: nuevos desafíos y prioridades de la cooperación internacional, José Antonio Ocampo (ed.), CEPAL/Siglo Veintiuno, Argentina, 2015, 286 p.
- *Decentralization and Reform in Latin America: Improving Intergovernmental Relations, Giorgio Brosio and Juan Pablo Jiménez (eds.), ECLAC / Edward Elgar Publishing, United Kingdom, 2012, 450 p.*
- Sentido de pertenencia en sociedades fragmentadas: América Latina desde una perspectiva global, Martín Hopenhayn y Ana Sojo (comps.), CEPAL / Siglo Veintiuno, Argentina, 2011, 350 p.

Coediciones / *Co-editions*

- Perspectivas económicas de América Latina 2016: hacia una nueva asociación con China, 2015, 240 p.
  Latin American Economic Outlook 2016: Towards a new Partnership with China, 2015, 220 p.
- Perspectivas de la agricultura y del desarrollo rural en las Américas: una mirada hacia América Latina y el Caribe 2015-2016, CEPAL / FAO / IICA, 2015, 212 p.

Documentos de proyecto / *Project documents*

- Complejos productivos y territorio en la Argentina: aportes para el estudio de la geografía económica del país, 2015, 216 p.
- Las juventudes centroamericanas en contextos de inseguridad y violencia: realidades y retos para su inclusión social, Teresita Escotto Quesada, 2015, 168 p.
- La economía del cambio climático en el Perú, 2014, 152 p.

Cuadernos estadísticos de la CEPAL

42 Resultados del Programa de Comparación Internacional (PCI) de 2011 para América Latina y el Caribe. Solo disponible en CD, 2015.

41 Los cuadros de oferta y utilización, las matrices de insumo-producto y las matrices de empleo. Solo disponible en CD, 2013.

Series de la CEPAL / *ECLAC Series*

Asuntos de Género / Comercio Internacional / Desarrollo Productivo / Desarrollo Territorial / Estudios Estadísticos / Estudios y Perspectivas (Bogotá, Brasilia, Buenos Aires, México, Montevideo) / *Studies and Perspectives* (The Caribbean, Washington) / Financiamiento del Desarrollo/ Gestión Pública / Informes y Estudios Especiales / Macroeconomía del Desarrollo / Manuales / Medio Ambiente y Desarrollo / Población y Desarrollo/ Política Fiscal / Políticas Sociales / Recursos Naturales e Infraestructura / Seminarios y Conferencias.

Revista CEPAL / *CEPAL Review*

La Revista se inició en 1976, con el propósito de contribuir al examen de los problemas del desarrollo socioeconómico de la región. La *Revista CEPAL* se publica en español e inglés tres veces por año.

CEPAL Review first appeared in 1976, its aim being to make a contribution to the study of the economic and social development problems of the region. CEPAL Review is published in Spanish and English versions three times a year.

Observatorio demográfico / *Demographic Observatory*

Edición bilingüe (español e inglés) que proporciona información estadística actualizada, referente a estimaciones y proyecciones de población de los países de América Latina y el Caribe. Desde 2013 el Observatorio aparece una vez al año.

Bilingual publication (Spanish and English) proving up-to-date estimates and projections of the populations of the Latin American and Caribbean countries. Since 2013, the Observatory appears once a year.

Notas de población

Revista especializada que publica artículos e informes acerca de las investigaciones más recientes sobre la dinámica demográfica en la región. También incluye información sobre actividades científicas y profesionales en el campo de población.
La revista se publica desde 1973 y aparece dos veces al año, en junio y diciembre.

Specialized journal which publishes articles and reports on recent studies of demographic dynamics in the region. Also includes information on scientific and professional activities in the field of population. Published since 1973, the journal appears twice a year in June and December.

Las publicaciones de la CEPAL están disponibles en:
ECLAC publications are available at:

www.cepal.org/publicaciones

También se pueden adquirir a través de:
They can also be ordered through:

www.un.org/publications

United Nations Publications
PO Box 960
Herndon, VA 20172
USA

Tel. (1-888)254-4286
Fax (1-800)338-4550
Contacto / *Contact*: publications@un.org
Pedidos / *Orders*: order@un.org